*Ordinary Egyptians*

# Ordinary Egyptians

*Creating the Modern Nation*
*Through Popular Culture*

Ziad Fahmy

STANFORD UNIVERSITY PRESS

STANFORD, CALIFORNIA

Stanford University Press
Stanford, California

Library of Congress Cataloging-in-Publication Data

Fahmy, Ziad (Ziad Adel), author.
Ordinary Egyptians : creating the modern nation through popular culture /
Ziad Fahmy.
pages cm
Includes bibliographical references and index.
ISBN 978-0-8047-7211-2 (cloth) —
ISBN 978-0-8047-7212-9 (pbk.)
1. Nationalism—Egypt—History—19th century.  2. Nationalism—Egypt—
History—20th century.  3. National characteristics, Egyptian—History—19th
century.  4. National characteristics, Egyptian—History—20th century.
5. Popular culture—Egypt—History—19th century.  6. Popular culture—
Egypt—History—20th century.  I. Title.
DT70.F225 2011
962'.04—dc22
2011000517

Typeset by Bruce Lundquist in 10/12 Sabon LT Pro

*This book is dedicated to the memory of my grandfather,*
*Muhammad Abd al-ʿAziz Fahmy (1913–1978).*
*His wisdom, freethinking, erudition, and tolerance serve as*
*a model and inspiration for my life and scholarship.*

We cannot understand cultural and literary life and
the struggle of mankind's historic past if we ignore the
peculiar folk humor that always existed and was never
merged with the official culture of the ruling classes.
While analyzing past ages we are too often obliged to
"take each epoch at its word," that is to believe its official
ideologists. We do not hear the voice of the people and
cannot find and decipher its unmixed expression. All the
acts of the drama of world history were performed before
a chorus of the laughing people. Without hearing this
chorus we cannot understand the drama as a whole.
— Mikhail Bakhtin, *Rabelais and His World*

The intellectuals as such can do little politically unless
they attach themselves to a massive form of discontent.
The discontented intellectual with his soul searching
has attracted attention wholly out of proportion to his
political importance, partly because these searchings
leave behind them written records and also because
those who write history are themselves intellectuals.
— Barrington Moore Jr., *Social Origins
of Dictatorship and Democracy*

# Contents

# Illustrations

# Preface

> No prairie fire ever sped more swiftly than the hilarious tiding that Saad Zaglul [Sa'd Zaghlul], whose arrest had made him a national martyr, was free [April 7, 1919]. . . . Apparently the masses thought that independence had been granted to Egypt. There could be no doubt of the appeal of patriotism to the hearts of even the humblest. A man at a London desk might contend that the lower classes of Egyptians neither know nor care anything about nationalism, but no honest person looking upon the Cairo outburst would believe so for a moment.     —William T. Ellis, *Washington Post*, June 21, 1919

The 1919 Revolution, which erupted when the British arrested and exiled the Egyptian nationalist leader Sa'd Zaghlul, demonstrates the need to incorporate nonelites into the historical narrative. Thousands of Egyptians from all backgrounds took to the streets, protesting the exile of Zaghlul and demanding an end to British occupation. According to British Foreign Office reports, "Street boys, lower-class natives and seed vendors" publicly chanted new songs in colloquial Egyptian that insulted British officials and called for the immediate evacuation of the British from Egypt.[1]

Despite the obvious populist characteristics of the 1919 Revolution, the existing historiography places Egyptian nationalism primarily within the realm of elite politics. Missing from these narratives are everyday Egyptians and the colloquial language used to address them. In this book I investigate the agency of ordinary Egyptians in constructing and negotiating national identity. I challenge the idea that nationalism was disseminated predominantly by European-educated intellectuals. Certainly European conceptions of nationhood and the state had an important impact on the formulation of a "modern" Egyptian identity; however, to be effective, these "ideas" had to be reworked, reconstructed, and transformed into a form that was meaningful to a local Egyptian milieu, and equally they had to be in a language that everyone understood. A principal reason that the Egyptian urban masses are not well represented in the literature is the neglect of colloquial Egyptian sources. Unlike Fusha (Modern Standard Arabic), colloquial Egyptian is spoken and understood by all Egyptians regardless of class, literacy, or education level, making it a better, more comprehensive barometer of the cultural trajectory of Egyptian society as a whole.

For this reason, in this book I primarily focus on Egyptian mass culture and on works that were mostly written, performed, or recorded in colloquial Egyptian; these diverse works include the satirical press, vaudeville plays, recorded songs, and *azjal* (colloquial poetry).[2] By incorporating performance and sound media, especially the rising record industry, I strive to expand the historical study of this period beyond just the visual and the printed to include sound and aural/oral expressions of culture. This larger field allows for much wider audiences, because the vast majority of Egyptians who were illiterate had the potential at least of directly listening to and engaging with these songs and performances.

This book is not meant to be a comprehensive study of Egyptian nationalism, but I aim to examine the beginnings of territorial Egyptian national identity through a popular culture lens. In contrast to most studies on early Egyptian nationalism, intellectuals and the political elite, who wrote predominantly in Fusha, do not figure prominently in this book. Instead of intellectuals, such as Muhammad Husayn Haykal, Lutfi al-Sayyid, and Taha Husayn, I discuss the cultural contributions of musicians, singers, actors, and popular playwrights, such as 'Uthman Jalal, Badi' Khayri, 'Amin Sidqi, Najib al-Rihani, Sayyid Darwish, and Munira al-Mahdiyya. In other words, my book is about the dissemination of a nationalist ideology to the masses and how this ideology was translated and acted on in the streets and not about the intellectual debates surrounding the formation of Egyptian national identity. Not only were recorded colloquial music, vaudeville, *azjal*, and the popular press the most effective tools for the dissemination of nationalist ideas to the majority of Egyptians, but they also provided the space necessary for a nascent middle class to construct and maintain new, "modern" identities.

Finally, in this book I also engage with some of the theories of nationalism and test their applicability to Egypt and the Arab world. I introduce the concept of media capitalism, which expands the historical analysis of Egyptian nationalism beyond just print and silent reading through the incorporation of audiovisual, sound, and performance media. By integrating these new media, especially the burgeoning record industry, I attempt to make room for both the ear and the eye—for the aural and oral alongside the visual and written—and in the process provide a more comprehensive explanation for how individuals and communities digest and embody cultural information. Cultural productions, in any form, are not socially relevant unless they are communally and socially activated; they must be discussed, breathed, and animated in the routine of everyday life.

# Acknowledgments

This book took more than seven years to research and write and has passed through several stages of transformation. During this long process, I have benefited from the encouragement and ideas of countless colleagues, mentors, friends, and family members.

First, I would like to thank Charles D. Smith and Julia Clancy-Smith. Carl's and Julia's mentoring, insight, and engagement with my work were instrumental in seeing this project through. I will forever be in their debt. I would also like to thank Linda T. Darling. Linda is the consummate mentor; her office door was always open to me for endless academic questions and discussions.

I would like to thank Kate Wahl, the Stanford University Press executive editor, for taking a chance on my book and for her thoroughness and professionalism. The critical and encouraging comments of the SUP anonymous readers were extremely helpful in framing my revisions. My book is much better because of the readers' advice. I am especially grateful to Walter Armbrust, who meticulously examined and critiqued the entire manuscript. His insights led me to explore new paths I had not yet considered.

I am indebted to many colleagues, friends, and acquaintances: Donald Malcolm Reid, Tracy Gould, Julia Hutchins-Richards, and Christina Lindeman, for reading and commenting on an earlier draft of Chapter 2; Frédéric Lagrange, for sending me some relevant pages from the catalogs of Odeon, Columbia, and Baidaphon record companies; Munther Yunis, for allowing me to use his extensive library on linguistics; and Lauren Monroe, for reading and commenting on my introduction. I would also like to thank Deborah Starr and Vikash Yadav for sharing their book proposals with me and for their helpful advice on the publication process. Through the years, a great number of people have directly or indirectly contributed to my scholarship and intellectual growth. I benefited from the mentoring and advice of Richard Eaton, Leila Hudson, Michael Bonine,

Adel Gamal, Kamran Talattof, Amy Newhall, Richard Cosgrove, Kevin Gosner, Eric Davis, and Stephen Reinhardt.

Throughout the writing process, my colleagues and the academic staff in the Department of Near Eastern Studies at Cornell University were generous and unbelievably supportive. I am truly blessed to work in such a collegial and supportive atmosphere.

Financial assistance for the research and writing of this project came from a variety of sources. The bulk of the research for this book took place in Egypt and England, with the help of generous research grants from Fulbright-Hays and the American Research Center in Egypt. Cornell University's Society for the Humanities summer research grants in 2008 and 2010 helped me acquire additional resources, which were instrumental in the completion of this project. I am also indebted to the Cornell University Library and especially Ali Houissa, the Middle East and Islamic Studies librarian, for acquiring dozens of rare Arabic periodicals, which were extremely useful for my research.

A part of Chapter 5 and a section from the introduction are reprinted with permission from my previous work, "Media Capitalism: Colloquial Mass Culture and Nationalism in Egypt, 1908–1918," *International Journal of Middle Eastern Studies* 42(1) (February 2010): 83–103.

I am eternally grateful to my parents, Ferial Sammakia and Adel Fahmy, who sacrificed a lot for my education and helped instill in me a sense of historical and intellectual curiosity. Most of all, I would like to thank my wife, Kaila Bussert, who proofread countless incarnations of this manuscript and endured my endless obsessions with this book project. Her love and unfailing intellectual and emotional support made this book possible.

# Note on Transliteration

Fusha, or Classical Arabic, words have been transcribed according to a simplified system based on the *International Journal of Middle East Studies* (IJMES). All diacritical marks have been omitted except for the 'ayn ('), and the hamza ('). For texts, songs, and plays written or performed in colloquial Egyptian, I have slightly modified the transliteration system based on IJMES. Instead of jim (j), I use gim (g); instead of qaf (q), I use a hamza ('). Also, the definite article (al-) in Fusha is transliterated as (il-) in colloquial Egyptian. Because the term Fusha appears frequently in this study, it is important to note that it is pronounced as fuss-ha. The names of Egyptian authors writing in French or English have not been changed.

*Ordinary Egyptians*

## CHAPTER ONE

# Colloquial Egyptian, Media Capitalism, and Nationalism

Modern man is not loyal to a monarch or a land or a faith,
whatever he may say, but to a culture.
                    —Ernest Gellner, *Nations and Nationalism*

If the decoding of power relations depended on full access to the
more or less clandestine discourse of subordinate groups, students
of power—both historical and contemporary—would face an im-
passe. We are saved from throwing up our hands in frustration by
the fact that the hidden transcript is typically expressed openly—
albeit in disguised form. I suggest, along these lines, how we might
interpret the rumors, gossip, folktales, songs, gestures, jokes and
theater of the powerless as vehicles by which, among other things,
they insinuate a critique of power while hiding behind anonymity
or behind innocuous understandings of their conduct.
                    —James C. Scott, *Domination and the Arts of Resistance*

In Egypt, during the late nineteenth and early twentieth centuries, older,
fragmented, and more localized forms of identity were rapidly replaced
with new, alternative concepts of community, which for the first time
had the capacity to collectively encompass the majority of Egyptians. In
this examination of modern Egyptian history, I trace the development
of Egyptian national identity from the 1870s until the 1919 Revolution through the lens of popular culture. I seek to highlight and feature
the role and importance of previously neglected colloquial Egyptian
sources—be they oral, aural, or textual. This approach is crucial to any
attempt at capturing the voice of the majority of Egyptians. A second
objective is to document the influence of a developing colloquial Egyptian

mass culture as a vehicle and forum through which, among other things, "hidden transcripts" of resistance and critiques of colonial and elite authority took place.[1] Third, I engage with some of the theories of nationalism and test their applicability to Egypt and the Arab world. I introduce the concept of media capitalism to expand the historical analysis of Egyptian nationalism beyond print and reading, through the incorporation of audiovisual, sound, and performance media.

Until recently, scholars have almost entirely focused on the role of intellectuals in the formation of modern Egyptian identity. Jamal Mohammed Ahmed, Albert Hourani, Nadav Safran, Charles Wendell, Charles D. Smith, and Donald Malcolm Reid investigated the roots of Egyptian nationalism by examining the cultural influences of European ideas on the Egyptian intelligentsia.[2] Although the theoretical framework of Egyptian nationalism might have been formulated by these intellectuals, without the dissemination and the adoption of nationalist ideas by the masses, such politicized rhetoric remained an abstract notion without widespread resonance.[3] In the last couple of decades, more expansive studies have been conducted by Zachary Lockman, Joel Beinin, Juan Cole, and, later, John Chalcraft, who examined in part the street politics and the economic and political mobilizations of guilds and a growing labor movement.[4] More recently, several innovative studies have documented the literary and journalistic representation and often personification of the nation into "authentic" national archetypes. Eve Troutt Powell has examined the nationalistic "othering" of the Sudanese and Nubians in the Egyptian media. Beth Baron has described the changing personification of Egypt as a woman in Egyptian public monuments and the Egyptian illustrated press. Samah Selim and Michael Ezekiel Gasper have examined the urban intelligentsia's representations of the Egyptian fellahin (peasantry) in novels and the press and the role that these played in the creation of national identity.[5]

The most wide ranging study on early Egyptian nationalism is Israel Gershoni and James P. Jankowski's *Egypt, Islam, and the Arabs: The Search for Egyptian Nationhood, 1900–1930* (1986). The book's major contribution to the field is its use of new sources and its excellent discussion of the formulation of Egyptian national identity. Gershoni and Jankowski's study, however, neglects several issues that need to be addressed. For instance, despite the title of their work, most of their scholarship examines Egyptian nationalism from the post–World War I era. The critical period from the 1870s, when the nationalist press began to take shape, to 1914 is discussed only in their introduction and is rarely mentioned throughout the remainder of their study. A more comprehensive understanding of the genesis and growth of Egyptian nationalism, however, must begin with an analysis of this "period of preparation," as it is appropriately called by Jamal Mohammed Ahmed.[6] In addition, *Egypt, Islam, and the Arabs* focuses mainly on elite and intellectual-centered conceptions of nationalism, overlooking the important role of colloquial mass culture. Indeed, Gershoni and Jankowski themselves admit in the preface that their book "does not deal with the popular attitudes and opinions of the uneducated Egyptian masses."[7] The relationship and effects of popular culture and mass politics on the development of early Egyptian nationalism remain largely uncharted.[8]

## POPULAR CULTURE AND COLLOQUIAL EGYPTIAN

Here and elsewhere in this book I try to historicize and see beyond this currency, straining for a concept that can preserve culture's differentiating functions while conceiving of collective identity as a hybrid, often discontinuous inventive process. Culture is a deeply compromised idea I cannot yet do without.

—James Clifford, *The Predicament of Culture*

Anthropologists have long debated (and are still debating) the meaning and importance of culture. However, as Lila Abu-Lughod has argued, the concept of culture is often reified and essentialized as timeless, homogeneous, and perpetually coherent.[9] Consequently, I find James Clifford's ideas about culture to be especially constructive. Cultures are limited, time-specific constructs that are learned and constantly in a state of flux. In fact, in this book I document many changes in the Egyptian cultural landscape—changes that accelerated as a result of the introduction of new forms of mass communication at the end of the nineteenth century. Indeed, Egyptian mass culture at the turn of the twentieth century was persistently changing, adapting, and subverting.[10]

No consensus exists on the definition of "popular culture." In his classic work *Popular Culture in Early Modern Europe*, Peter Burke argues that popular culture is "perhaps best defined initially in a negative way as unofficial culture, the culture of the non-elite, the 'subordinate classes' as Gramsci called them."[11] This preliminary definition provided by Burke does not serve our purpose, because in Egypt at least, "popular culture," especially in its mass-produced form, was often consumed by "elite" and nonelite alike.[12] More recently, scholars have been advocating more expansive definitions. Harold Hinds, for instance, describes popular culture as "those aspects of culture, whether ideological, social, or material, which are widely spread and believed in and/or consumed by significant numbers of people, i.e., those aspects which are popular."[13] Or as Gary Fine succinctly put it, popularity is the sine qua non of popular culture.[14] Therefore, for the purpose of this study, I adopt these more wide-ranging definitions of popular culture, allowing for the inclusion of all disseminated cultural productions that directly or indirectly target the widest audience possible, regardless of literacy level or socioeconomic background. In other words, to be considered part of popular or mass culture, a cultural product must be accessible to all, which in Egypt requires it to be articulated in colloquial Egyptian Arabic.[15]

Late nineteenth- to early twentieth-century Egypt witnessed the unprecedented growth of an assortment of mass-mediated popular culture productions, and this growth coincided with the rise of modern Egyptian identification with the nation. Hundreds of periodicals and books were published; new theatrical plays and thousands of new songs were performed to increasingly larger and more politically discerning audiences. Most of these new productions were created in Cairo, enhancing the capital's political and cultural control and contributing to the formation of an increasingly homogeneous Egyptian national culture that eventually reached the national periphery. The Cairene, and to a lesser extent the Alexandrian, base of this new mass culture gave national dominance not only to Cairo's urban culture but also to Cairo's Egyptian dialect, effectively making Cairene colloquial Arabic the "unofficial" spoken language of Egypt.

Indeed, the colloquial language used in the thousands of new Egyptian songs, theatrical plays, and satirical periodicals was exclusively Cairene, transforming it into the de facto Egyptian dialect and provoking the gradual decline of other provincial dialects. Despite the importance of mass culture and the vital role of colloquial Egyptian as its primary linguistic vehicle, only recently have scholars begun to pay attention to the cultural and historical significance of vernacular Egyptian culture, especially *azjal* (colloquial poetry). Kamal Abdel-Malek and Marilyn Booth examine the written colloquial prose of Ahmad Fu'ad Nijm and Bayram al-Tunsi, two of Egypt's most important twentieth-century colloquial poets. Walter Armbrust analyzes the "split vernacular" between colloquial and Fusha (Modern Standard Arabic) and discusses the impact of modern colloquial Egyptian cultural production, especially film. Niloofar Haeri offers an important analysis of colloquial Egyptian culture in modern Egypt, examining the sociopolitical ramifications of the split between Fusha and *'ammiyya* (colloquial Arabic) cultures. Eve Troutt Powell has examined the racial and nationalist implications of the colloquial comedic theater of 'Ali al-Kassar; Beth Baron, Lisa Pollard, and most recently Michael Ezekial Gasper have made use of the colloquial Egyptian press.[16] Through their pioneering analyses of colloquial Egyptian sources, these scholars have begun the process of incorporating more voices into the historical narrative. Accordingly, in this book I hope to expand on these recent efforts by examining late nineteenth- to early twentieth-century Egyptian history almost entirely through a colloquial Egyptian popular culture lens.

## EGYPTIAN IDENTITY BETWEEN FUSHA AND 'AMMIYYA

Popular Culture has been linguistically important in Egypt because it has historically been a qualitatively different vehicle for establishing national identity than official discourse.                    —Walter Armbrust, *Mass Culture and Modernism in Egypt*

In all Arab countries today, there are unresolved linguistic tensions between everyday spoken colloquial variations of Arabic and Fusha, or Modern Standard Arabic (MSA), which is the predominant language of written discourse. According to the linguist Clive Holes, MSA is an imprecise term used by linguists to denote modern written Arabic "from about the middle of the nineteenth century, when concerted efforts began to modernize it lexically and phraseologically."[17] Holes elaborates that MSA is "the modern descendant of Classical Arabic, unchanged in the essentials of its syntax but very much changed, and still changing, in its vocabulary and phraseology."[18] In the Arab world both MSA and Classical Arabic are simply identified as *al-'arabiyya al-fusha* (the clear/ eloquent Arabic), or just *fusha* for short. Colloquial Arabic is referred to as *al-lugha al-'ammiyya* (the common people's language) or *al-lugha al-darija* (the widespread/popular language). The intrinsic definitional hierarchy differentiating Fusha and *'ammiyya* is quite clear: Fusha is reified as a clear (pure) and eloquent language with a Qur'anic and classical pedigree, whereas *'ammiyya* is regarded as the common language of the masses and everyday life.[19] This Bourdieuian hierarchy between a "high" and "low" language or dialect is very much as alive today as it was at the turn of the twentieth century.

In Egypt today, Egyptian Arabic is the predominant language of daily communication, songs, jokes, cartoons, movies, television serials, and most other audiovisual and sound media. Fusha is more formalized and is largely the domain of the vast majority of print media, newspapers, school textbooks, official speeches, and television news broadcasts. This linguistic equation, however, was drawn slightly differently in Egypt at the turn of the twentieth century. For instance, although by the end of the twentieth century no "purely" colloquial periodicals were in print, from the 1870s to the early 1940s newspapers and magazines using a significant amount of colloquial material were quite common (see Chapters 4–6).[20] Charles Ferguson described this linguistic division in the Arabic-speaking world as diglossic, with a clearly defined, rigid distinction between Fusha and *'ammiyya.*[21] However, linguists have since shifted away from explaining this phenomenon as diglossia, emphasizing that this "split" in the language is not rigidly fixed but flexibly defined along a linguistic continuum, with *'ammiyya* and Fusha continually "bleeding" into each other. Depending on the context, some Fusha words can be used in everyday speech just as varying degrees of colloquialisms are often incorporated in printed Modern Standard Arabic.[22] In more formalized settings—for example, an interview—educated individuals may inject Fusha vocabulary into their speech, although they rarely incorporate Fusha grammatical constructions. Speaking on the current linguistic situation, Clive Holes elaborates that because of the "enormous economic and demographic changes that have occurred in the Arab world in the last two to three decades," linguistic borrowing and hybridization between Fusha and *'ammiyya* is increasing.[23] Thus, in part because of satellite television, the Internet, and increased transnational migration and travel and, more important perhaps, because of dramatic increases in levels of literacy and education, this linguistic hybridization of Fusha words into *'ammiyya* speech is much stronger today than it was just a century ago.[24] In 1917, for example, only 6.8% of the Egyptian population was literate, and hence knowledge of Fusha vocabulary and construction was limited, allowing only a small percentage of the population the capacity to effortlessly code-switch any significant Fusha vocabulary in everyday *'ammiyya* speech.[25] For the most part, even this small literate percentage of the population communicated in almost all their daily interaction in various forms of colloquial Egyptian. Although respected and revered by Egyptian Muslims as the linguistic heir to the language of the Qur'an, Fusha is not a spoken language, and as such it is severely limited in expressing everyday conversational discourse. This reality was bluntly, though accurately, expressed by the linguist T. F. Mitchell.

MSA is not a *spoken* language; it is nobody's mother-tongue, and the man who wants to talk at all times like a book or newspaper is a decided oddity. Many, perhaps most of the purposes of speech, including notably the familial, homely, and casual, are served for the people of a particular Arab country by their own regional vernacular or "colloquial" Arabic and, in the important case of Egypt, the colloquial usage of the cultured classes of the capital city provides spoken norms for the whole country.[26]

Indeed, because of its lack of use in everyday normal conversation, Fusha alone is incapable of accurately conveying the ordinary nuances and color of daily Egyptian interactions: It would be almost unimaginable for anyone to successfully communicate a joke to an Egyptian audience using Fusha. The only laughter this experiment would produce would be the audience snickering at the futility of the attempt.[27] Only colloquial Egyptian possesses the linguistic flexibility and the tools necessary to articulate wit and humor to all Egyptians regardless of education or class. This was the primary reason for the popularity and political effectiveness of the comedic theater, recorded popular music, and the satirical press at the turn of the twentieth century and the continuing need for an outlet for colloquial Egyptian culture today. As Mikhail Bakhtin has shown, the vernacular is "the language of life, of material work and mores, of the 'lowly,' mostly humorous genres (*fabliaux, cris de Paris,* farces), the free speech of the marketplace."[28]

Appropriately, I draw on Bakhtin's theories on popular culture and the sociopolitical function of humor, which was ever present in the satirical press and the Egyptian vaudeville theater. In late nineteenth- to early twentieth-century Egypt, laughter and satire played an important counter-hegemonic role. As Bakhtin effectively demonstrated in his work on Rabelais, "Not only does laughter make no exception for the upper stratum, but indeed it is usually directed toward it. Furthermore, it is directed not at one part only, but at the whole. One might say that it builds its own world versus the official world, its own church versus the official church, its own state versus the official state."[29] As I argue in this book, the rich satirical material that filled these cultural productions created virtual carnivalesque spaces, providing an egalitarian tool of subversion that was regularly and effectively used by the rising middle and working classes to participate in and consequently modify official discourses and practices.[30]

However, despite the popularity of the colloquial press at the turn of the twentieth century, publishing colloquial Egyptian texts in any forum was always a controversial proposition. The idealism surrounding Fusha as the perceived direct descendant of the language of the Qur'an made it extremely difficult to print colloquial Egyptian without incurring the wrath of cultural and religious traditionalists. The use of colloquial Arabic (especially in the written form) was and still is deemed by most as a direct assault on Arab and Islamic culture. Many distinguished Egyptian intellectuals, including Muhammad 'Abduh, Taha Husayn, and Najib Mahfuz, who by most definitions are considered modernists, vigorously attacked the use of colloquial Egyptian in any written discourse.[31] And yet, only colloquial cultural and communicative forms can effortlessly straddle both oral and written culture and consequently are equally appealing to the literate and illiterate. Even Azhari sheikhs, who theoretically at least have mastered Fusha like no other segment of Egyptian society, speak colloquial Egyptian in their daily interactions.[32] Accordingly, despite the relatively high prestige of Fusha, the Egyptian masses are/were typically not moved or affected in their day-to-day lives by the iconic and well-respected writings of Taha Husayn and Lutfi al-Sayyid or the high poetry of Ahmad Shawqi. On the other hand, the colloquial newspapers of Muhammad Tawfiq and Ya'qub Sannu', the songs of Munira al-Mahdiyya and Sayyid Darwish, the *azjal* of Badi' Khayri and Bayram al-Tunsi, or the comedic plays of Najib al-Rihani and 'Ali al-Kassar were comprehensible and culturally accessible to all Egyptians, regardless of class or education. In other words, to fully grasp the growth of national identity in Egypt, we cannot solely rely on the official Fusha discourses of the state and the intellectual elite.

## LINGUISTIC REGIONALISM AND THE
## DOMINANCE OF THE CAIRENE DIALECT

All nations possess multiple colloquial dialects that reflect regional pronunciation differences. Egypt is no exception, with several different, though mutually understandable, regional dialects. According to linguists, the two most divergent Egyptian Arabic dialect groups are the Northern, or Delta, dialects (from Cairo northward) and the Southern, or Nile Valley, dialects (from Giza southward). The Arabic letter *qaaf*, for instance, is pronounced as a hard *g* (as in *get*) in upper Egyptian and as a hamza (or glottal stop) in Cairene Arabic. The letter *jim* is pronounced as a hard *g* in Lower Egypt and as a *j* (as in *jet*) in Upper Egypt.[33]

Partly because of the prevalence of advanced transportation and communication technologies and a growing national education system, these dialects are less widespread today than they were in the nineteenth century. Since the 1870s, almost all the printed colloquial texts appearing in newspapers in the form of *azjal*, comedic dialogues, and cartoons were in the colloquial Cairene dialect. The colloquial dialogues and the colloquial cartoons of the Egyptian press often represented the urbanite and "intelligent" *bint* or *ibn al-balad* (daughter or son of the country) character as always speaking fluent Cairene Egyptian.[34] This predisposition to use only the Cairene Egyptian dialect did not stop with print but continued with all other performed cultural productions. In mass-produced songs and theatrical plays at the turn of the twentieth century, it was colloquial Cairene that was represented as the mainstream dialect of all Egyptians. By the start of the twentieth century, most purported representations of the "typical Egyptian" dialect were written, recorded, or performed in the Lower Egyptian Cairene dialect.

Facilitating the hegemony of the Cairene dialect, and, more important, Cairene culture, was the systematic representation of what I would call the internal "other." Upper Egyptian Sa'idi characters, with exaggerated Southern dialects, were often portrayed as dimwitted and backward and were usually contrasted with a "normal" Lower Egyptian–speaking urbanite. This can still be observed in most jokes circulating in northern Egypt, which often portray Upper Egyptians as unintelligent, hardheaded, and culturally inferior. When Sa'idi jokes are "performed," the Upper Egyptian accent is mimicked for added humor and contrasted with the "normal" Egyptian accent of a Cairene. In most Egyptian films and television miniseries today, the negative portrayal of Sa'ayyda (pl.) continues. Thus in the popular imagination the Sa'idi's accent was and is still associated with backward feeblemindedness, whereas the Cairene accent is portrayed as conventionally "Egyptian" and is often linked with positive or, at the least, neutral qualities.[35]

For example, in *al-Kashkul al-Mussawwar* (The illustrated notebook), a 1920s satirical periodical, the Southern Sa'idi dialect was always cast in a negative light.[36] A January 2, 1925, colloquial Egyptian sketch depicting an Egyptian parliamentary session features two members of the Egyptian parliament: a witty Ni'man Bey al-'A'sar speaking in a fluent Cairene dialect and his colleague Doctor al-Dab' from the south of Egypt speaking with a heavy Sa'idi accent. The two parliamentary colleagues start a friendly conversation about the proper uses of classical Arabic, which turns into a heated argument.

NI'MAN BEY AL-'A'SAR (in colloquial Cairene Arabic): And you, what do you know about classical Arabic . . . oh you people from the Sa'id [*Ya btu' al-Sa'id*]. Classical Arabic belongs more to us and came to us from the land of the Arabs [*bilad al-'Arab*] through the Suez road as far as the island of Roda [southwest of Cairo]. . . . If your uncle Rashid Rida didn't come this way to Cairo to "smell the smell" of classical Arabic [*sham rihtu*], then he wouldn't be able to write the few words that he fills *al-Manar* with.[37]

DOCTOR AL-DAB' (in a heavy Sa'idi accent): All the Arab tribes are in the Sa'id, not in Buhayra [in the Delta]. What do you think the tribe of Guhayna is? Aren't they Arab, or you don't read about history?

NI'MAN BEY AL-'A'SAR: What is this history that you want me to read? The situation does not require history or any such rubbish [*hiyya al-'ibara 'ayza tarikh wala hibab* (soot)]. Here are my words and here are your words. You understand me and I don't understand a word you are saying. Who then is speaking Arabic, and who is speaking *barbari* [Nubian]?[38]

Another colloquial sketch satirized the anachronistic incomprehensibility of elevated Fusha to the average Egyptian. In a similar fictionalized parliamentary session, to the horror of all who were present, the erudite Wahid Bey al-'Ayubi addressed the other parliamentary members in exaggeratedly antiquated Fusha, despite the fact that some of those present urged him to "speak in the normal colloquial that we speak every day." Nevertheless, al-'Ayubi continued to speak in Fusha as the puzzled parliamentary members misunderstood most of his speech and continually interrupted him with questions and requests for clarification. In the middle of the speech, a parliamentary member whispers in low colloquial Egyptian: "Is he done speaking? Please [*wa hayat waldak*] Amin Bey, translate for me what he just said because I didn't understand a word."[39] Al-'Ayubi continues with his speech and is again interrupted by Amin Bey Wassif, who shouts sarcastically: "Bravo Wahid Bey, but I have a small suggestion. Could you please do us a favor [*i'mil ma'ruf*] and write for us a small pocket dictionary with some of the words and expressions that you used tonight, so we can consult it and understand your beautiful [-sounding] words?"[40]

In Egyptian mass media, only the Cairene dialect was portrayed as understandable to all Egyptians and hence familiar and "normal." Speaking in Fusha was and still is portrayed as not only haughty but also incomprehensibly distant from everyday Egyptian life. The Sa'idi dialect, on the other hand, was not only marginalized but also deemed alien and was "insultingly" classified as "Nubian." Thus, according to the discourse of Egypt's new vernacular mass culture, the primary prerequisite of Egyptian identity or Egyptianness was/is speaking flawless Cairene Egyptian Arabic.

The creation of internal "others" is in no way unique to Egypt but is common in other national contexts. Still today in Italy the less developed south is depicted with the same denigration as the Egyptian Sa'id, and in the United States, the American South is viewed as backward by many northerners.[41] This political regionalism creates what Antonio Gramsci labels the Southern Question, which according to Gramsci can be necessary in the establishment of nation-state hegemony. Gramsci argues that the northern ruling class and the southern landowners conspire by playing off the "modern" northern worker against the backward southern farmer, in the process distracting the workers from class conflict.[42] However, whether such a deliberate conspiracy between northern and southern elites existed is not as important as the fact that the existence of a Southern Question facilitated the hegemony of a Cairene-based national culture. Unlike Fusha, the spread of colloquial Cairene Arabic as the "unofficial" national colloquial dialect was not necessarily supported or pushed by the state or the ruling elite but was a natural by-product of the overwhelming cultural production emanating from an ever-expanding and increasingly urban north—imposing its culture and dialect on the rest of the nation.[43] In fact, as we will see here and in later chapters, some of the Egyptian cultural and religious elite were staunchly against many forms of popular colloquial media. It appears that in the Egyptian case, no state institutions supported the "hegemony" of Cairene colloquial

Egyptian culture. Rather, it was the developing popular culture market, propagated and supported through the successive introduction of new forms of mass media, and the incessant demand for colloquial cultural expressions, that drove this Cairene-based cultural hegemony.

## THEORIES OF NATIONALISM AND THE EGYPTIAN CASE

Intellectual debates over nationalism abound, with many varying and sometimes conflicting explanations about the origins of national identity. Three major theoretical positions attempt to explain nationalism. The primordialists view nationalism as a natural (i.e., quasi-biological) and direct continuation of a shared historical and cultural identity rooted in the deep past.[44] The perennialists agree with the primordialists on the foundational antiquity of nations, although in their view nations are not "natural" but are a by-product of social organization.[45] And last, there are the modernists, who regard nationalism as an invented or imagined by-product of modernism.

Overall, the modernists provide the most convincing argument. When examining the Egyptian case, it is apparent that, indeed, territorial nationalism would not have materialized without modernist institutions and transportation and communication technologies (see Chapter 2). The modernists, however, also differ greatly in their approaches, emphasizing different dynamics and catalysts in their accounts of nationalism. For instance, John Breuilly and Paul Brass emphasize the political transformations of the modern state; neo-Marxists such as Michael Hechter and Tom Nairn stress the importance of economics; and Benedict Anderson and Ernest Gellner highlight the role of culture.[46]

Of the modernist theories of nationalism, the culturist approach is the most productive, primarily because the role of culture and especially language is often (although not always) central to the creation of national identities. Although I adopt the culturist approach of Anderson and Gellner, some of their "universalist" assumptions about nationalism simply do not fit when applied to Egypt. The primary reason for this incompatibility between theory and practice is an overreliance on Western Europe and the Americas as the exemplary model for their theorizing about nationalism. As Partha Chatterjee has eloquently stated, "If nationalisms in the rest of the world have to choose their imagined community from certain 'modular' forms already made available to them by Europe and the Americas, what do they have left to imagine?"[47] Through examining the particulars of the Egyptian case, I challenge some of these universalist assumptions while expanding on the works of Gellner and especially Anderson.

In examining the particularities of the Egyptian case, I find several incongruities and contradictions in both Gellner's and Anderson's theories. An important component of Anderson's theory is an emphasis on the vernacularization of the liturgical language, which, with the help of print technology and mass education, is transformed into the unifying secular language of the nation. According to Anderson, the demotion of Latin in favor of the various European vernaculars "exemplified a larger process in which the sacred communities integrated by old sacred languages were gradually fragmented, pluralized, and territorialized." This shift from sacred language to profane vernacular(s) was indispensable to the development of territorial nationalism, and "print capitalism" was the primary catalyst for this transformation.[48] As discussed earlier, however, this "larger process" has not occurred in the same way in the Arab world, where the "sacred language"—albeit in its modern standard form—still officially reigns supreme as the written language of most Arab intellectuals and is the predominant language of most print culture today.[49] As Niloofar Haeri has noted, Fusha "continues to separate the sacred from the profane, writing from speaking, and prescribed religious rituals from personal communication with God."[50]

If Anderson is correct about the necessity of vernacularizing and hence secularizing the liturgical language—and print media in the Arab world is predominantly in Fusha—then how could territorial nationalism exist in Egypt or for that matter anywhere in the Arab world? To answer this question, one simply needs to look elsewhere. Instead of just focusing on the Fusha texts of novels, newspapers, and other print media, we must also examine the nonprint, mostly colloquial Egyptian domain of audio, audiovisual, and performance media. There one finds the secular, universally understood, vernacular cultural expressions of which the theorists of nationalism speak, amply providing the "necessary shared medium" required for territorial nationalism to grow.[51]

This ongoing tension between Fusha and *'ammiyya*, however, creates another unresolved dilemma: With two effectively coexisting languages and hence two cultures, the dynamics of identity in modern Egypt, and by extension the Arab world, share an ongoing duality. At the least, this perceived duality makes it difficult to fit the Egyptian case within the universalizing framework of Anderson's or Gellner's theories. For instance, Gellner states that for nationalism to emerge in a given society, it must be within the same shared culture, and "moreover, it must now be a great or high (literate, training-sustained) culture."[52] The Egyptian case, as I will detail in this study, challenges this assumption. Aside from the duality of Egyptian cultural expressions, the predominant Egyptian national culture is/was not "high," "literate," or "training-sustained." It is colloquial Egyptian culture that played the predominant role of supplying a distinctly Egyptian middle-class culture that is relationally different from and more directly relevant to the average Egyptian than high culture, which was exclusively expressed in Fusha. Thus, in the Egyptian case at least, it was not a high culture but what I would label a middle culture, which is expressed in colloquial Egyptian and disseminated mainly by audio and audiovisual mass media, that provided what Gellner calls the "necessary shared medium" where all could "breathe, speak and produce."[53]

This does not mean that Fusha texts were unimportant; in fact, the overwhelming majority of academic and intellectual discussions about Egyptian nationalism and most other pertinent political and economic issues in Egypt were written and printed in Fusha. And it is a dead certainty that these Fusha discourses and the discussions arising from them heavily influenced the political content of most colloquial mass media. However, because during the period under study the overwhelming majority of Egyptians were illiterate, it was practically impossible for the Egyptian masses to directly gain access to these Fusha discourses. Thus for most Egyptians their exposure to nationalist ideas and rhetoric was primarily acquired through colloquial mass culture and especially through performance and audiovisual and sound media.

### BEYOND "READING":
### ACCOUNTING FOR HEARING AND SPEECH

The modern sensorium remains more intricate and uneven, its perceptual disciplines and experiential modes more diffuse and heterogeneous, than the discourses of Western visuality and ocularcentrism allow. —Leigh Eric Schmidt, *Hearing Things*

Benedict Anderson's framing of print culture and print capitalism as the primary factor in creating the "possibility of a new form of imagined community" also does not fully apply to the Egyptian case.[54] Not only does Anderson's overemphasis on print ignore the relationship between the written and spoken word—especially in turn-of-the-twentieth-century Egypt, where texts were often read aloud—but, as we will examine later, it also misses the disseminating efficacy of performance and audiovisual and sound media, which unlike print media have the instant advantage of more directly reaching illiterate and semiliterate people.[55] As Tim Edensor has noted, Anderson's analysis "remains rooted in a historical perspective which reifies the sources (literature) through which the nation is (re)produced and thereby reduces the rich complexity of cultural production to one field."[56]

Moreover, Anderson's representation of the mechanics of reading in *Imagined Communities* is implicitly colored by a modernist ocular-centric framework. Ocularcentrism, as popularized by Walter Ong and Marshall McLuhan's "great divide" theory, reifies sight and visualism at the apex of a sensory hierarchy, explaining what they deem as the detached, objective "superiority" of Western modernity, while contrasting this to more "primitive" oral and illiterate cultures.[57] Recently, however, many scholars from a variety of disciplines have convincingly challenged these binary ocularcentric views, for example, Alain Corbin, Leigh Eric Schmidt, Mark M. Smith, and Charles Hirschkind, to name a few.[58] Indeed, when humanists and social scientists have closely examined diverse early modern and modern societies, they discover that "hearing and sound remained critical to the elaboration of modernity." As Mark Smith explains in his most recent work on sensory history, "Virtually all the evidence produced by the historians of aurality and hearing of the modern era points to the continued importance of hearing and, implicitly at least, heavily discounts the effect print had on diluting aurality in favor of sight."[59]

In *Imagined Communities*, however, Anderson focuses almost exclusively on reading and print; the type of reading he depicts is private, meditative, and unequivocally ocular, or as he describes it, "performed in silent privacy, in the lair of the skull."[60] As Peter Wogan elegantly explains, "Anderson paints a ghostly picture of silent, atomistically isolated readers who come to recognize national bonds through purely visual experiences, i.e. imagining ('image-ing') the nation by perceiving juxtaposed images on a single newspaper page or within the flaps of a book."[61] This entirely visual and cerebrally meditative depiction of the act of reading does not reflect the complexity of the reading process in most, if not all, cultures. Reading is not always a silent and private experience, as described in *Imagined Communities*. Newspapers are often read in public places in full view of passersby, and as I discuss in Chapter 2, in Egypt at the turn of the twentieth century, it was common for the latest news to be read aloud in crowded cafés.[62] If the news was not directly read aloud, current events printed in the newspapers were certainly discussed and debated in the public sphere. Yet in Anderson's devocalized imagined communities, there is no place for the spoken word.

Dismissing orality and direct social interactions ignores a critical component of the digestion and integration of news, rumors, gossip, and culture. Indeed, engaging in or merely listening to or observing a conversation or a performance in the urban public sphere creates real and physically embodied (unimagined) communal identities, informing and structuring perhaps the grander, more idealized imagined communities described by Anderson. In other words, our very understanding of what we read, and whatever we may "imagine" because of it, is largely grounded on our own lived experiences. Thus print is important, yet we must not ignore that it is often digested in a living (embodied) communal context and hence is very much enmeshed within a framework of orality. Human beings are not automata, silent, visual producers and consumers of print; they consume, synthesize, share, and propagate the printed information orally and communally.[63]

## MEDIA CAPITALISM: ENGAGING THE SENSORIUM

The other main development in the West that serves not only to illustrate the importance of sound and hearing under modernity but, in fact, suggests the increasing instability of the eye at the end of the nineteenth and early decades of the twentieth centuries concerns recorded sound.                    —Mark M. Smith, *Sensing the Past*

The introduction of sound-recording technologies and audiovisual media further complicate Anderson's print-centric thesis. Sound and audiovisual media, musical and theatrical performances, and later on radio, film, television, and the Internet, like the novels and newspapers described by Anderson, can also provide the "technical means for 're-presenting' the kind of imagined community that is the nation."[64] Yet they are nowhere to be seen in Anderson's thesis and do not fit his print capitalism model. For this reason, I believe that the term *media capitalism* is more appropriate for examining the cultural processes taking place; it is wide enough to incorporate all forms of mass media, including print, performance, recording, and broadcast media, and allows everyone, regardless of class, education, or literacy level, to aurally and visually participate in the nationalist project. Media capitalism broadens the scope of Anderson's print capitalism not only by including other forms of media in addition to print but also by making room for the aural and oral alongside the visual and, in the process, providing a more comprehensive explanation for how individuals and communities process cultural information. In other words, by allowing performance and sound media into the equation along with print, both the eye and the ear can participate in those nationalist imaginings. By accommodating the ongoing technological complexity of culture, media capitalism allows for, among other things, the incorporation of printed texts, sounds, moving and still pictures, music, and the recorded (or live) human voice within its framework (see Figure 1).

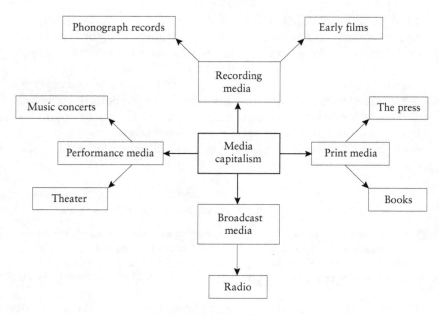

FIGURE I. *Media capitalism in Egypt.*

Like print capitalism, media capitalism describes the commodification of mass media, including print, and their function as a part of a media market. Indeed, as examined in later chapters, the demand for colloquial Egyptian cultural expressions drove the record companies and the theater troupes to fill this almost limitless market, largely at the expense of the Fusha media championed by many in the intelligentsia. Certainly in the Egyptian case, and I suspect in other cases as well, a synergetic combination of all available media, from print to sound recordings, simultaneously helped to shape the "modern" identities of cultural consumers. It is important to reemphasize that all the media forms, including print, functioned as an integrated "media system" competing, echoing, and supplementing each other.[65] By relying mainly on colloquial Egyptian, these media had a tremendous influence on public opinion. The increasing availability in Egypt of audio and audiovisual transmission media, such as the theater and a profit-motivated music industry, contributed more to the molding of national tastes and the creation of a national culture than just print media alone.

Music and the recording industry played a vital role in the formation of this new Egyptian middle culture. By the 1910s, record sales were increasing, as mass-scale manufacturing of phonographs and discs made them cheaper and more accessible to a greater number of Egyptians (see

Chapter 4). Most of these records featured colloquial Egyptian songs, which aided their popularity and accessibility. The speed with which some of these songs turned into national hits was unprecedented. Indeed, this was only the beginning of a growing and constantly changing repertoire of Egyptian songs—a sort of national anthology of songs heard and, more important, sung by most Egyptians.

This would not have been possible without the recording industry, which emerged in 1904, making recording media at least as important as print media in transforming the way Egyptians perceived their identity. More important, with the transformation of songs into a mass medium, discourse and practice often converged, in the sense that unlike novels, newspapers, and other forms of written discourse, listeners often participated in the experience of discourse dissemination by the simple act of singing along. Although periodicals, especially colloquial satirical newspapers, were often read out loud in coffee shops—dramatically increasing their reach—songs were directly consumed by their listeners without intermediaries or translators. In addition, because of simple melodies and lyrics, literate and illiterate alike could easily memorize and redisseminate songs, reaching a potentially much larger audience.

To be sure, most of the people who worked on the front line of the Egyptian entertainment industry were literate, and the writers of these songs, *azjal*, and plays were certainly exposed to and influenced the discourses emanating from the nationalist intelligentsia. At the same time, the form, content, and language of most vernacular media were inspired by, and to a large extent reflected, the concerns and the diversity of everyday Egyptian life. The demand from below was for media products that were entertaining, accessible, socially relevant, and culturally and linguistically comprehensible. Indeed, the economic success of these media depended to a large degree on their accessibility and relevance to the greatest number of consumers possible. With illiteracy rates near 93% (in 1917), the market potential and hence ideological reach of recording and performance media were exponentially greater than any print media.[66] This does not mean that print was not important, just that audio and audiovisual media had a more direct reach to a greater number of potential consumers.

Before continuing with the analysis of Egyptian popular culture, I must detail the building of Egypt's modern cultural infrastructure. In Chapter 2 I discuss the formation of a "modern" centralized Egyptian state and the effects that such political and economic changes had on Egyptian cultural transformation. The impact of the printing press, the subsequent explo-

sion of newspapers, the increasing utilization of the expanding railroad
network, and the introduction of modern centralizing state institutions,
from a national post office to a standardized educational system, are analyzed. The effects of these new technologies and national institutions were
enormous, as they utterly transformed the Egyptian sociocultural and
political landscape, allowing for new forms of collective identity.

In Chapter 3 I cover the beginnings of mass culture in Egypt, from the
pioneering plays of Ya'qub Sannu' (1839–1912) in the early 1870s to
the 'Urabi revolt a decade later. The chapter traces the precedent-setting
newspapers, plays, and *azjal* of Sannu', 'Uthman Jalal (1828–1898), and
'Abdallah Nadim (1845–1898), who simultaneously dabbled in several
colloquial Egyptian media. The groundbreaking work of these three men
left a noticeable imprint on the next generation of writers, cartoonists,
and playwrights. Near the end of Chapter 3, I demonstrate how these
early colloquial media had an important impact on mobilizing the masses
during the 'Urabi revolt.

In Chapter 4 I investigate the growth and effects of the Egyptian mass
media from the beginning of the British occupation in 1882 until the
aftermath of the 1906 Dinshaway incident. I examine the satirical press,
the developing Egyptian theater, and the increasing popularity of the phonograph and its effects on the commercialization of colloquial Egyptian
music. In the middle of the chapter I focus on the counterhegemonic elements of the colloquial press and the resulting "vulgarization" and repression of the satirical press by the British and the Egyptian elite. The
Egyptian political, religious, and cultural elite were particularly threatened by the mass appeal of colloquial cultural production and repeatedly
attacked it as morally inferior to Fusha elite culture. Finally, I historicize
the impact of Egyptian mass culture by revisiting the Dinshaway incident
exclusively through the lens of mass culture.

Chapter 5 begins with an examination of the explosion of urban mass
politics from 1907 until the beginning of World War I. I then analyze the
war period strictly from a mass culture perspective. Vaudeville plays and
recorded colloquial songs, which became extremely popular during this
period, expressed the Egyptian street's frustrations with the economic and
political hardships caused by the war. The growth of these media industries was instrumental in the creation of an increasingly homogeneous
Egyptian mass culture, which had unprecedented power over the street.

The focus of Chapter 6 is the street politics of the 1919 Revolution,
and I cover as much as possible the lives of ordinary Egyptians who acted
en masse during the spring of 1919. Accordingly, Egypt's streets and, by
extension, its many public squares, cafés, bars, theaters, mosques, and
churches served as centers of most of the events covered in this chapter. I

also examine the role of illicit publications and circulars on the Egyptian streets, especially in light of the tight censorship of the officially recognized press by the British and the palace. Finally, I scrutinize the almost instantaneous celebrations and depictions of the revolution in theater and in song and the role that these mass media played in the actual revolution and, more important, in shaping its memory in the Egyptian national imagination.

Overall, in this book I trace how Egyptians resisted elite and then British domination from the 1870s until the eve of the 1919 Revolution by analyzing the often hidden transcripts of newspapers, recorded songs, jokes, satire, vernacular poetry, and plays. Not only were these varied media extremely entertaining—explaining their popularity and commercial success—but they also offered a highly accessible creative outlet for national discussions and even sociopolitical resistance. As I argue throughout this book, the developing mass media facilitated a sense of collective camaraderie, which was an instrumental component in the development of a national imagined community. The steady homogenizing influence of a de facto national media, speaking in a language that all Egyptians could understand, was/is the most important factor in the construction, maintenance, and mobilization of an Egyptian national identity. Through shifting the scholarly focus from the abstract discourses of the elite intellectuals to wider and more expansive social "ideas" and "practices," I hope to more fully account for the politicization of the growing literate middle classes and bring the semiliterate and illiterate urban masses more fully into the historical narrative.

## CHAPTER TWO

# Political Centralization to Cultural Centralization

> Changes in the media system also need to be related to changes in the transportation system, the movement of goods and people in space, whether by land or water (river, canal and sea). The communication of messages is, or at any rate was, part of the system of physical communication.
>
> —Asa Briggs and Peter Burke, *A Social History of the Media*

Late nineteenth- to early twentieth-century Egypt witnessed unprecedented infrastructural and institutional changes. The introduction of the printing press, with the subsequent explosion of newspapers, an expanding railroad network, and the building of modern centralizing state institutions, from a national post office to a standardized educational system, set the groundwork for a dramatic transformation of Egypt's economic, political, and cultural landscape.[1] The effects of these new political, economic, and cultural institutions played an important role in the gradual identification of more and more Egyptians with a sense of territorial national identity.

In this chapter I place Egyptian nationalism in its late nineteenth- and early twentieth-century geopolitical context. After a brief overview of early nineteenth-century state centralization, which provided the political and economic means for the construction of modern state institutions, I examine the sociocultural effects of these newly introduced transportation and communication technologies. Next I analyze the cultural and economic implications of Egypt's dramatic rise in urbanization, which was due in part to the demand for labor in the northern towns and cities and was facilitated by the growing network of rails and roads connecting the periphery to the urban centers. This increased connectivity was multidirectional, allowing for a continual national circulation of people, goods, and ideas from the center to the periphery and from the periphery back to the center. At the end of the chapter I discuss the development and the growing effects of urban-based colloquial Egyptian mass culture, which was a natural by-product of the mixing of peoples and cultures that was taking place mostly in the rapidly expanding northern urban centers. It was this circulating colloquial mass culture, incubated in Cairo and Alexandria, that was the primary catalyst for the eventual establishment of a widely accepted sense of Egyptian national identity.

## STATE CENTRALIZATION

The physical geography and topography of a nation has a substantial effect on the character and degree of socioeconomic and cultural centralization imposed by the capital on the "national" periphery. For instance, despite their relatively small size, nation-states with a mountainous terrain, such as Lebanon and Switzerland, have a natural resistance to state centralization, and thus their populations exhibit above-average cultural and religious heterogeneity. The topography of Egypt, on the other hand, with most of its inhabitants living in an easily accessible thin strip of land stretching from Aswan to the Mediterranean, has historically facilitated centralization efforts from the capital and simultaneously aided in the relative cultural homogenization of Lower Egyptian society. However, because of its distance from Cairo, its hilly terrain, and the periodic influx of tribal migrants from Arabia, the *Sa'id*, the southern half of Upper Egypt (from Asyut to Aswan), was usually beyond the direct reach of the capital and to some degree was more culturally distinct than the north.[2]

Before the nineteenth century, Egypt tended to shift cyclically from relatively short periods of strong governmental control from Cairo to longer periods of relative decentralization. Typically, when a strong political regime controlled Cairo, the strategic location of the capital at the mouth of the Nile Delta and the relatively easy navigation up and down the Nile aided in the administrative centralization of most of the country. Taxes were regularly collected, and with the surplus, basic agricultural projects, such as canals, were constructed or maintained.[3] Consistent with this cycle, 'Ali Bey al-Kabir (r. 1760–1766) took over Cairo in 1760, expelled the Ottoman governor from Egypt, centralized and took control of tax collection, and largely succeeded in subduing rebellious Mamluk factions. Perhaps more significantly for Cairo's ascendancy as the unrivaled power center in Egypt was 'Ali Bey's defeat of the Hawwara tribal confederation at Girga, which was until then a thriving cultural and economic center in Upper Egypt. This significant although rarely examined event paved the way for Cairo's political, economic, and, more important for our purposes, cultural ascendancy.[4] Long-lasting political centralization of Egyptian society, however, did not fully take place until a half century later with the reforms and political consolidations of Muhammad 'Ali (r. 1805–1848).[5]

In the first decade of his reign, Muhammad 'Ali forcefully consolidated his regime by controlling the *'ulama* (religious scholars), defeating the Mamluks, and bringing most of Upper Egypt under Cairo's sphere of influence. A strong and loyal military was vital to maintaining Muhammad 'Ali's grip on power, which made modernizing the army his first priority after securing his rule. To fund the military and other ambitious state projects, 'Ali set out to transform Egypt's agricultural production through the aggressive introduction of a variety of exportable cash crops. He expanded the infrastructural capacity of Egypt's ports and other transportation networks and executed significant public works projects to maximize Egyptian agricultural yields. To further boost the state coffers, 'Ali took control of all Egyptian farm production. This essentially meant that the government dictated to the peasants the type and quantity of crops to plant, directly bought the harvest at artificially low prices, and then sold the goods to Europe at market price.[6]

## The Expanding Bureaucracy

The changes wrought by the massive influx of revenues from this developing cash crop economy were significant. A modern conscript army was created by 1820 along with a growing military industrial complex, which included factories for guns, ammunition, and military uniforms, tanneries, and iron foundries. Hospitals, schools, and a host of modernizing social and bureaucratic institutions were constructed, planting the seeds, for better or worse, of a complete socioeconomic transformation of Egyptian society.[7] However, the military-industrial infrastructure and the agriculture monopoly set up by Muhammad 'Ali did not survive his reign. Although initially his new military machine defeated his Ottoman overlords and expanded Egyptian territory into greater Syria, the Hijaz, and southward into the Sudan, overexpansion and pressure by the European powers forced his signing of the London Treaty of 1840.[8] Egypt was forced to reduce its armed forces to 18,000 men, cede all its newly conquered territories except for the Sudan, and adopt the 1838 Anglo-Turkish Commercial Convention, which banned all monopolies in Ottoman territory. In one stroke Egypt lost its new military-dependent industrial complex and the state's agricultural monopoly.[9]

In return, however, Muhammad 'Ali was guaranteed the continuation of his dynastic line, with recognition of his family's hereditary rights to rule Egypt as Ottoman governors. Despite the blow given to his military, the smaller army of 18,000 troops proved more than adequate in preserving 'Ali's grip on power. His centralized bureaucracy remained intact and continued to maintain and expand national public works projects. This unprecedented centralization of political power in Egypt was secure enough to continue after the death of 'Ali in 1849. Aided by the introduction and expansion of new communication and transportation technologies, 'Ali's successors solidified the centralizing grip of Cairo on Egyptian society. During his reign, 'Ali had created fifteen separate centrally controlled administrative units, including departments for civil affairs, war, finances, public education, industry, and foreign affairs.[10] By Isma'il's reign (r. 1863–1879) the government had added departments of interior, religious endowments (Awqaf), public works, agriculture, justice, and railway (Maslahat al-Sika al-Hadid). These large governmental institutions and bureaucracies became a permanent fixture of the Egyptian geopolitical landscape, and with time they structurally knitted together a new culturally and economically centralized Egyptian society with Cairo at its center.

These rapid infrastructural changes, however, took a heavy political and financial toll. Isma'il especially was guilty of unchecked borrowing and was notorious for his spending on expensive infrastructural projects.[11] The cost for these projects, with the Suez Canal topping the list, along with Isma'il's personal extravagance, led to a skyrocketing foreign debt and the eventual bankruptcy of the Egyptian economy.[12] In 1876 these events brought about the direct control of Egyptian finances by the French and the British through the newly set up Caisse de la Dette (Debt Commission). This financial instability would lead to the 'Urabi revolt and subsequently to the 1882 British occupation (see Chapters 3 and 4).[13]

## Public Education and the 'Afandiyya Class

As with many other "modern" Egyptian institutions, Muhammad 'Ali founded the Ministry of Education and state schools to help meet the immediate demands of his military and the newly established administrative bureaucracies. He established the first system of public primary and secondary schools and opened more specialized technical schools for accounting, administration, and engineering. Initially some of 'Ali's advances in education were reversed by his immediate successors. 'Abbas (r. 1849–1854) closed many schools and cut back funding for state-sponsored public works projects. Sa'id (r. 1854–1863) also neglected public education, although he encouraged the growth of private foreign schools, which, for the time being, became the primary educational outlet for the children of the Egyptian elite.[14] In the mid-1860s public education expanded rapidly. The Ministry of Education was established, and dozens of public schools opened, including primary, secondary, and professional schools and colleges. Tens of thousands of new students entered the growing school system to feed the emerging governmental bureaucracies.[15]

Graduates of these schools would gradually fill the ranks of the ever important *'afandiyya* class. The *'afandiyya* were literate Egyptian urbanites who often wore *tarabish* (fezzes; sing. *tarbush*); they donned Western-style clothes and typically worked in the civil service and in "the free professions." As has been discussed elsewhere, the role that the *'afandiyya* played in the making of modern Egypt is significant.[16] For instance, most of the journalists, writers, playwrights, actors, singers, and songwriters discussed in this book belong to the *'afandiyya* class.

During the first decade of the British occupation, state educational spending declined, although over the long run the upsurge in the number of schools and students continued.[17] By 1915 the total number of schools and *katatib* (religious schools; sing. *kuttab*) reached 9,060, with more than 543,000 students (80,000 of whom were female).[18] This dramatic rise in the number of students not only increased Egypt's literacy rate, which slowly inched to 6.8% by 1917 (see Table 4 later in this chapter), but also simultaneously exposed tens of thousands of students every year to a standardized curriculum, which in most cases included the history and geography of Egypt.

The overall political, economic, and administrative centralization of Egyptian society continued under the British, and in some cases the bureaucracy became more efficient. According to Robert Tignor, during the British occupation, the Egyptian central government increased its control over rural Egyptian society, where "rural officials, through regulations from the central government and through special training, were gradually becoming more the agents of the central government than an extension of the village community and kinship system."[19] This level of control would not have been possible without the help of centralizing communication and transportation technologies.[20]

## NATIONALISM AND
## "CENTRALIZATION TECHNOLOGIES"

The greatest of these public works and the most deserving of public funding are the railroads and the Egyptian telegraph system. . . . Extensive utilization of these works and the maximization of their countless benefits did not take place till the reign of his Excellency the Khedive Isma'il Pasha. . . . He devoted all of his energies and thoughts to the organization of the Egyptian telegraph and railway systems through . . . expanding the reach of their services throughout the land, until all could benefit.

—'Ali Pasha Mubarak, *al-Khitat al-Tawfiqiyya*

This boastful declaration by 'Ali Pasha Mubarak—who during his long public service career held the posts of minister of public works, of rail-

ways, and of education—elaborates on the ever increasing political centralization of Egyptian society, which became even more efficient as new
communication and transportation technologies were introduced. The
physical connection of vast distances economically, politically, and culturally linked Egyptian territories as never before. Armies, people, goods,
and, more important for our purposes, new "cultural products"—from
newspapers to recorded songs—quickly and efficiently circulated between
the capital and the national periphery, creating for the first time the necessary conditions for the development of a national identity. The introduction of printing, railroads, telegraphs, and other communication and
transportation technologies had obvious wide-ranging political, cultural,
and economic implications.

### The Egyptian Railroads

There could be no national unity before there was national circulation.
                            —Eugen Weber, *Peasants into Frenchmen*

Perhaps the most important of the transforming technologies was the
railroad. It was first introduced into Egypt, with a 209-kilometer line connecting Cairo with Alexandria, in 1856 during the reign of Sa'id. In 1858
Suez was connected with Cairo, and by 1861 several towns in the Delta
were linked by rail. It was not until the reign of Khedive Isma'il, however, that the railroad system expanded into Upper Egypt, totaling 2,112
kilometers (1,325 miles) by 1876.[21] By the eve of World War I, Egypt
had approximately 2,600 kilometers of government-controlled railroads
crisscrossing the Delta and extending southward to the Sudan. During the
British occupation, government railroads were supplemented by a number of private companies, which built light-railway lines to link the small
agricultural towns of the Delta with the main railway arteries. Economically, the speed of transporting crops by rail from the fields of the Delta
and Upper Egypt to Egypt's ports and population centers dramatically
increased as the price of transport decreased. Conversely, inexpensive
manufactured products, mostly made in Europe, were rapidly transported
from Egypt's ports to the countryside.[22] In 1880, 1,145,000 tons of cargo
were transported by rail in Egypt, and the amount continued to rise each
year, doubling to 2.2 million tons in 1892 and nearly doubling yet again
to 4.2 million tons by 1907 (see Appendix A, Table A.1).[23] The immediate
ramification of these dramatic transformations was an increase in the pe-
ripheralization of the Egyptian economy as a producer of raw materials,
mainly long-staple cotton, for European factories. The growing economic
dependence on foreign economic and political centers, which started

decades earlier, led eventually to Britain's 1882 military occupation of Egypt and the subsequent acceleration of that economic dependence.[24]

The economic repercussions of the expanding Egyptian railroad system are evident; the sociocultural implications of such a drastic change, however, are less visible and have been largely overlooked. One of the most important social ramifications of the new railway system was the noticeable increase in the physical connectedness of the national population, expanding the geographic worldview of the average Egyptian from a village or regional perspective to an increasingly national one. Statistics compiled by Maslahat al-Sika al-Hadid (the Egyptian Railroad Department) show that the annual number of passengers skyrocketed from roughly 2 million in 1877 to more than 30 million in 1920 (see Appendix A, Table A.1).[25] Like the spokes of the wheel, all rail lines led to Cairo, and to a lesser degree Alexandria and the newly established canal cities, where most rural Egyptian migrants and seasonal workers headed in search of work. In turn, Cairo's cultural influence radiated outward to the national periphery using these same arteries. This nationwide circulation of people, goods, and culture was instrumental in creating the beginnings of a national consciousness. It is important to emphasize, however, that one need not be a passenger on the train to be culturally or economically affected by the railroad system. Railway stations within a reasonable distance of a village physically linked that area to the rapidly expanding national transportation and communication network, systematically exposing the nearby population to Cairene mass culture. For instance, as I discuss in later chapters, traveling theater and music troupes relied heavily on the railroad networks to travel and perform throughout the Egyptian countryside from the Delta to Aswan (see Chapter 5).[26] Also, this cultural diffusion was enhanced by the nearly symbiotic relationship between the railroad system and the developing Egyptian postal system.

### The Egyptian Postal System

The Egyptian post office contributed greatly to Egypt's increasing cultural centralization by becoming the primary carrier of "cultural materials," especially newspapers, to thousands of households and institutions in Egypt. The first organized postal service in Egypt was established early during the reign of Muhammad 'Ali, although at first it limited its services to governmental use only. Sheikh Hassan al-Badily established the first "regular" courier service for public use in the 1820s. This was followed by Carlo Merati's 1843 opening of the first post office in Alexandria and the establishment of a regular postal service between Cairo and Alexandria. This postal service, which was later called the Poste Européenne, gradually established post offices throughout the Delta and later Upper Egypt. In January 1865 the Egyptian government bought the network of nineteen post offices of the Poste Européenne for 950,000 francs and incorporated them into an official "Egyptian Post Office."[27]

By 1913 there were 427 large post offices and 1,477 smaller postal stations spread throughout Egypt's cities and villages, with roughly 51 million pieces of "internal" mail delivered every year.[28] Illiterate migrant workers in Cairo or Alexandria could correspond with their illiterate families in the countryside of the Sa'id or the Delta through the use of literate acquaintances or the services of professional readers and writers for a small fee. The number of social and cultural exchanges taking place in those millions of yearly correspondences contributed to the gradual standardization of Egyptian culture by increasing the systemic national circulation of news, gossip, and culture, and in the process it exposed the periphery to the developing culture of the national core.

Aside from the delivery of personal mail, the Egyptian postal system was instrumental in the national distribution of periodicals, which were mostly printed in Cairo and delivered to thousands of subscribers in the towns and villages of Egypt (see Appendix A, Table A.2). In 1913, of the 51 million pieces of mail delivered nationally, 17 million pieces were newspapers and magazines. On average, roughly one-third of all national mail consisted of periodicals. This large-scale distribution of newspapers radiating from Cairo to the national periphery is crucial in understanding the reach and consequently the transformative role of periodicals in Egyptian society.[29]

### URBANIZATION AND NATIONAL IDENTITY

The native Muslim inhabitants of Cairo commonly call themselves "El-Masreeyeen" [the Egyptians], "Owlad-Masr" [the children of Egypt] (or "Ahl-Masr" [the people of Egypt]), and "Owlad-el-Beled" [children of the country] which signify people of Masr, Children of Masr, and children of the town: the singular forms of these appellations are "Masree," "Ibn-Masr," and "Ibn-el-Beled." Of these three terms, the last is most common in the town itself.

—Edward William Lane, *An Account of the Manners and Customs of the Modern Egyptians*

The Arabic word *al-Qahirah* (Cairo) is rarely used in colloquial Egyptian Arabic; instead the Egyptian capital was and still is simply referred to as *Misr* (Egypt) by all Egyptians. The synonymous identification of Cairo with Egypt demonstrates the city's importance as the national political and economic center.[30] Cairo's demographic and economic significance increased even more by the turn of the twentieth century, mostly because of a dramatic increase in migration from the Egyptian countryside (see Appendix A, Table A.3). The mass migration of peasants into the cities was fueled by the impoverishment of Egypt's rural society, which was in part due to overtaxation, the absence of land reform, a rapid increase in population, and the shifting of Egyptian farm production from subsistence to cash crop farming. Starting in the mid-nineteenth century, thousands of migrants left the countryside for the cities in the north, with hopes of finding economic opportunity.[31]

In 1907 more than 243,000 (38.3%) of the inhabitants of Cairo were born outside the capital and 128,350 (35%) of Alexandria's residents migrated there (see Appendix A, Table A.3).[32] The demographic pressures of such a dramatic population shift and the resulting urban problems associated with it were reflected in British consular reports.

Between 1897 and 1907 Cairo increased by 84,414 persons and Alexandria (with Ramleh) by 50,243; that is to say, Cairo has added to its inhabitants at the rate of 14.8 percent during these ten years and Alexandria at the rate of 15.7 percent. . . . The two cities of Egypt have, it will be seen, increased at a rate higher than that of any of these urban areas with the exception of Calcutta and Berlin, a surprising result in view of their comparatively non-industrial character.[33]

The full implication of this dramatic population shift is beyond the scope of this book, although for our purposes I briefly examine some of the cultural ramifications of this sudden demographic change, especially as it relates to issues of identity.[34] Although most of the subsistence migrants arriving from the Egyptian countryside were illiterate and professionally untrained, their mere presence in the urban milieu gradually integrated most of them into urban living and in the process exposed them to a new urban culture, especially performance and sound media (see Chapters 4–6).

In addition to the internal migration, the cultural clout and importance of Cairo and Alexandria was enhanced and fueled by the large influx of human capital migrating to both cities from overseas, mainly from southern Europe (Greece, Italy, and Malta) and greater Syria. In 1907, 11.5% (75,000) of Cairo's population and 17.6% (65,000) of Alexandria's population were foreign-born.[35] This relatively large number of foreigners migrating to Egypt throughout the nineteenth and early twentieth centuries lived mostly in urban areas, and as a whole they played an important role in creating these rapid infrastructural and cultural transformations. In addition, such a large "non-Egyptian" population, interacting daily with Egyptians, automatically contributed to the development of Egyptian identity simply by reinforcing the differentiation between the "other" and the "native." The perceived differences between a native Egyptian (*ibn al-balad*, or literally "son of the country") and the foreign (*khawaga*) "other" were often strengthened by the deliberate portrayals of this dynamic in colloquial culture.[36] As we will see in later chapters, contrasting the habits, demeanor, and, most important, the accent of the native Egyptian urbanites with those considered "foreign" was often dramatized in the latest jokes, in the cartoons and dialogues of the satirical press, and later in the theatrical sketches and plays of the developing comedic theater.

Many of these cultural productions emphasized the accented non-Egyptian pronunciations of Syrian, Sudanese, Greek, English, and other foreign residents and contrasted them with the fluency of a native Egyptian. In all these representations, fluent speakers of Cairene Egyptian Arabic were represented as de facto Egyptian and were automatically imbued with certain qualities, such as patience, goodness, resilience, perseverance, and intelligence. They were contrasted with the nonfluent, accented speakers, who were often characterized with opposing negative values, such as exploitative greed, laziness, disloyalty, and naïveté. Thus, through the continual contrast between the representation of Egyptian characters and a host of external "others," a distinct Egyptian identity began to form in the popular imagination. However, not all foreigners were portrayed in the same manner.

Lower- and lower middle-class Maltese, Greeks, and Italians who worked as waiters, dock workers, and laborers were portrayed much more positively in the media than wealthy bankers, entrepreneurs, and speculators, who were often depicted as sucking the economic lifeblood of everyday Egyptians. In fact, the vast majority of the foreign residents and their descendants were from a lower middle-class background, and many lived and worked in the same neighborhoods and institutions as native-born Egyptians. Many of the sons and daughters of the thousands of Levantine, Maltese, Italian, and Greek immigrants were so thoroughly integrated culturally and linguistically into Egyptian society that they considered themselves de facto Egyptians. During the first third of the twentieth century, these *mutamassirun* (Egyptianized foreigners) fully participated in Egyptian cultural and economic life; some were fervent Egyptian nationalists, and in the 1920s many acquired Egyptian citizenship.[37]

## PRINT CAPITALISM AND THE EXPANSION
## OF URBAN CULTURE

In Egypt, literary work is daily on the increase. New printing-offices, new books, new periodicals, and new men follow one another with a rapidity that is surprising in an Oriental country.     —Martin Hartmann, *The Arabic Press of Egypt*

The explosion of print in Egypt at the turn of the twentieth century is accurately described in the quote from Martin Hartmann's 1899 study. In the decade after Hartmann wrote his book, no fewer than 270 new

Arabic periodicals were printed, more than doubling Hartmann's 1899 estimate of 168 existing Egyptian newspapers (see Table 1). The earliest "national" Egyptian newspaper was the official government journal *al-Waqa'i' al-Misriyya*. First published in 1828, *al-Waqa'i'*'s audience was limited to the Egyptian government's growing public sector employees and consisted mainly of official government reports and news with little cultural content. From the first publication of *al-Waqa'i'* in 1828 until the 1860s, there were no new newspapers in Egypt. It was not until the reign of Isma'il that private newspapers and magazines were published for an increasingly literate Egyptian audience. By the end of Isma'il's tenure, there were eleven Arabic newspapers and sixteen European language newspapers, including some that relied on colloquial Egyptian. Unlike *al-Waqa'i'*, with its mostly dry government announcements and statistical reports, the new semi-official and private periodicals were more entertaining and contained a host of varied cultural materials, ranging from literary essays and short stories to songs and *azjal* (colloquial poetry).

By providing an increasingly politicized Egyptian public sphere with unprecedented large-scale access to new forms of printed cultural material, these new types of periodicals began instilling a growing sense of civic consciousness among literate and semiliterate Egyptian urbanites.[38] In the first five years after Isma'il's reign, Arabic periodicals tripled, with

TABLE 1. *Establishment of new Egyptian periodicals,*
*1828–1929*

| Years | Newspapers | Magazines | Total |
|---|---|---|---|
| 1828–1879 | 16 | 3 | 19 |
| 1880–1884 | 16 | 5 | 21 |
| 1885–1889 | 15 | 13 | 28 |
| 1890–1894 | 16 | 37 | 53 |
| 1895–1899 | 70 | 40 | 110 |
| 1900–1904 | 78 | 51 | 129 |
| 1905–1909 | 86 | 63 | 149 |
| 1910–1914 | 19 | 25 | 44 |
| 1915–1919 | 17 | 19 | 36 |
| 1920–1924 | 119 | 99 | 218 |
| 1925–1929 | 98 | 126 | 224 |
| Total | 550 | 481 | 1,031 |

SOURCE: *Dar al-Kutub al-Misriyya*. All statistical information is based solely on the periodical collection available at Dar al-Kutub. The actual number of periodicals is likely to be higher. The decline in new periodicals between 1909 and 1919 is primarily due to the 1909 reapplication of the press law of 1881 and stringent British press censorship during World War I.

twenty-one new magazines and newspapers. In the 1890s more than 163 new Arabic periodicals were printed in Egypt (mostly in Cairo). In the first decade of the twentieth century more than 280 new periodicals appeared on the scene, and during the 1920s newly published periodicals surpassed 450 (see Table 1). These figures, however, are highly deceptive, because many of these new periodicals did not last more than a few issues before closing for political or financial reasons. Nevertheless, the continual growth of new magazines and newspapers in the Egyptian marketplace of ideas is indicative of the growing consumer demand for this new form of urban-based cultural expression.

The overwhelming majority of newspaper and magazine production in Egypt was urban-based. In the first 130 years of the existence of a "national press," 78.6% of all of Egypt's magazines and newspapers were published in Cairo, with Alexandria running a distant second with 9.2% of periodical production (see Table 2).[39] Cairo's virtual monopoly of the press dramatically increased the cultural influence of the capital city through its domination of the production and delivery of new mass culture. This is consistent with other forms of late nineteenth- to early twentieth-century cultural production. For instance, the developing Egyptian music industry and the theater, which will be discussed in more detail in later chapters, were almost entirely based in Cairo and Alexandria.

TABLE 2. *Egyptian (Arabic) periodicals by publishing location,*
*1828–1958*

| Place of publication | Newspapers | Magazines | Total | Publication percentage |
|---|---|---|---|---|
| Cairo | 584 | 870 | 1,454 | 78.6 |
| Alexandria | 110 | 60 | 170 | 9.2 |
| Tanta | 33 | 9 | 42 | 2.3 |
| Asiut | 6 | 15 | 21 | 1.1 |
| al-Mansura | 12 | 5 | 17 | 0.9 |
| al-Fayum | 9 | 6 | 15 | 0.8 |
| Miniyah | 12 | 0 | 12 | 0.6 |
| Damanhur | 8 | 2 | 10 | 0.5 |
| Mit Ghamr | 6 | 2 | 8 | 0.4 |
| Benha | 5 | 1 | 6 | 0.3 |
| Giza | 3 | 2 | 5 | 0.27 |
| Damietta | 5 | 0 | 5 | 0.27 |
| Beni Sueif | 3 | 2 | 5 | 0.27 |
| Rest of Egypt | 38 | 42 | 80 | 4.3 |
| Total | 834 | 1,016 | 1,850 | 100 |

SOURCE: *Dar al-Kutub al-Misriyya.*

## Books, Literacy, and Communal Reading

Most printing presses in Egypt were located in Cairo and Alexandria, making book production, like newspaper production, an overwhelmingly urban enterprise. Although, as mentioned earlier, books had a smaller influence on the masses than newspapers, they were still an accurate barometer of the radical cultural changes taking place in Egypt in the second half of the nineteenth century. As Table 3 demonstrates, the number of printed books and authors dramatically spiked from the beginning to the end of the nineteenth century; this uptick was partly an expected outcome of the gradually increasing literacy rate. The increase in the number of private presses, compared to government presses, in the second half of the nineteenth century was also dramatic. The privatization of printing and journalism allowed for more editorial freedom, and the inevitable competition between periodicals and presses led to a simplification of language and the streamlining of newspaper and book content to attract an increasingly nonspecialized readership.[40]

Books were not just more numerous and available than ever before; they were becoming more affordable as well. Book prices in Egypt ran counter to normal inflationary trends; in fact, the average price of a book decreased from 25 piasters in the first half of the nineteenth century to 16 piasters in the second half of the century. This almost 40% decrease in the average price of a book was partly due to the decrease in paper prices and the increase in the number of competing printing presses.[41] More important for our purposes, books were becoming more affordable to increasingly literate consumers. Egypt's overall literacy rates gradually increased from 4.8% in the late 1890s to 6.8% in 1917. Within the next decade the Egyptian literacy rate nearly doubled, reaching 11.8% by 1927 (see Table 4). In the

TABLE 3. *Books and authors in nineteenth-century Egypt*

| Years | Number of titles published | Number of published authors | Government-owned presses | Privately owned presses | Number of books printed |
|---|---|---|---|---|---|
| 1820–1829 | 105 | 13 | 1 | 0 | 60,000 |
| 1830–1839 | 358 | 31 | 7 | 5 | 208,000 |
| 1840–1849 | 404 | 36 | 6 | 2 | 229,500 |
| 1850–1859 | 443 | 62 | 0 | 9 | 221,500 |
| 1860–1869 | 1,391 | 206 | 2 | 22 | 695,500 |
| 1870–1879 | 1,597 | 176 | 1 | 22 | 1,295,000 |
| 1880–1889 | 3,021 | 444 | 4 | 17 | 2,406,500 |
| 1890–1899 | 3,086 | 369 | 0 | 41 | 2,416,000 |
| Total | 10,405 | — | 21 | 118 | 7,532,000 |

SOURCE: Nussayr, *Harakat Nashr al-Kutub*, 54–80, 131–32, 176, 410–46.

TABLE 4. *Egyptian literacy rates*

|      | Male literacy (%) | Female literacy (%) | Total literacy (%) |
|------|------|------|------|
| 1897 | 9.1  | 0.7  | 4.8  |
| 1907 | 9.7  | 1.1  | 5.4  |
| 1917 | 11.9 | 1.8  | 6.8  |
| 1927 | 19.6 | 3.9  | 11.8 |

SOURCE: *Annuaire statistique de l'Egypte*, 1914, 24; *Annuaire statistique de l'Egypte*, 1918, 15; *Annuaire statistique de l'Egypte*, 1928–1929, 30.

urban areas, where most of the cultural production took place, the literacy rates were significantly higher than the national average. In 1917 Cairo and Alexandria's total literacy rates were about 21% and the national average was only about 6.8%. In just a decade the two cities' literacy rates jumped to 33%, with the national rate increasing to 11.8%. Thus, on average, the literacy rates in the cities were three times the national average. This critical mass of consumers and creators of cultural production gave Cairo, and to a lesser extent Alexandria, an unprecedented cultural influence over the entire country.[42]

After the introduction of modern printing in Egypt, book production exploded, but it was newspapers and magazines that had the most profound cultural impact. Magazines and other periodicals were often filled with poems, *azjal*, plays, scientific essays, and serialized books and novels. Many, especially the satirical and literary periodicals, were collected and bound in book form by their readers. In addition, unlike books, dailies and other periodicals were much more accessible to the average Egyptian. Their availability in coffee shops, barbershops, shoe-shining shops, and other public and private institutions, where a typical periodical was read by several readers, greatly increased their "circulation" figures.[43] Indeed, to understand the effect of these periodicals on Egyptian readers in the late nineteenth and early twentieth centuries, we must consider that readership figures differed considerably from circulation figures, with at least five different people typically reading a single issue of a given publication. This was especially true in late nineteenth- and early twentieth-century Egypt, when the borrowing and exchange of newspapers was common.[44]

In addition, the availability of public reading areas during this period allowed for easy access to books, magazines, and newspapers, which were typically reused by countless readers. Coffeehouses, which were, and still are, located on almost every street corner of Egypt's major towns and cities, played the greatest role in the oral diffusion of mass culture. For the price of a cup of tea or coffee, readers had access to many newspapers and magazines. If the clientele happened to be illiterate, their mere presence in a crowded coffee shop exposed them to an unlimited amount of oral discourse, from the reading aloud of newspapers to conversations, songs, and theatrical performances.[45]

## The Satirical Press and Reading Newspapers Aloud

Satirical periodicals played a significant role in late nineteenth- to early twentieth-century Egyptian urban culture, and the satirical press was extremely popular because of its reliance on colloquial Egyptian and its forceful satirical content; but it also functioned as a repository and catalyst for other forms of vernacular expressions. Colloquial poetry, colloquial songs, and satirical dialogues were often printed in the pages of the satirical periodicals, and this content exhibited and publicized the full range of what would soon become a national mass culture.

The colloquial press contained a significant admixture of colloquial Egyptian material within its pages. The amount of colloquial material varied from one periodical to the next. *Al-Khala'a al-Misriyya* (Egyptian loose behavior), *al-'Arnab* (The rabbit), and *Humarit Munyati* (The idiocy of my desires), for example, were written almost entirely in colloquial Egyptian; others, such as *al-'Arghul* (The reed flute) and *al-'Ustadh* (The teacher), filled about a quarter of their pages in colloquial Egyptian, usually in the form of *azjal* or colloquial dialogues. Almost all the colloquial content of these newspapers was satirical or humorous, primarily because the everyday vernacular was more suited to comedy and satire than Fusha was. Contributing to the vitality of the Egyptian satirical press was its unique straddling of oral popular culture and print culture. Unlike the relative inaccessibility of Fusha, with its clear divergence from the everyday language of all Egyptians, the uncomplicated colloquial writings of the satirical press allowed for a complex set of exchanges between written and oral dissemination.

Reading segments from the colloquial press aloud was quite common, because its witty contents were understood by all; moreover, *azjal*, a common feature of satirical newspapers, were intended to be read aloud. In his extensive study on the history of the press in the Arab Middle East, Ami Ayalon elaborates that reading newspapers "was not necessarily an individual act of receiving information. . . . The public places that offered wide accessibility to newspapers, created a pattern of reading papers as a collective experience. Reading aloud, an old practice that converted a text of any kind to the property of a circle of listeners, was extended to journals."[46] According to Ayalon, in the Arab world, early periodicals were initially at least "written so as to be transmitted to an 'audience' in the literal sense of the term—a listening, not reading, public."[47] This, I would argue, was especially true for texts that were printed in *'ammiyya*; these materials were especially well suited for oral dissemination. Aside from the obvious advantages of having the spoken language read aloud, many of the *'ammiyya* pieces were dialogues, depicting everyday conversations. They were written with an inherent potential for oral dissemination, or as described by Walter Ong, they contained a great deal of "oral residue," facilitating their oral broadcast.[48]

This interaction between print and orality is similar to Jürgen Habermas's description of the developing public sphere in eighteenth-century England.

The periodical articles were not only made the object of discussion by the public of the coffee houses but were viewed as integral parts of the discussion. . . . The dialogue form too, employed by many of the articles, attested to their proximity to the spoken word. One and the same discussion transposed into a different medium was continued in order to reenter, via reading, the original conversational medium.[49]

Ample evidence suggests that in Egypt during this period parts of periodicals were indeed read aloud in cafés and other public spaces. For example, in an 1883 essay, John Ninet observed the novelty and influence of printed, easier-to-understand colloquial Egyptian on the Egyptian masses: "Some of these sheets were especially addressed to the fellahin, and were written in their own patois, an idea absolutely new to the oriental mind, and one which had an extraordinary effect upon the popular imagination."[50] The reading aloud of the satirical press at the turn of the twentieth century was also repeatedly documented by the contemporary Egyptian chronicler Mikha'il Sharubim (b. 1854).[51] In the later parts of his multivolume work, which chronicles historical and social events occurring during his lifetime, Sharubim writes many detailed accounts of the public readings of satirical newspapers from the 1880s until the end of his account in 1910. As Sharubim recounts, the habitual reading aloud of satirical newspaper articles took place not just in cafés but also in other public areas: "People were greatly attracted to these sorts of papers . . . to the extent that if you walked by a workshop, a low class café, or a carriage/transportation stop, you inevitably see someone surrounded by a crowd, and reading aloud from one or more of these newspapers. The listeners often laugh out-loud and uncontrollably pound the floor with their feet, while repeating the rude and vulgar words and phrases read out to them."[52]

This does not necessarily mean that most of those who consumed such newspapers listened to them; I doubt that to be the case. It is probable that most of the contents of these newspapers were read individually, but in late nineteenth- and early twentieth-century Egypt it was not uncommon for selections from these newspapers to be publicly and communally read aloud. Although many of those who listened to the public readings of these newspapers were literate, it is likely that many illiterates were exposed to these writings as well. Also, aside from the direct reading aloud of newspapers, the contents of these newspapers were certainly debated, digested, and discussed in the public sphere. Indeed, the importance of simple oral communication should be discounted, especially when conducted en masse in urban settings.

The flow of information also went in the other direction, from oral to written. Many readers of the satirical press submitted *azjal* for publication, which they either composed themselves or heard in public. This cyclical flow of information between written media and oral/aural dissemination (or redissemination) increased the reach and efficacy of the political messages contained therein. In addition to the populist appeal of colloquial Egyptian, the language's flexibility facilitated the use of linguistic subterfuge, metaphor, and satire, endowing it with an indirect yet effective avenue for dissent and subversion. As discussed in Chapter 1, these active public readings and the inevitable conversations and discussions such readings were bound to trigger contrast rather vividly with the more cerebral, silent, and entirely visual type of reading described by Benedict Anderson in *Imagined Communities*. Thus cafés and other urban meeting places became important oral communication centers and were intimately connected with newspapers and, later, newly introduced sound media. Or as Jürgen Habermas elaborates in his study on the public sphere, cultural consumers verbalized and analyzed the meanings of newspapers, books, and other newly accessible cultural commodities "on their own (by way of rational communication with one another)." In other words, "readers, listeners, and spectators could avail themselves via the market of the objects that were subject to discussion."[53] These embodied public readings, conversations, and debates were an important part of the complex urban soundscape of late nineteenth- to early twentieth-century Egyptian towns and cities.[54]

## PERFORMANCE AND SOUND MEDIA

By the first decade of the twentieth century, another layer was added to the cultural soundscape of Egyptian towns and cities. The sounds of recorded music emanating from phonograph records could increasingly be heard in cafés, enhancing the accessibility of a growing vernacular national culture to more and more Egyptians. This of course only supplemented the live café and street musicians and performers, who were already an important part of Egyptian urban life. Professional theater troupes and especially the developing colloquial theater were also fast becoming an important and effective form of mass culture, which synergistically fed into both the Egyptian music industry and the burgeoning national press. Newspapers, for example, advertised, promoted, critiqued, and publicly discussed most of these new songs and plays.

Traditional forms of Egyptian popular culture had been a part of Egypt's urban culture for centuries. Singers, *zajjalun* (colloquial poets; sing. *zajjal*), storytellers, and traveling puppet (*'aragoz*) and shadow theater (*khayal al-zil*) performers were for hundreds of years a part of Egypt's urban environment, entertaining the masses in an easy-to-understand everyday colloquial language (see Chapter 3).[55] What began to change, starting in the last quarter of the nineteenth century, was the gradual systematization and professionalization of these art forms and the literal transformation of colloquial popular culture into new genres of colloquial mass culture. The increasingly popular colloquial theater and the record industry permitted the semiliterate and illiterate public to absorb and digest this new urban mass culture and in the process to participate in an increasingly national culture.

However, the introduction of new media did not necessarily dictate the demise of old media, as they were often not abandoned but "coexisted and interacted with the new arrivals."[56] As Peter Burke points out, "Manuscripts remained important in the age of print, like books and radio in the age of television." For this reason, the "media need to be viewed as a system, a system in perpetual change in which different elements play greater or smaller roles."[57] Only then can there be a more realistic balance in evaluating the cultural impact of the oral, the aural, and the visual.

## CONCLUSION

The conjunction of secondary [rail] lines and of the roads built to serve them resulted in a crash program of national integration of unparalleled scope and effectiveness; a program that could operate on this scale only because, for the first time, economic and technological conditions offered the possibility of radical cultural change. Before culture altered significantly, material circumstances had to alter; and the role of road and rail in this transformation was basic.

—Eugen Weber, *Peasants into Frenchmen*

The infrastructural and institutional changes of late nineteenth- to early twentieth-century Egypt were essential to the materialization of the ensuing cultural transformations. Without the increasing physical interconnectedness of Egyptian society, a result of the rapid introduction of communication and transportation technologies, the diffusion of a colloquial mass culture would hardly have been possible. Indeed, the eventual commercialization of Egyptian cultural production was partly due to the modernization of communication technologies, which allowed for the rapid and unprecedented large-scale distribution of new cultural products. Advances in printing and photography and the invention of the telegraph and phonograph dramatically changed the way cultural materials were disseminated and digested. For instance, the telegraph, which was introduced in Egypt in the mid-nineteenth century, allowed newspapers to gather news more rapidly and widely than ever before, permitting the rise of daily newspapers. Photography gave rise to illustrated periodicals, which dramatically democratized the press by making it a more accessible tool of entertainment as well as news.

In addition to newspapers and other periodicals, the colloquial comedic theater and, more important perhaps, the developing music recording industry dramatically transformed how Egyptians consumed cultural information. The development of a national Egyptian music industry, which almost exclusively produced colloquial songs for popular consumption, was an influential component of this new urban-based culture. Most of these new media were nurtured in Cairo, although these media were certainly influenced and even shaped by the cultural impact resulting from the mass of human capital that migrated there from all over Egypt and beyond.

The colloquial language used in the thousands of new Egyptian songs, theatrical plays, and the popular satirical periodicals was almost exclusively Cairene, encouraging the emergence of Cairene colloquial as the de facto Egyptian dialect. Because these materials were meant to be heard and viewed, colloquial Egyptian performances and recording media had the potential to reach the vast majority of Egyptians who were illiterate. These urban-based colloquial media were increasingly connected with a national audience and consequently were beginning to (re)shape Egyptian perceptions and identities.

## CHAPTER THREE

# Print Capitalism and the Beginnings of Colloquial Mass Culture, 1870–1882

Late nineteenth-century Egypt experienced many sociopolitical and cultural transformations that affected nearly every aspect of Egyptian society. Although these changes were more acutely felt in urban areas, the Egyptian countryside was increasingly becoming more connected to the urban centers, in part because of the telegraph, the post office, and the extensive railroad system. New national media, primarily centered in Cairo, were being introduced, profoundly changing how Egyptians were entertained and informed. The most important of these media, owing to their increased accessibility and popularity with the Egyptian public, were the colloquial press and the burgeoning comedic and musical theater.

The parameters, tone, and direction of colloquial Egyptian mass culture were arguably formulated as early as the 1870s by the precedent-setting newspapers, plays, and *azjal* of 'Uthman Jalal (1828–1898), Ya'qub Sannu' (1839–1912), and 'Abdallah Nadim (1845–1898), who simultaneously worked in several colloquial media. All three men edited newspapers and wrote *azjal* and colloquial Egyptian plays.[1] Not only were these three pioneers the first to popularize a new type of mass-produced colloquial culture, but, more important, they created media templates that were emulated by countless other colloquial writers for at least half a century. The characterizations, techniques, and methods used in Sannu''s cartoons and colloquial prose, Nadim's *azjal* and colloquial dialogues, and Jalal's Egyptianization of European plays had a noticeable influence on the next generation of writers, song lyricists, cartoonists, and playwrights. Accordingly, in this chapter I examine the critical beginnings of Egyptian mass culture by focusing primarily on the early works of Sannu', Nadim, and Jalal and their effects on late nineteenth-century Egyptian society.

## TRADITIONAL POPULAR CULTURE AND
## THE ROOTS OF EGYPTIAN MASS CULTURE

I witnessed the magicians and the storytellers in the coffee shops and the rababa singers[2] . . . and I heard the phonograph when it was first introduced . . . and I watched
historical plays in the Arabic theater and watched the shadow and puppet theater . . .
all this before I was ten years old.     —Muhammad Lutfi Jum'a, *Shahid 'Ala al-'Asr*

Traditional forms of popular culture undoubtedly left an imprint on the
development of colloquial mass culture. For instance, the early colloquial
comedic theater borrowed heavily from traditional street performers and
puppet theater. Prototypical puppet theater (*'araguz*) characters, such as
the wise *ibn al-balad* persona, the conniving *khawaga* (foreigner), and the
menacing mother-in-law, were readapted later in 1920s comedic theater,
and by the late 1930s they were reflected in the budding Egyptian movie
industry. Some traditional *zajjalun* (colloquial poets; sing. *zajjal*) shifted
to writing short colloquial songs to fill the needs of the growing music
industry, and many started their own colloquial newspapers to publish
their prose and expose their work to thousands of readers and listeners. This relative continuity in some of the forms of colloquial culture
from the "traditional" to the mass-mediated variety helped guarantee the
popularity of their works.[3]

Colloquial proverbs, perhaps the oldest medium of popular culture,
express the daily realities and concerns of the masses in a tacit yet powerful way. Proverbs were assimilated into the new mass media by novelists,
journalists, and playwrights, who often inserted popular proverbs into
their work to add authenticity. Colloquial sayings commented on everyday life and often reflected the political and social state of affairs, with
some sayings directly dealing with injustices experienced by the masses.
These sayings provided an immediate, spontaneous form of mundane
resistance, helping the masses cope with injustices by publicly expressing a shared sense of oppression. To be sure, some of these proverbs also
reflected a certain xenophobic fear of those who were deemed outsiders.

An entire lexicon of proverbs focused on the Turks (*Ghuz*), who more
or less had composed the ruling elite of Egypt since the thirteenth century. Most, if not all, of these proverbs portrayed the Turks as unjust
oppressors who continually exploited native Egyptians. For instance, the
proverb *'Akhir khidmat al-ghuz 'al'a* (Working for the Turks will only
lead to being beaten) reflects the perceived aggressiveness of the Turkish
soldiery against the native population. Relying on scatological humor,
the proverb *Shukhakh 'inhadar 'ala khara 'al marhaban kurdash* (Urine
ran into some excrement and greeted it by saying, "Hello, *kurdash*")[4] de-

bases the Turks as unclean. Another proverb addressed the threat of rape of local women by outsiders, which was commonly used to dehumanize the "other": *Rahit min al-ghuz harba 'abluha al-magharba* (She escaped, running away from the Turks, and she was greeted by the Moroccans/ northwest Africans).[5] The Moroccan community was also stereotypically viewed as lacking in civility and manners, as expressed in this proverb: *'Alit il-magharba li-'ahl masr: "laysh ma tihibbuna?" 'Aluh min il-'akhla' il-radiyya* (The Moroccans asked the Egyptians, Why don't you care for us? On account of your poor character, they replied).[6] Besides the *Magharba* (Moroccans or northwest Africans) and the Turks, the Bedouins (*il-'arab* or *il-badu*) also earned their fair share of negative proverbs, reflecting the unease felt by sedentary Egyptians toward those who lived outside what was deemed to be the geographic, cultural, or social boundaries of Egyptian society. For example, the saying *Gur il-turk wala 'adl il-'arab* (The oppression of the Turks is better than the justice of the Arabs [i.e., Bedouin]) reflects the fear of Bedouin raids and potential anarchy; also, the perceived deceitfulness of the Bedouin is reflected in the proverb *Dayyif il-badawi yisra' thiyabak* (Invite the Bedouin over and he will steal your clothes).[7]

Some proverbs addressed the perceived injustices and corruption of the ruling class. For example, proverbs that are still as popular today as they were when they first appeared a few hundred years ago include *Hamiha haramiha* (Those who are supposed to protect the country [i.e., the rulers] are those who rob it); *Yibni 'asr wi yihdim masr* (He builds a palace and ruins Cairo [the city]); *'Ur'us lil 'ird fi dawlitu* (When the monkey reigns, dance before him); *Diyar misr khirha li-gharibha* (also *li-ghirha*) (The riches of Egypt belong to the foreigners [the others]); and *Il-hitan liha widan* (The walls have ears).[8] Other, more dated sayings expressed the general sense of injustice and fear felt by the masses toward their rulers: *'Ili yishrab min mar'it il-sultan tinhara' shifitu* (He who drinks from the Sultan's broth will burn his lips);[9] *Ya wali la tigur, il-wilayya la tidum* (Oh governor, don't tyrannize—your dominion will not last forever); *Il-lissan 'aduw il-'afa* (The tongue is the enemy of the back of the neck [i.e., if you speak freely, you will be beaten]); and *Dar il-zalim kharab wala ba'd hayn* (The abode of the oppressor will eventually be destroyed).[10]

This counterhegemonic spirit also extended to traditional street theater, which in its many forms has been an integral part of urban Egyptian street life for hundreds of years. Traditional storytellers, shadow and puppet theater performers, and monodrama satirists, who made audiences laugh by mimicking authority figures, such as tax collectors or the ruling elite, gave voice to the masses through the acting out of grievances and perceived injustices.[11] As Edward William Lane observed in the early 1830s:

The Egyptians are particularly prone to satire, and often display considerable wit in their jeers and jests. Their language affords them great facilities for punning, and for ambiguous conversations, in which they very frequently indulge. The lower orders sometimes lampoon their rulers in songs, and ridicule those enactments of the government by which they themselves most suffer.[12]

Lane later gave an example of this political satire by detailing the plot of an 1833 street play in which the protagonist was a fellah who could afford to pay only 5 piasters out of the 1,000 piasters he owed the government. Because of his inability to pay the taxes, he was severely beaten and imprisoned, which motivated his wife to use bribery and to later resort to seducing a government official to release her husband from prison.[13]

Corruption and the abuse of authority were also common themes in traditional *azjal*. Before they were transformed through colloquial newspapers and the music industry into a mass culture, *azjal* were primarily spread through oral dissemination. These colloquial poems were typically recited out loud for small groups of listeners at coffee shops, barbershops, and other urban meeting places. In the early to mid-nineteenth century, several well-known *zajal* celebrities had a following among some of the urban masses. Many attended certain coffee shops to hear some of the latest colloquial poems. Hassan al-'Allati (Hassan the instrumentalist), for example, was widely known throughout Alexandria and Cairo for his irreverent and humorous *azjal* and had a large following in both cities. In 1889 he published *Tarwih al-Nufus wa Mudhik al-'Ubus* (The promenade of the souls and the laughter of the melancholic), in which he documented dozens of comedic and often sarcastic poems, *azjal*, and other colloquial prose that he and his contemporaries wrote and/or performed during their nightly "literary" meetings. The participants in these meetings, as implied by al-'Allati, were often under the influence of alcohol or hashish, which undoubtedly added to the entertainment value of these comedic gatherings. In the book's introduction, al-'Allati describes how these meetings began.

Nightly, we used to frequent each other's houses, losing ourselves in oceans of thoughts. . . . However when our numbers dramatically increased and our houses became too small, we picked out a new safe center to continue our meetings. This was a pleasant coffeehouse in Khalifah Street. And when we re-established our meeting in this new place, we called our gathering *al-Mudhikana al-Kubra* [the grand factory of laughter].[14]

These literary meetings were attended by the next generation of *zajal* writers, such as 'Abdallah Nadim, Muhammad al-Najar, Ahmad 'Ashur,

Muhammad Tawfiq, 'Isa Sabri, Husayn Shafiq al-Misri, and Muhammad Fahmi Yusuf, who would soon transform colloquial cultural production into a mass culture. These new colloquial poets were literally transformed into newspaper editors and owners overnight; in fact, as we will examine in Chapter 4, most colloquial periodicals were established by *azjal* writers (see Appendix B).[15]

In addition, many colloquial writers and poets took advantage of the increase in consumer demand for popular entertainment and the overall changes in the cultural landscape by simultaneously expanding into many different media. This demand for colloquial production also gave writers an unprecedented flexibility in working with multiple media. 'Uthman Jalal, for example, who is mainly known for his theatrical contributions, published a book on *azjal* and proverbs called *al-'Uyun al-Yawaqiz fi al-'Amthal wa al-Mawa'iz* (Awakened eyes for proverbs and wisdom). The book is full of colloquial poetry with lines of traditional sayings embedded within.[16] Over the next four decades the mass printing of *azjal* along with the rapidly developing music industry, which relied on *zaj-jalun* to write colloquial songs, would transform colloquial poetry into a national mass culture.[17]

## JALAL AND SANNU': THE BEGINNINGS OF "MODERN" COLLOQUIAL THEATER, 1870–1880

Street theater performances in colloquial Egyptian were always a part of Egypt's urban fabric. However, it was not until the last third of the nineteenth century that more professional theatrical troupes began forming.[18] The roots of the professional colloquial theater were laid by pioneers such as Ya'qub Sannu' and 'Uthman Jalal, who established certain artistic templates and mores that would be emulated by later theatrical writers such as Muhammad Taymur (1892–1921) and Badi' Khayri (1893–1966). However, as I examine in Chapters 5 and 6, professional colloquial Egyptian theater did not become a truly popular medium of expression in Egypt until World War I, when the comedic theaters of Najib al-Rihani and 'Ali al-Kassar revolutionized Egyptian entertainment.

The birth of modern colloquial Egyptian theater is often solely attributed to Ya'qub Sannu'.[19] Although it is true that the first documented performance of a professionally cast and scripted colloquial Egyptian play was written and produced by Sannu', the influence that Muhammad 'Uthman Jalal had on the development of Egyptian theater was arguably more lasting. Among other things, Jalal provided an extensive library of translated European plays, all in an easy-to-understand colloquial Egyptian. Most of these works were continually performed after his death by many different theatrical troupes.

Jalal and Sannu' came from different social and cultural backgrounds, but they both had similar professional careers as language teachers and translators. Jalal was born in 1828, more than a decade before Sannu', in a village near Bani Suwayf in the Egyptian Delta. He received his primary education in the Qasr al-'Aini khedival school and afterward attended Rifa'a al-Tahtawi's School of Foreign Languages (Madrasat al-'Alsun) in Cairo, perfecting Turkish and French. Upon graduation in 1845, Jalal worked first as a French teacher and later as a translator at Diwan al-Tarjama (the Translation Bureau). Although he translated some scientific books and manuals, Jalal was mostly interested in translating European literary works, specializing in the translation of Molière's plays.[20]

The earliest appearance of colloquial Egyptian in a printed periodical is probably the 1871 serialized printing of Jalal's translation of *Le médecin malgré lui* (The doctor in spite of himself) by Molière in *Rawdat al-Madaris al-Misriyya*. *Rawdat al-Madaris* was a biweekly government publication started by Rifa'a al-Tahtawi (1801–1873) on April 17, 1870, and lasting until 1877. It was essentially a publication for "public" education in Egypt and contained primary and secondary school lesson plans in a variety of disciplines, educational essays, exam samples, and general education news. It catered to Egyptian educators and to students, and with the exception of Jalal's play, it was written exclusively in Fusha. The characters in Jalal's *al-Fakh al-Mansub Lil-Hakim al-Maghsub* (The entrapment of the doctor in spite of himself) were thoroughly Egyptianized and spoke in a matter-of-fact Cairene street language with an abundance of realistic swearing. For example, the play's main character, Fatuma, responded to her husband Ibrahim's threats of beating her by yelling at him, "How dare you try to hit me! You are a Gypsy-like, thieving, drunk, pimping, hashish-addicted dog."[21] Perhaps because of the excessive swearing, or the general controversy over the use of colloquial Egyptian in an official educational publication, the printing of Jalal's serialized play lasted for only a few weeks and was abruptly canceled after the printing of only five sections.[22]

Jalal later published some of his plays in five books, with the publication of *al-Shaykh Matluf* (an Egyptianized translation of Molière's *Tartuffe*) in 1873, followed by *al-Arba' Riwayat Min Nikhb al-Tiyatrat* (The four novellas from the theater) in 1890, which again included his translation of *Tartuffe* along with Molière's *Les femmes savantes*, *L'école des maris*, and *L'école des femmes* (*al-Nisa' al-'Alimat*, *Madrasit al-Azwag*, and *Madrasit al-Nissa'*).[23] After translating Molière's comedies, Jalal translated a few of Racine's and Corneille's tragedies, including *Le cid* and *Les trois Horaces*.[24] The uniqueness and importance of Jalal's work, however, lay in the fact that many of his translations (mainly the comedies) were free adaptations of the European originals, reset completely in an Egyptian setting. Jalal's "translations" of Molière's plays were entirely Egyptianized, from the Egyptian names and accents of the characters to the social and geographic milieus of the plays. For instance, Molière's Tartuffe is expertly transformed from a pious Catholic layman into the Muslim sheikh Matluf. Molière's anticlerical message is also represented, as Matluf is shown to be a hypocritical alcoholic who does not practice what he preaches.[25]

All of Jalal's theatrical translations were in colloquial Egyptian, including his translations of the tragedies. The difference between his translation of comedies and tragedies was that with the tragedies he did not Egyptianize the setting and the characters.[26] Jalal's work, especially his Egyptianization of European plays, led to the popularity of his translated adaptations, which were performed by several theatrical troupes at the turn of the twentieth century. These works established the model for later translators and playwrights for creating thoroughly Egyptian theatrical performances.[27]

Whereas Jalal only translated and wrote plays, Sannu' started his own theatrical troupe and was the first to create a functioning modern colloquial Egyptian theater. Sannu' was the eldest son of an Italian Jewish father and an Egyptian Jewish woman named Sarah.[28] Because of his eclectic and multicultural upbringing, by the time he was 12 years old Sannu' was fluent in Arabic, Hebrew, Italian, French, and English. Prince Ahmad Pasha Yeken, his father's employer, was apparently so impressed by the young Sannu' that he fully sponsored his education in Livorno, Italy, from 1852 until 1855, where he studied fine art, science, political economy, and international law. Considering the relatively young age of Sannu', this European excursion surely had a tremendous impact on him. Italy, on the verge of unification, was at the time teeming with nationalistic discourse and propaganda, which must have affected Sannu''s perceptions of nationhood and national identity.[29] Upon returning to Egypt, Sannu' worked as a private tutor until 1863, when he was employed as a language teacher at the military Polytechnic Institute. In 1870 Sannu' became a makeshift playwright and with the financial support of Khedive Isma'il (r. 1863–1879) established Egypt's first Arabic theater company.[30] Sannu''s theatrical troupe even performed on the khedive's private stage at Qasr al-Nil, and he was reportedly labeled *Molière Misr* (the Egyptian Molière) by Isma'il.[31]

All of Sannu''s plays were performed in colloquial Egyptian and contained subtle nationalistic themes and a significant amount of social criticism. For instance, *al-Duratayn* (The co-wives) openly criticized polygamy. In *al-'Amira al-'Iskandaraniyya* (The Alexandrian princess) Sannu' warned middle-class Egyptians against blindly imitating European customs and habits, a cause championed later by 'Abdallah Nadim and other nationalists. In *al-'Alil* (The sick man), Sannu' expressed a more modernist theme by supporting modern medicine against traditional medicine, stereotypically represented by a Moroccan religious quack who summons spirits.[32]

Sannu''s plays were heavily influenced by traditional *'araguz* (puppet) theater scenarios, where language play and misunderstandings frequently take place for comedic effect. Like the *'araguz* theater, most of Sannu''s plays had the clever and resourceful *ibn* or *bint al-balad* (son or daughter of the country) persona encountering his or her nemeses, who are often foreigners or religious sheikhs. Sannu''s most important contributions to the colloquial Egyptian theater were his creation and reification of archetypical non-Egyptian personalities and his expert portrayal of their accents. The use of colloquial Egyptian diction provided the necessary linguistic flexibility to mimic the stereotyped speech of foreigners, creating in the process timeless characterizations of the "other" in the Egyptian comedic theater.[33] For added effect, the accents and personalities of these non-Egyptian characters were typically contrasted to the "accent-free" Cairene colloquial Egyptian pronunciations of *'awlad al-balad*.

For example, the prototypical character of the Nubian servant, almost always represented as simultaneously trustworthy, kindhearted, and impulsive, was first introduced in Sannu''s *al-Bursa* and *Abu Rida al-Barbari wa Ka'b al-Khayr*. This character was perfected later in the plays and movies of 'Ali al-Kassar (see Chapter 5).[34] Also represented in Sannu''s plays were Greek-Egyptian characters, often merchants, tavern owners, or waiters who, although familiar with Egyptian culture, spoke in a distinctively comedic accent. Syrians, European tourists, Moroccans, and other foreigners with their distinctive accents were also represented and were contrasted with native Egyptians and their familiar accents.[35] Sannu' continued his linguistic portrayals of the "other" in his pioneering colloquial newspaper, and his style was copied by most future editors of the satirical colloquial press.

As the subject matter of Sannu''s plays became more critical of Egyptian elite society, his theatrical activities were banned by the government in 1872.[36] No longer allowed to have his plays performed publicly, Sannu' promptly found other outlets for his nationalistic discourse. He formed two secret societies. The first organization, Mahfal al-Taqadum (The Circle of Progress), founded in 1872, was later banned by the Egyptian government, after which Sannu' established his Jam'iyat Muhibi al-'Ilm (The Society of the Lovers of Knowledge). Colonel Ahmed 'Urabi, who would soon burst onto the Egyptian political stage, attended some of those meetings; the featured topics of discussion ranged from politics and current events to critiques of Isma'il's domestic policies. Soon, however, the government discovered the existence of this organization and banned it as well.[37]

Sannu''s and Jalal's activities transformed the colloquial Egyptian theater into an important forum for the expression of ideas in Egyptian society. Their precedent-setting plays and characters created functional templates that inspired other writers and playwrights. More important, perhaps, because of the ever-present controversy over the use of colloquial Egyptian rather than Fusha (classical Arabic), Jalal and Sannu''s colloquial adaptations facilitated the work of such future playwrights as Muhammad Taymur, Tawfiq al-Hakim, and Badi' Khayri in presenting their colloquial works to audiences and critics.[38]

## PRINT CAPITALISM: NADIM, SANNU', AND THE EARLY SATIRICAL PRESS, 1877–1881

The first satirical colloquial Egyptian newspaper in Egypt was Ya'qub Sannu''s *Abu-Naddara Zarqa'*, first published in 1877, followed a few years later by 'Abdallah Nadim's *al-Tankit wa al-Tabkit*, which appeared in 1881.[39] The overwhelming success and popularity of these early satirical newspapers created an ongoing demand for similar productions and set the tone for all future colloquial periodicals. The pioneering roles of Nadim and Sannu' initiated a satirical periodical craze, which lasted well into the first half of the twentieth century. Such periodicals had mass appeal not only because a significant portion of their material was written in colloquial Egyptian but also because of the heavy reliance on humor and satire. Sannu' and Nadim's journals were not merely newspapers recounting current events; they contained fictional dialogues, drama, and in the case of Sannu''s *Abu-Naddara*, visually rich cartoons depicting the Egyptian nation and often satirizing the Egyptian ruling family and, later, British authority.

After his theater was closed and restrictions were placed on his political activities by the Egyptian government, Sannu' became an active Freemason. In 1875 he joined the British-affiliated lodge Kawkab al-Sharq (Star of the East), allowing him to continue some of his nationalistic activities. The role of Freemasonry in early Egyptian nationalism was substantial; their semisecret organizational structure provided an unrestricted forum for the discussion and exchange of ideas between Egyptians from varied socioeconomic backgrounds and some of the European residents of Egypt. Recognizing the advantages of such an organization, the Iranian reformer Jamal al-Din al-Afghani (1838–1897) also became a Mason and joined the Kawkab al-Sharq lodge along with Muhammad 'Abduh, 'Abdallah Nadim, and an entourage of Egyptian and Syrian followers. By 1878, the number of prominent Egyptians in Kawkab al-Sharq reached 300, with al-Afghani emerging as the leader of the lodge.[40]

Perhaps motivated by al-Afghani's encouragement, Sannu' began to publish anonymously printed sheets in which he allegorically attacked the khedive's government. The relative success of this venture led to the establishment of his weekly satirical journal *Abu-Naddara Zarqa'*, in March 21, 1877.[41] The format and content of Sannu''s paper was heavily influenced by his early theatrical activities. Every issue of *Abu-Naddara* contained a small theatrical sketch, usually in the form of a colloquial Egyptian dialogue in which the characters satirically comment on the government as well as the khedive. This was the last straw for Isma'il, and he ordered the exile of Sannu' to France on June 22, 1878.[42] Sannu''s exile, however, did not stop the distribution of *Abu-Naddara* in Egypt. Almost immediately after his arrival in Paris, Sannu' recommenced printing his journal and successfully smuggled it into Egypt.[43]

Sannu''s illustrated newspaper was relatively popular in late nineteenth-century Egypt. This was likely due to its novelty, the uniqueness of its illustrations, and its uncompromising tone. However, because it was printed in Paris and smuggled into Egypt from 1878 onward, its circulation figures are hard to determine.[44] Sannu' maintained in his introduction to the 1889–1890 *Abu-Naddara* album that "no less than fifteen-thousand copies of every edition were printed."[45] However, taking into consideration Sannu''s tendency to exaggerate, the true circulation figure was certainly less than 15,000. In March 1885, the London *Times* correspondent in Paris estimated the number of *Abu-Naddara* issues sent to Egypt at 7,000, with "the expectation being that though many will be seized a large number will reach their destination."[46]

Most of the *Abu-Naddara* journals consisted of only four pages printed on two double-sided sheets of paper. If shipped en masse, the diminutive size of the journal would have facilitated its transportation without detection. If mailed individually, the journal's concealment in virtually any small package was entirely possible. In fact, according to Irene Gendzier, Sannu' revealed in his memoirs "that he had smuggled his newspaper into Egypt by hiding copies in the pages of larger illustrated reviews, books, art albums, and other respectable documents."[47] Whatever methods Sannu' used to smuggle his journal into Egypt, it is certain that *Abu-Naddara* regularly reached its subscribers in Egypt from its first Paris publication date in August 1878 to the last issue published in December 1910. This can be demonstrated by the frequent letters written to Sannu' by the Egyptian readers of *Abu-Naddara*, which Sannu' often printed in his magazine. One such letter to the editor, written fluently in French by a teenage Egyptian boy named Muhammad Sabri (who would later become a well-known Sorbonne-educated Egyptian historian), was published by Sannu' in the November 1907 edition of *Abu-Naddara*. In his letter, Sabri proudly announces to Sannu' that he has collected the complete thirty years of his journal and includes his own nationalistic theatrical sketch, which Sannu' features in *Abu-Naddara*. The fact that a boy born in the early 1890s collected all of the *Abu-Naddara* issues from 1877 to 1907 is a clear testament to the availability and accessibility of Sannu''s journal in Egypt.[48]

Although Sannu' continued to publish his newspaper until December 1910, by the mid-1890s *Abu-Naddara* was competing with many other locally printed satirical newspapers. Because of this and because of Sannu''s distance from the political situation in Egypt, his newspaper would gradually lose much of the novelty and the political relevance that it had during its first two decades. In part because of these realities, by the 1890s Sannu' shifted his primary political priorities toward making the case for Egyptian nationalism in Europe. Working toward this end, beginning as early as 1882, Sannu' started to gradually add a small French section to his newspaper. At first the French sections were simply handwritten translations of political cartoons or some of his small Arabic articles; however, by 1885 *Abu-Naddara Zarqa'* was almost equally divided between a French section and an Arabic section.[49]

After Sannu''s banishment, another one of al-Afghani's disciples began to pursue a similar career path. Although 'Abdallah Nadim came from an entirely different background than Sannu', their ideologies, writing styles, and journalistic techniques have many similarities. Born in 1845 into an impoverished family in Alexandria, Nadim empathized with the needs of the Egyptian masses.[50] At a young age, he attended a traditional *kuttab*, were he memorized the Qur'an at the age of 9, and in 1855 he continued his religious education at the local al-'Anwar mosque. Nadim, however, did not like the antiquated and dry learning style of the traditional religious school and quit his studies to pursue his real love—literature. During this period, he frequented literary salons and coffeehouses, where he developed and sharpened his writing and oratory skills by reading, listening, and participating in debates and *azjal* contests. After discovering his son's "trivial" pursuits, Nadim's father stopped supporting him financially, which quickly forced Nadim to find steady employment. At the age of 17, he began working as a telegraph operator and eventually earned a job at the telegraph office of al-Qasr al-'Ali (the high palace), the residence of Khedive Isma'il's mother. This job allowed Nadim to mingle in some of the literary circles in Cairo and to attend some lectures at al-'Azhar University.[51] This ideal combination of financial security and intellectual stimulation lasted for only a few years. Unexpectedly fired from his job at the palace, Nadim was unable to find employment in Cairo, compelling him to travel around the country in search of work. For a while, Nadim worked as a private tutor for the children of the *'umda* (village chief) of Bidawy in the province of al-Daqahliyya.[52] After wearing out his welcome in Bidawy, Nadim left for Mansura, where a well-to-do businessman with an appreciation for literature and poetry hired him to manage his linen boutique, which like many other small businesses of the period also served as a meeting place for local literary and political figures.[53]

This period of leisurely literary exploration ended for Nadim in 1878, when he returned to Cairo and thrust himself into the intensifying political situation, reuniting with al-Afghani's social circle at the Masonic lodge of Kawkab al-Sharq (which included Sannu' until his exile in June of the same year). Responding to the deterioration of Egypt's financial position and the increasing interference by European powers, al-Afghani's rhetoric became more aggressive. He urged his followers to agitate for active resistance and to promulgate the values of national unity to the Egyptian masses. Influenced by al-Afghani's arguments, Nadim left for Alexandria and began writing some articles for the newspapers *al-Tijara* (Commerce) and *Misr*. He later joined the secretive Misr al-Fatah (Young Egypt) organization, which called for extensive judicial reforms, an end to absolutist rule, and the introduction of an Egyptian parliament. However, he soon left Misr al-Fatah and started his own educational organization, al-Jam'iyya al-Khayriyya al-'Islamiyya (the Islamic Philanthropic Society). Through this association Nadim founded a school and became its active principal, and, like Sannu', he wrote two nationalistic theatrical plays performed by the students.[54]

The success of Sannu''s *Abu-Naddara*, with its easy-to-understand colloquial prose, undoubtedly influenced Nadim's decision to start his own satirical newspaper. On June 6, 1881, Nadim began publishing his weekly journal, *al-Tankit wa al-Tabkit* (Humor and criticism), which was subtitled "a literary, satirical national weekly newspaper" (*Sahifa Wataniyya 'Usbu'iyya, 'Adabiyya Hazaliyya*). Unlike *Abu-Naddara*, *al-Tankit wa al-Tabkit* did not include any cartoons and was written in both Fusha and *'ammiyya*. The *azjal*, jokes, and theatrical dialogues were in colloquial Egyptian, but Nadim's long essays, often social commentaries on Egypt's deteriorating economic situation, were written in Fusha. Nadim's newspaper had roughly the same circulation figures as *Abu-Naddara*. The first issue of *al-Tankit wa al-Tabkit* sold 3,000 copies, which was a large circulation figure for Egypt in 1881. According to Nadim, only five issues remained from the more than 3,000 printed copies. These two critical newspapers, written in a language and manner that were highly accessible to listeners and readers, had a significant social effect and played a key role in garnering mass support for the 'Urabi revolt.[55]

### ABU-NADDARA AND AL-TANKIT WA AL-TABKIT: SELLING THE 'URABI REVOLT, 1879–1882

Egypt's increasing state centralization, urbanization, and infrastructural modernization created unprecedented socioeconomic and cultural changes. These conditions provided the necessary climate for social mobilization and, as Juan Cole has shown, were an essential ingredient in the fermentation of the 'Urabi revolt.[56] One of the most important yet understudied catalysts of social mobilization in this period was the early use of colloquial mass culture in all its varying forms. In the period leading up to the 'Urabi revolt, *al-Tankit wa al-Tabkit* and *Abu-Naddara Zarqa'* were influential in focusing the public's anger on Egypt's deteriorating economic position, the corrupt ruling regime, and foreign economic interference. The papers played a crucial role in actively mobilizing support for the 'Urabi movement.

Isma'il's financial negligence had led to the bankruptcy of the Egyptian economy and the 1876 establishment of the Caisse de la Dette (Debt Commission), which essentially gave control of Egyptian finances to European creditors. The mismanagement of Egypt's finances decreased Isma'il's popularity in the eyes of the Egyptian masses. This situation was aggravated by the appointment of European officials to the Egyptian cabinet and an increase in taxes on ordinary Egyptians. These events were masterfully satirized by Sannu''s newspaper in a series of irreverent political cartoons, which proved to be extremely popular, as a London *Times* correspondent related.

M. Sanua [Sannu'] now added point to his attacks by availing himself of the French talent for caricature. He gave pen-and-ink cartoons of the subjects of his diatribes. These were far behind the brilliant drawings published by his London *confrere*; but, being a novelty in Egypt, whither the journal found its way under cover, they formed an attraction to natives and foreigners alike.[57]

The combination of biting vernacular humor and satire, geared for oral (re)transmission, and new visually stimulating cartoons greatly enhanced the popularity and political effectiveness of these journals. Their novelty, entertainment value, and accessibility to the masses greatly contributed to the delegitimization of the ruling regime and helped to focus Egyptian anger on foreign interference and economic inequity. An early cartoon (October 1878) by Sannu' accurately portrayed the national mood over the bankruptcy of the Egyptian economy and the perceived exploitation of the fellahin with excessive taxation (see Figure 2).

The cartoon depicts a fat Khedive Isma'il at the center with an emaciated and starving fellah on the right and his minister (Nubar) holding baskets full of food and drink on the left. As with all of Sannu''s cartoons, a short dialogue in colloquial Egyptian accompanies the illustration.

COMMENTATOR [SANNU']: O Muslims! The fellah is dying of hunger and his oppressor [i.e., Isma'il] is getting fatter . . .

ISMA'IL: My dear minister, I am terrified that these people will defeat us and that I might lose all this weight that I gained from eating [pork] and drinking alcohol.

THE MINISTER: Oh, don't worry, they are all in my pocket [*kuluhum fi gaybi*]. . . . Just stay behind me, master, and don't worry. You will get the freshest and most delicious foods and drinks and your [personal] savings are plentiful as always.

Sannu''s frequent cartoon assaults on Isma'il and the khedival cabinet in the pages of *Abu-Naddara* served to focus the public's anger on their economic condition while simultaneously delegitimizing khedival

FIGURE 2. *Isma'il's corruption. From* Abu-Naddara Zarqa', *October 22, 1878.*

authority. The effects of these images should not be underestimated, as the captions and dialogues were frequently read out loud not only in Cairo and Alexandria but also, as the Egypt correspondent of the London *Times* relates, "in many a village in Egypt."[58] John Ninet, a contemporary Swiss observer and a sympathizer with Egyptian nationalist aspirations, observed that "there was hardly a donkey boy of Cairo, or of any of the provincial towns, who had not heard them read, if he could not read them himself; and in the villages I can testify to their influence, for I was myself a diligent *colporteur* of Sanua's [Sannu''s] lucubrations wherever I went."[59] In his account of the events leading to the 'Urabi revolt, the contemporary Egyptian chronicler Mikha'il Sharubim corroborates these reports by describing how "those who were illiterate among the common people [*al-'amma*] relied on those who can read, and you saw them congregate in the streets of old and new Cairo, surrounding a man or a boy of these newspaper stands, who proceeds to read to them." On another day Sharubim recounts how he personally witnessed a "boy who works in a grain/bean store . . . standing outside the store . . . surrounded by a common low class crowd who were intently staring at him as he read aloud the latest news from an Arabic newspaper."[60]

The degree to which Egyptians valued the entertainment and information in the satirical press, the practice of communal reading, and the effortless shift from the written to the aural/oral is illustrated by an incident that took place at a public music concert in Cairo. According to the Cairo correspondent of *L'Europe diplomatique*, at a June 1879 concert of the "famous Cairene singer" Ahmad Salim, a newspaper seller was able to sell 300 copies of the recently outlawed *Abu-Naddara Zarqa'* to the audience, who completely ignored the singer and proceeded to read and discuss the newspaper in small groups. Finally, members of the audience convinced the singer to sing an anti-Isma'il *zajal* from *Abu-Naddara*. The end result of this audience-coerced group improvisation was the arrest and imprisonment of Ahmad Salim and his entire band for ten days.[61]

These continuing criticisms of Isma'il further delegitimized his authority, and by early 1879 the political situation in Egypt deteriorated even further. Because of Egypt's worsening debt problem, Nubar Pasha's cabinet, acting on a recommendation from its European cabinet members, began to implement a sharp decrease in public spending complemented by an even greater increase in taxation rates. These harsh methods alienated virtually every segment of Egyptian society, increasing the level of general discontent. The winter and spring of 1879 witnessed several demonstrations and riots. In February 18, 1879, a group of military officers surrounded the carriage of the Egyptian prime minister, Nubar Pasha, yelling obscenities at him and "screaming in his face: 'Oppressor! You don't deserve to live in such luxury while we are dying of hunger!'"[62] Isma'il was similarly accosted at a Cairene *mulid* (religious festival) when a crowd publicly insulted him by announcing his arrival with chants of "the dog has arrived" (*al-Kalb gih*) and cursing him for being the cause of their poverty.[63]

Behind the scenes, Isma'il attempted to channel the public's anger over the country's overall economic stagnation toward the European powers and the debt commission, by encouraging a group of influential Egyptians to draw up a petition.[64] Conveniently for Isma'il, the National Manifesto (*al-La'iha al-Wataniyya*) demanded the dismissal of the European cabinet members and the organization of an exclusively Egyptian parliament. The petition was signed by 329 Egyptian notables and was delivered to the representatives of the European powers and Isma'il on April 7, 1879. Isma'il of course immediately complied with those demands in a last ditch effort to regain some of his sovereignty. However, the khedive's machinations backfired and provoked England and France into forcing Sultan 'Abdul-Hamid to depose him in June in favor of his more malleable 27-year-old son Tawfiq.[65] Late in August 1879, perhaps fearing further political agitation, Tawfiq expelled al-Afghani from Egypt. Yet this move had little impact; al-Afghani's political philosophies were already deeply entrenched in his disciples, who had begun to form secret organizations and to publish independent newspapers to publicize their cause to an increasingly aroused and more politically aware Egyptian populace.[66]

Tawfiq fared no better than Isma'il, and the public's distrust and aggression was redirected toward his reign. In his newspaper, for example, Sannu' almost never used Tawfiq's real name but called him *al-Wad al-'Ahbal* (the dimwitted kid). In one of his brief theatrical sketches, Sannu' introduced the character of Tawfiq as "the kid well known for his dimwittedness, may the lord enlighten him and cure him of his mental condition." The major theme of this theatrical piece was that Tawfiq was merely a figurehead and that the real power behind the throne was in the hands of his prime minister Riyad Pasha—dubbed *Halik Wadi al-Nil* (tormenter of the Nile Valley) by Sannu'—who ruled by British decree. Adding to the comedic effect of the sketch was the condemnation and reproach directed at Tawfiq by his sister Wahida, who, unlike her brother, was represented in a positive light. Upon hearing that Tawfiq was traveling to Alexandria, Wahida tells her brother in colloquial Egyptian:

I heard that you are going on a trip, imbecile . . . so I came to see you off. By God what the hell are you going to do up north? Now I do believe it when they say that dimwits are in utter bliss. Riyad [Abu al-Rida] is getting rid of you politely so he can take care of his business without you looking over his shoulder. I wish that our father would have known before conceiving you what you were going to be like, and maybe then he would have never put you in this world and ruined our family name with your stupidity. . . . If only I were the man and you the woman, then maybe things would have worked out for the both of us.[67]

The sketch concluded in typical puppet theater fashion with Tawfiq's sister beating Riyad Pasha with her horsewhip while declaring, "Rise up, fearful Egyptians! Don't be scared and celebrate the beating of the enemy of all Muslims. . . . Be joyful *'afandiyya*, Beys, Pashas, and soldiers, for the Little Kid's minister wants to sell us and sell our nation to his English friends."[68]

This increasing interference by the European powers, coupled with overtaxation and the loss of financial independence, contributed to an overall sense of instability that affected all branches of Egyptian society. The military was not spared from these socioeconomic conditions, and budget cuts and perceived discrimination against "native" Egyptian officers by the Turkish and Circassian officers set into motion the spark triggering the rebellion. At the end of January 1881, a group of junior Egyptian officers led by Colonels Ahmad 'Urabi, 'Abd al-'Al Hilmi, and 'Ali Fahmi petitioned the government of Riyad Pasha to discontinue its policy of discrimination against "native" Egyptians. On the morning of February 1, 'Urabi, Hilmi, and Fahmi were stripped of their rank and arrested by direct orders of Riyad Pasha and placed in solitary confinement in the basement of the Diwan al-Jund (Ministry of the Soldiery) in Qasr al-Nil.

Immediately upon hearing the news, officers and soldiers of the Khedival Guard (Haras al-Khidiywi) led by an officer named Muhammad 'Ubaid, marched from 'Abdin to Qasr al-Nil and forcibly freed the officers. All the officers, the soldiers, and a gathering mass of civilians, who tacitly gave their support to the rebellion, proceeded to march and surround the khedival palace in 'Abdin. 'Urabi then delivered a public speech in 'Abdin Square, thanking the soldiers for freeing him from captivity and demanding that the khedive reinstate him along with Fahmi and Hilmi into the military ranks. Finally, he asked for the replacement of 'Uthman Pasha Rifqi as the minister of war. Tawfiq fulfilled all these demands, and 'Urabi made sure to receive further concessions from the khedive with regard to the military. Military salaries were increased, food quality improved, and the soldiers and officers received other fringe benefits ranging from paid vacations to discounted train tickets. This shrewdly made 'Urabi even more popular in the military and guaranteed its support.[69]

After securing the allegiance of the military, 'Urabi did his best to win over the Egyptian masses. In this effort he relied on 'Abdallah Nadim, who by June 6, 1881, had started publishing *al-Tankit wa al-Tabkit*. *Al-Tankit wa al-Tabkit* was less direct than *Abu-Naddara* in its critiques of the khedive and his ministers and initially focused on ameliorating social problems through a combination of serious essays in Fusha and humorous dialogues in colloquial Egyptian. Almost immediately after the initial military rebellion, Nadim supported the 'Urabists and used his magazine and his oratorical skills to popularize their cause with the Egyptian masses. According to the contemporary chronicler Mikha'il Sharubim, 'Urabi personally appointed Nadim as the movement's propagandist.

At that time Ahmad 'Urabi Bey assigned 'Abdallah Nadim, the owner of a newspaper called *al-Tankit wa al-Tabkit*, to roam the country's northern and southern districts to convince the people to support the leaders of the military faction ['*isabit al-jund*] and coerce the people into demanding the formation of a Representative Council [Majlis al-Nuwwab]. . . . 'Abdallah Nadim was strong willed, smooth-tongued, charismatic, easily understood by all, and an excellent motivator of people. He knew how the masses thought and catered his speeches to them, traveling to cities, towns, and villages to address the people and convey to them the latest news and convince them to take action against the injustice, and the [economic] deterioration they were experiencing.[70]

Nadim provided a glimpse of his travels throughout the Egyptian countryside and gave some accounts of what he encountered in *al-Tankit wa al-Tabkit*.[71] Indeed, as Sharubim indicates, Nadim's influence on the masses during the 'Urabi revolt was considerable. His revolutionary *azjal* and speeches were an integral component of propagandizing the 'Urabi movement.[72] On the suggestion of 'Urabi, Nadim changed his journal's name after its eighteenth weekly edition to *al-Ta'if* (The voyager) and edited it exclusively in Fusha, making it the official newspaper of the 'Urabi revolt. 'Urabi's decision to change Nadim's *al-Tankit wa al-Tabkit* from a satirical newspaper with a significant portion of its content in colloquial Egyptian into a newspaper written entirely in Fusha was a reflection of the consolidation of 'Urabi's movement from a counterhegemonic movement to, for the time being at least, the de facto governing force in Egypt. Colloquial Egyptian was, in everyone's view, "not serious enough" for an official newspaper.[73]

Partly because of Nadim's propaganda campaign, the Cairene urban masses supported the military demonstration of September 9, 1881, when, in a similar fashion to the events of February 1, a coordinated march of thousands of Egyptian troops headed to the khedival palace in 'Abdin. The three most important demands presented to the khedive were (1) the firing of the Riyad government, (2) the reconstitution of the Chamber of Delegates (Majlis al-Nuwab), and (3) the restoration of the Egyptian army to 18,000 men. Eventually all these demands were met, as yet another government was set up with Sharif Pasha at its head. Elections were held and the Chamber of Delegates was reinstated. This, however, did not end the reshuffling of the cabinet; Sharif's government fell on February 2, 1882, because of his refusal to bow to the demands made by 'Urabi and the Chamber of Delegates over control of the nation's budget. A new cabinet was soon assembled with the pro-'Urabi Mahmud Sami al-Barudi at its head. To win over the allegiance of the Egyptian army, al-Barudi promoted 'Urabi to major general and appointed him minister of war.[74]

Nadim was not the only propagandist for 'Urabi; throughout the events of 1881 Sannu' gave his full support to the officers' movement, filling his newspaper with cartoons and theatrical sketches designed to appeal to the Egyptian masses. For instance, after the dismissal of Sharif's cabinet and the appointment of 'Urabi as minister of war, Sannu' printed the cartoon shown in Figure 3 on the front page of *Abu-Naddara*.

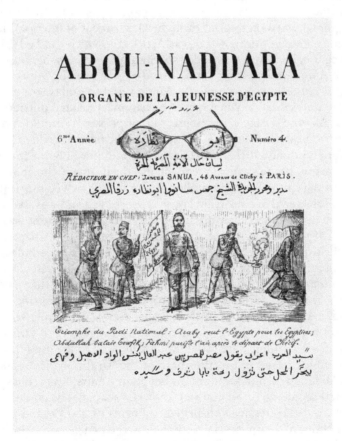

FIGURE 3. *Egypt for the Egyptians. From* Abu-Naddara Zarqa', *February 1882.*

In a clear attempt to justify the pushing aside of the Sharif government and legitimize the new pro-'Urabi cabinet, Sannu' depicts a proud
'Urabi in the center, holding a flag with the slogan "Egypt for the Egyptians" (*Misr lil-Misriyyin*). To the left and right of 'Urabi are Colonels 'Ali
Fahmi and 'Abd al-'Al Hilmi, who are forcing Tawfiq and Sharif Pasha
out of the room. The cartoon's caption reads: "The master of all Arabs,
'Urabi, says that 'Egypt is for the Egyptians' as 'Abd al-'Al sweeps out
the dimwitted kid [Tawfiq] and Fahmi lights some incense to remove the
smell of Sharif Pasha [*baba Sharaf*] and his master [Tawfiq]."[75]
    It was mainly because of cartoons and press attacks such as these by
Nadim and Sannu' that, months before the replacement of Sharif's government, a new press censorship law was drawn up, on November 26,
1881. The press law of 1881 primarily attempted to control all Egyptian
periodicals through the forced implementation of a number of regulations.
For instance, all new and existing newspapers were required to register
and acquire permission to print from the Department of Interior. The most
intriguing clause in this new law was Article 17, which can be labeled the
Sannu' clause, because it was added specifically to address the smuggling of
Sannu''s *Abu-Naddara* from Paris. It reads: "The Interior Minister [*Nazir
al-Dakhiliyya*] of this government is empowered to outlaw the entry, distribution, and sale of any newspaper or pamphlet printed outside Egypt's
borders. All who smuggle, distribute, sell, or possess a forbidden newspaper or periodical published outside Egypt will be fined anywhere from 1 to
25 Egyptian pounds." This article demonstrates not only the importance
and popularity of the satirical press but also the degree of threat and suspicion with which the Egyptian authorities and elites viewed satirical newspapers. However, this censorship law was short-lived and was shelved after
the British occupation. Three decades later, as the satirical press was boom-
ing, the 1881 press law was controversially reinstated (see Chapter 5).[76]
    The British, who would soon be directly involved in the administration
of the country, were also quite alarmed by the Egyptian press. Describing
*Abu-Naddara*, the London *Times* correspondent stated that its "worst
feature . . . is the extremely hostile tone which it is adopting towards
England." *Abu-Naddara*'s hostile tone, he added, "is in the worst taste,
the object being to render England ridiculous in the eyes of Orientals."[77]
The attacks on Sannu' were rather mild compared to the ones directed at
Nadim, which began in the aftermath of the 'Urabi revolt. In an article
titled "Abdallah Nedim [Nadim] on Egyptian Affairs," the *Times* quoted
translated segments of Nadim's *al-Ta'if* newspaper. The correspondent
chose the most aggressive anti-British segments of *al-Ta'if* and presented
them without any context. Directly below the article, a patriotic poem
about the reawaking of the British Empire was printed.[78]

Immediately after the new Barudi cabinet took the reins of power, the political situation began to deteriorate. Fearful of the pro–native Egyptian direction of the new cabinet, some Circassian and Ottoman notables ended their support for 'Urabi. A constitutional crisis ensued among Tawfiq, the Barudi cabinet, and the Chamber of Delegates. Before a diplomatic resolution could take place, the British and French, fearful of losing their debt payments, sailed their gunboats to Alexandria and, on the morning of May 25, demanded the immediate dismissal of the Barudi cabinet. This classic gunboat diplomacy was quite effective; Tawfiq quickly complied and sacked the Barudi cabinet, which provoked anti-foreigner riots throughout the city of Alexandria. The riots of June 11, which killed 250 Egyptians and 50 Europeans, sparked a chain of events leading to the British occupation of the country.[79] Thus in the summer of 1882, the British bombarded Alexandria and routed 'Urabi's forces at the battle of Tal al-Kabir, beginning an occupation that would last for more than seven decades.

### CONCLUSION

During the late nineteenth century, more than 94% of the Egyptian population was illiterate, underscoring the importance of satirical periodicals and *azjal*, which were written in an easily understood everyday Egyptian language.[80] Printed humorous vernacular sketches and catchy colloquial poems and jingles were orally transmitted in the same manner as jokes, or popular Egyptian proverbs, usually spreading like wildfire with the aid of urban communal meeting places, such as coffeehouses, marketplaces, barber shops, and mosques and Coptic churches. The use of the vernacular undoubtedly contributed greatly to the popularity of these journals and especially enhanced their potential for being read aloud.

Sannu''s *Abu-Naddara Zarqa'* and Nadim's *al-Tankit wa al-Tabkit* were not only unprecedented in their accessibility to a large readership and listenership but were also specifically designed to move the masses into action against the Turko-Circassian Egyptian elites and increasing European economic influence. As we have seen, both periodicals played a significant role in creating a counterhegemonic atmosphere that allowed Egyptians to question authority by encouraging and providing a forum of critical discussion. It is also clear that *al-Tankit wa al-Tabkit* and *Abu-Naddara Zarqa'* were instrumental in motivating and agitating Egyptian public opinion into supporting the 'Urabi revolt.

These new tools of mass culture reflected and articulated the frustrations of the Egyptian masses in an easy-to-understand and popular manner, supplying them with a sense of collective participation in national events and, in the process, giving rise to both a national public opinion and, by association, the beginnings of proto-national awareness. These urban-based cultural productions, which were predominantly written and performed in colloquial Egyptian, would soon develop into a national popular culture, transforming Cairene Egyptian for all intents and purposes into the de facto national dialect. This growth of a "popular" Egyptian-centric national culture, articulating itself almost exclusively in colloquial Egyptian, is the linchpin in a comprehensive understanding of the eventual rise of territorial Egyptian nationalism. This is especially true when calculating the impact of new recording technologies, such as the gramophone, which would be increasingly used in the first two decades of the twentieth century (see Chapters 4–6). Accordingly, in the remainder of the book I examine the implications of this "national" upsurge in colloquial Egyptian-centric cultural productions, especially as they relate to the formation of Egyptian national identity.

## CHAPTER FOUR

# New Media

## *Laughter, Satire, and Song, 1882–1908*

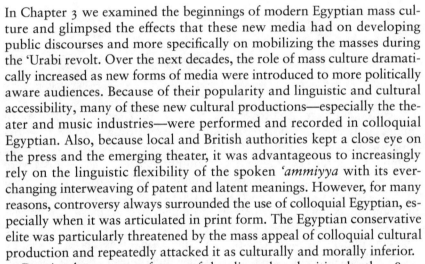

In Chapter 3 we examined the beginnings of modern Egyptian mass culture and glimpsed the effects that these new media had on developing public discourses and more specifically on mobilizing the masses during the 'Urabi revolt. Over the next decades, the role of mass culture dramatically increased as new forms of media were introduced to more politically aware audiences. Because of their popularity and linguistic and cultural accessibility, many of these new cultural productions—especially the theater and music industries—were performed and recorded in colloquial Egyptian. Also, because local and British authorities kept a close eye on the press and the emerging theater, it was advantageous to increasingly rely on the linguistic flexibility of the spoken *'ammiyya* with its ever-changing interweaving of patent and latent meanings. However, for many reasons, controversy always surrounded the use of colloquial Egyptian, especially when it was articulated in print form. The Egyptian conservative elite was particularly threatened by the mass appeal of colloquial cultural production and repeatedly attacked it as culturally and morally inferior.

Despite the protests of some of the elite cultural critics, by the 1890s several small improvisational theater troupes, performing comedic sketches and short *'ammiyya* one-act plays, crisscrossed Egypt—although professional colloquial Egyptian plays would not take off as an important medium until the middle of World War I. Commercial recordings of colloquial Egyptian songs and the establishment of a music industry began to take shape during the first decade of the twentieth century, inaugurating the transformation of colloquial Egyptian songs into a national mass medium. The cultural implications of recording sound and playing it on demand to mass listeners were immense. Unlike print, new recording technologies captured the aural nuances of sound and of the human voice, equally registering the emotional subtleties and tonal resonance of words as well as wordless vocalizations.[1]

In this chapter I follow the changes and effects of the Egyptian mass media from the beginning of the British occupation until the aftermath of the Dinshaway incident. In the process I examine the satirical press, the developing Egyptian theater, and the beginnings of the music recording industry. After briefly outlining the relative national inactivity during the first decade after the British occupation, I examine the sudden reawakening of the local satirical press in the 1890s and the political implications of this revival. The middle of the chapter focuses on the counterhegemonic elements of the colloquial press and the resulting "vulgarization" and repression of the satirical press by the British and the Egyptian cultural conservatives. Finally, I historicize the impact of Egyptian mass culture by examining the Dinshaway incident exclusively through the lens of mass culture.

### EARLY BRITISH OCCUPATION AND COLLOQUIAL CULTURE, 1882–1892

*Ya Kharabi, Ya 'Urabi!* (O, my ruin, o, 'Urabi!)                    —Egyptian proverb

The colloquial Egyptian proverb *Ya kharabi, Ya 'Urabi!* was likely born immediately after the bombardment of Alexandria and the British occupation of Egypt.[2] It reflects the sense of universal shock felt by average Egyptians over the occupation of the country. Most of the 'Urabists were arrested, and the key conspirators, including 'Urabi himself, were exiled to the island of Ceylon (Sri Lanka). 'Abdallah Nadim, however, fled to the Egyptian countryside, where he hid undetected for close to ten years until his capture and brief exile to Haifa on October 3, 1891.[3] These changing dynamics, coupled with a sort of national mass shock caused by the British occupation, forced a temporary hibernation of overt nationalist activity, as reflected by the relative decline of subversive press activity.

In the first few years of the British occupation, the British were still determining their overall Egyptian policy. Initially, the British intended to stay for only a few years until Egyptian economic and political stability could be established. To achieve this stability, the British attempted to strengthen traditional Egyptian ruling institutions and, as much as possible, used those institutions to camouflage their firm control of Egyptian affairs. Restoring khedival authority after it was severely shaken by the 'Urabi revolt was by far the most important British policy goal. However, the goal was almost impossible to achieve, for the simple reason that Tawfiq was viewed by many as a traitor for siding with the British against the 'Urabists.[4] The continuing satirical attacks by Sannu', who was still able to smuggle his newspaper into Egypt, also played a role in sabotaging khedival authority. Indeed, Tawfiq could not escape his characterization as *al-Wad al-'Ahbal* (the dimwitted kid) in the Egyptian national consciousness.[5]

With Nadim in hiding during the first decade of the British occupation, only Sannu''s *Abu-Naddara* provided sustained counterhegemonic attacks on the British and the Egyptian regime. The British were Sannu''s favored target; the depiction of the faulty Arabic pronunciation of "John Bull" and other English characters became his trademark and was copied by later satirists. Many of his dialogues contained different layers of meaning, skillfully interwoven with similes and double entendres. At times, Sannu' comically exploited the linguistic miscommunication that inevitably took place between Egyptians and British administrators. In one of the dialogues, an English government official catches an Egyptian in the act of reading *Abu-Naddara*, resulting in a heated debate. As the debate develops, the Egyptian yells "*Misr lil misryin*" (Egypt for the Egyptians), and the Englishman angrily responds in English, "Goddamn you bloody fool!" The Egyptian, thinking that the Englishman was still speaking to him in broken Arabic, wrongly hears this last statement as *bilad al-ful* (the land of fava beans, meaning Egypt) and quickly interrupts, "*Bilad al-ful* is our country. You should go back to your country, the land of potatoes, and leave us our precious *ful*."[6]

Adding to Sannu''s humor was his seemingly unlimited selection of comedic nicknames with which he unmercifully tagged his political enemies. Because Sannu''s British characters often began their sentences by shouting "Goddamn" (in transliterated Arabic), they were labeled *al-goddam* (the goddamns).[7] Another name used for the British was *al-humr* (the reds), referring to the redness of their faces from exposure to the Egyptian sun. Sannu' also frequently associates *humr* with *himir* (jackasses). In colloquial sketches in which Sannu' portrayed the British exploitation of Egyptian farmland and the fellah, they were dubbed *al-garad al-'ahmar* (the red locusts).[8] Britannia, representing Great Britain, was labeled *al-'aguz al-shamta'* (the mindless old lady)[9] and was usually conspiring against *abu al-ghulb* (the father of misery; i.e., the Egyptian fellah) with her son *al-mister bul* (John Bull).[10] Rounding out the list of English characters was Lord Cromer, the British consul-general in Egypt, usually labeled as *al-lurd kurunb* (Lord Cabbage.) Also, as we saw in Chapter 3, Sannu' did not spare Egyptian rulers and government officials, as the Egyptian prime minister Nubar Pasha became *ghubar basha* (Dirt Pasha).[11]

In the first decade of the British occupation, the "organized" Arabic theater slowly continued to take root as an entertainment outlet not only for the elite but also for the rising middle class. By the mid-1870s, enterprising Syrians such as Salim Khalil al-Naqqash, Adib Ishaq, and Yusif al-Khayat started their Arabic theaters in Egypt. Unlike Sannu''s and Jalal's plays, however, most of these plays were in Fusha, and thus their audiences were limited to the educated elite.[12] Of these three men, only al-Khayat continued his theatrical activities well into the 1880s, and to attract larger audiences, he had to resort to scheduling comedic sketches in colloquial Egyptian after the performance of the main play, which was typically a Fusha translation of a European play.[13] This set a precedent, and Egyptian audiences attending large Fusha productions came to expect a colloquial Egyptian comedic sketch at the end of the main performance. For this reason, theater advertisements in the local press almost always mentioned the name of the colloquial sketch that was to be performed.[14] In addition, to help sagging ticket sales, most Syrian theatrical troupes incorporated popular Egyptian singers into their plays. For instance, Salama Hijazi, the famous turn-of-the-century Egyptian singer, became a permanent addition to the Sulayman al-Qirdahi troupe.[15] Indeed, some of the reviews of the local press reveal that to most of the theater audiences at the time, the main event was the singing and not the acting. A theater review in the November 19, 1888, issue of *al-Qahira* newspaper stated that the performance of a Sulayman al-Qirdahi play was "ashamedly flawed in multiple ways. If it wasn't for the singing of the talented Sheikh Salama Hijazi, this night would have been akin to a funeral."[16] This formula of including colloquial sketches and a famous singer became a necessary prerequisite to achieving any success with late nineteenth-century theater audiences.

## THE RETURN OF NADIM AND THE REVIVAL OF THE NATIONALIST MOVEMENT, 1892–1895

The fact that the rabid utterances of the native press continue unchecked is causing anxiety, and surprise is felt that England, who is responsible for the maintenance of order in the country has not authoritatively interfered to stop this source of danger. The worst offender is the *Ustadh*, a paper started by Abdallah Nedim ['Abdallah Nadim] shortly after his pardon and return from banishment, to which he was sentenced as one of the most violent incendiary orators during Urabi's revolt.

—*The Times* (London), May 29, 1893

The death of Khedive Tawfiq on January 4, 1892, shook the Egyptian political status quo. Although Tawfiq had been compliant with most British demands, his 18-year-old son, 'Abbas Hilmi II, incessantly challenged British authority for most of his twenty-two-year reign. From the beginning of his rule, 'Abbas II needed a counterweight against British influence; reaching out to Egyptian nationalists, early on at least, adequately served this purpose. Even Sannu', who made a living out of unmercifully satirizing the Egyptian khedival family, always held back his satirical punches when portraying the young khedive. This can be seen in a cartoon that appeared in the May 1, 1893, issue of *Abu-Naddara* just five months after the inauguration of the young khedive (see Figure 4).

The cartoon, which was titled "*Namradit wa 'Inad 'Ingiltira al-'Aguz*" (The hardheadedness and transgressions of the aged Britannia), depicts Egypt as the sphinx, with Great Britain as the "old Britannia" riding on its back with whip in hand. As the Egyptian fellahin attempt to dismount Britannia from the sphinx (Egypt), Wilfred Blunt, pictured on the right, forcefully reasons with her: "Get down from there! The sphinx of Giza is not your mount. You are dishonoring this noble representation of ancient Egyptian glory. It is enough that he has to witness his country in the hands of foreigners!" Meanwhile 'Abbas II is on the left observing what is taking place with visible concern.[17] Although only Wilfred Blunt, the British pro-Egyptian activist, and the Egyptian fellahin are actively opposing British rule, 'Abbas II at least is portrayed as concerned with British action and, unlike Tawfiq, is not actively supporting it.[18]

One of the first conciliatory gestures of 'Abbas II toward the Egyptian nationalists was the pardoning of 'Abdallah Nadim, who was allowed to return to Egypt from his brief exile just one month after 'Abbas II assumed the reins of power. Almost immediately upon his return Nadim began publishing *al-'Ustadh* (The professor, or teacher).[19] The first edition of *al-'Ustadh* came out on August 23, 1892, duplicating the half-Fusha, half-colloquial Egyptian format of his *al-Tankit wa al-Tabkit*. As demonstrated by the quotation from *The Times*, *al-'Ustadh* not only retained

FIGURE 4. *The hardheadedness and transgressions of the aged Britannia. From* Abu-Naddara Zarqa', *May 1, 1893.*

the same style of Nadim's earlier journal but also continued with the same political agitations. This greatly alarmed the British authorities, who closely watched him.[20]

Nadim's most effective tool was Egyptian colloquial dialogues, which he undoubtedly learned from Sannu', although he used noticeably different subject matter. In his dialogues, Nadim frequently conversed with a representative of the masses and not with a famous political figure, as typically done by Sannu'. Because, unlike Sannu', Nadim published his paper in Cairo, he was greatly restricted by the censors and had to be much more cautious in his journalistic approach.[21] In one of his own colloquial Egyptian dialogues, Nadim hinted at these restrictions by declaring to a character named Habib:

We have nothing to do with politics, which confuses the mind and causes frequent headaches. Politics has its own type of people; I, on the other hand, am a person who is only interested in jokes, amusements, and leisurely pursuits. Moreover, this paper is a paper of knowledge, comedy, entertainment, and the teaching of proper etiquette. So, if you want to talk about proper manners, then I am your man, but if you want to talk about politics, then find someone else.[22]

Although Nadim never complied with this statement, he did make some halfhearted attempts at concealing the political nature of his discourse. In *al-'Ustadh* he mainly dealt with the loss of traditional Egyptian values to the "corrupting" influences of the West. Nadim was troubled by everything from the Westernization of clothing styles to the decrease in economic opportunity; his portrayal of economic anxiety reflected the loss of traditional Egyptian handicrafts with the advent of an ever-increasing amount of European manufactured goods.[23] Not surprisingly, because of similarities in style, subject matter, and readership, the circulation of *al-'Ustadh* was similar to that of *Abu-Naddara*. In January 1893 Nadim calculated the circulation of his *al-'Ustadh* at 2,288 copies per edition. This made *al-'Ustadh*'s distribution second only to *al-Ahram*, estimated to be 2,775 by Nadim.[24] Although the British were unable to stop the smuggling of Sannu''s *Abu-Naddara*, they continued to pressure 'Abbas II until he yielded and ordered the shutting down of *al-'Ustadh* and the re-exile of Nadim from Egypt. Sannu' continued to smuggle *Abu-Naddara* into Egypt until his retirement from journalism in December 1910.[25] Sannu''s and Nadim's newspapers were only the beginning of a tidal wave of similarly designed satirical periodicals that flooded the Egyptian public sphere in the early decades of the twentieth century. In the two decades from 1890 until 1910, more than 400 new periodicals were introduced to Egyptian readers. At least one-quarter of these periodicals had substantial colloquial Egyptian content (see Table 5 later in this chapter).[26]

It is no coincidence that political agitation and resistance to British rule increased dramatically after the brief return of Nadim on the political stage. Nadim's journal was quite popular among Egyptian students who were looking for a forum to express their nationalist aspirations. The influence that Nadim had on a generation of young literate students was substantial.[27] For example, evidence points to a close, yet brief mentorship of the young Egyptian nationalist Mustafa Kamil (1874–1908) by Nadim.[28] Mustafa Kamil was entirely the product of a new and growing upwardly mobile and literate Egyptian middle class. Kamil's father, an Egyptian army engineer of modest means, encouraged his son to continue his education. While still in high school, Kamil had an early interest in Egyptian politics and journalism and founded several student organizations, the most important of which was Jam'iyat 'Ihyia' al-Watan (Society for the Revival of the Nation). After his graduation from high school in the spring of 1891, Kamil decided to go to the khedival law school and continued his nationalist activities there.[29]

In February 1893, Kamil began publishing a monthly student magazine, *al-Madrasa* (The school). *Al-Madrasa*'s slogan was "Love your school, your people, and your country," and it contained nationalistic chants and educational dialogues, usually between students and their teacher. The inclusion of a written educational dialogue was likely inspired by Nadim's *al-'Ustadh*. Nadim noticed Kamil's new magazine and in his February 28, 1893, issue of *al-'Ustadh* proudly announced the creation of "*al-Madrasa*, edited by the cultured Mustafa Kamil." Nadim took the young Kamil under his wing and advised him not to repeat the mistakes of the 'Urabi revolt. He urged him to never make use of the army, to rely exclusively on the power of public opinion, and to forge a strong alliance with the khedive in order to strengthen his position in relation to the British.[30]

'Abbas II also developed a close bond with Mustafa Kamil. It was as a politically active law student that Kamil attracted the attention of the young khedive, who was perpetually out of favor with the British and wanted to regain more of his khedival authority. He was well aware that to accomplish this task, he had to gain the trust and support of the Egyptian people, and to this end he labored to mobilize Egyptian nationalist feelings to counter British colonial authority.[31] 'Abbas II first met with Kamil in an official visit he made to the khedival law school on November 28, 1892.[32] Noticing the potential usefulness of the young Kamil, 'Abbas II established a strong bond with him and supported many of his nationalist efforts.[33] 'Abbas II sponsored Kamil's continuing law education in Toulouse, where he received his law degree in November 1894.[34] Upon his return to Egypt in December 1894, Kamil did not practice law but devoted his full attention to politics. He immediately wrote several articles in *al-Ahram*, attacking the British and calling for their evacuation.[35] Kamil would define and symbolize Egyptian nationalism and anti-British resistance until his premature death in 1908.

COLLOQUIAL THEATER AT THE TURN OF THE
CENTURY, 1890–1910

During the 1890s and the first decade of the twentieth century, large Syrian theatrical companies continued to perform plays mostly in Fusha. When al-Qirdahi's troupe, in an effort to expand his audience, performed 'Uthman Jalal's colloquial translation of Molière's *L'école des femmes* (*Madrasat al-Nisa'*), he encountered strong opposition from Egypt's conservative elite.[36] On the other hand, unofficial and smaller traveling troupes that performed plays almost exclusively in colloquial Egyptian were able to resist these critiques because of their "low" status on the Egyptian culture scale. A contemporary playwright lists the troupes of Ahmad al-Shami, 'Abd al-'Aziz al-Jahili, Mikha'il Jirjis, 'Awad Farid, Ibrahim Hijazi, and Husayn al-Kafuri as the most popular with the masses at the turn of the twentieth century.[37] During the last decade of the nineteenth century, the Mikha'il Jirjis troupe was especially popular, and it uninterruptedly performed colloquial Egyptian plays throughout Egypt.[38] Attracting largely a lower- and lower middle-class audience, Jirjis's troupe performed many of their plays during Egypt's many *mawalid* (religious festivals) and typically performed in coffee shops and makeshift outdoor theaters.[39] As with many Egyptian theatrical troupes, Jirjis's company often traveled and performed in Alexandria, in many of the Delta towns, and in Upper Egypt. To be sure, these traveling theatrical troupes were small and semiprofessional, and their plays were overwhelmingly improvisational; nonetheless, because of their linguistic facility and their use of humor and satire, they were quite popular with the urban and rural masses.[40]

In an attempt to draw wider audiences and attract some of the mass appeal of these smaller troupes, the larger theater companies increasingly incorporated more colloquial Egyptian comedic sketches into their acts, although they never truly resorted to the performance of colloquial plays wholesale. These colloquial comedic sketches were popular during this period, and many minitroupes and one-man shows specialized in performing these types of productions. Most of these small troupes were named after their star comedian, who typically had a comedic stage name and performed largely improvised sketches. Muhammad Salama al-Qutt (The Cat), for example, in addition to closing for large theatrical troupes, performed his own sketches in the popular theaters of Dar al-Salam and al-Klub al-Misri in the popular Cairene district of al-Sayyida Zaynab. His performances, representative of the comedic sketch genre, were similar in style and content to the traditional puppet theater. These simple sketches derived most of their comedy from physical humor, the mimicking of foreign and local accents, and counterhegemonic power reversal roles in which an *ibn al-balad* character, often a servant, outwits a king or a pasha.[41]

Other comedians, such as Muhammad Farid al-Majnun (The Insane One) specialized in comedic musical performances and in theatrical monologues. According to 'Ali al-Ra'i, al-Majnun would perform an entire play on his own, specializing in the plays of Salama Hijazi.[42] Ahmad Fahim al-Far (The Rat) was another one-man show performer who played multiple musical instruments, sang, acted, and performed comedic monologues and short plays. Al-Far's sketches and songs had typical farcical names, such as "*Ziribat al-Bahayim*" (The farm animals' barn), where among other things he would mimic animal sounds using a Scottish bagpipe.[43] Al-Far had a traveling troupe of about a dozen actors, and according to Jacob Landau, the "mimetic farces performed by his troupe were immensely popular."[44]

Al-Far and Muhammad Nagi, another well-known comedian and actor, joined the large Qirdahi troupe as it toured the Egyptian countryside. The inclusion of these two comedians in the Qirdahi troupe was advertised in the press, demonstrating their importance to the success of the tour.[45] Nagi was also a regular with the Salama Hijazi troupe and later on with the Sheikh 'Atiyya troupe. When not opening or closing for large troupes, these comedic stars performed in coffee shops, weddings, and *mawalid*—traveling throughout the Egyptian countryside. Other famous comedic sketch artists included Muhammad al-Maghribi (with the stage name of Rih-Rih Bey) and Muhammad Kamal al-Misri, who had the stage name of Sharafantah (a comedic nickname with no meaning).[46]

These comedic troupes had a large fan base and were able to attract large audiences. As demand increased, many of the popular theater houses would feature comedic sketches as the main event, with one or more comedic artists performing in succession.[47] Aside from the short improvised colloquial sketches, longer colloquial comedic plays began to play in reputable theater houses such as Salama Hijazi's Dar al-Tamthil al-'Arabi.[48] 'Aziz 'Id specialized in making short plays inspired by comedic sketches and consisting of three acts, which would set a precedent for the later comedic theater.[49] In September 1907 'Id established his own semiprofessional comedic troupe, the Arabic Comedy Troupe, which played in some of the mainstream theaters of Cairo. The titles of 'Id's plays best illustrate the type of comedy that was performed by his troupe. He premiered with his *Darbit al-Maqra'a* (The cane's wallop), which played for several weeks, and followed it with *Mubaghatat al-Talaq* (The abruptness of divorce), *al-Ibn al-Khariq lil-Tabi'a* (The paranormal son), and *al-Malik Yalhu* (The king is frolicking about).[50]

'Id seemed to test the limits of theatrical and social norms by constantly pushing the envelope. He readapted *Romeo and Juliet* into a farcical colloquial Egyptian comedy, titled *Shuhada' al-Gharam* (The martyrs of passion), which greatly infuriated classicists and theater critics. Although these burlesque plays were similar in style to the typical comedic sketches, they had more structured plots. To be sure, like all Egyptian comedic plays, the actors had an improvisational license, and often the audience vocally participated in the play, in literal dialogical exchanges. By the start of World War I, colloquial Egyptian theatrical productions began playing regularly in Cairene and Alexandrian theaters, and they forced out of business many of the Fusha troupes, which struggled to attract a regular audience. 'Id regularly performed his plays until the end of 1909, when he virtually disappeared from the pages of the Egyptian press, reappearing more permanently on the Egyptian scene in 1916 with a number of even more controversial and groundbreaking plays (see Chapter 5).[51]

## LAUGHTER AND RECORDED COMEDIC SKETCHES

Colloquial comedic sketches reached an entirely new milestone in popularity and accessibility with the introduction of gramophone technology in Egypt. The record companies in Egypt recognized the mass appeal of these sketch comedies and recorded dozens of monologues, dialogues, farcical songs, and *'afiya*s (linguistic duels) by the top comedic artists in Egypt. An *'afiya* (*qafiya*) is a form of formulaic verbal duel between two comedians or *zajjalun* who repeatedly exchange cutting taunts and insults, using double entendres and plays on words. Traditionally these duels took place in coffee shops, and the winner, the one judged to be the "wittiest," was declared by the spectators.[52] Many of the early comedic recordings consisted of *'afiyya*s. Typically, after the two participants introduced themselves and the subject matter of their comedic "debate," they took turns in formulaically setting the other up for alternating punch lines. After the delivery of each punch line, both participants along with any "audience" members who may have been present at the recording session "spontaneously" laughed aloud. According to sound media scholar Jacob Smith, this recorded "sound of uninhibited laughter, produced both by the performers and by audiences, was an important index of authentic presence used to bridge the gap between recorded sound and the listener."[53] Recorded laughter was also intended to draw in the listeners and entice them to laugh on cue along with the recorded punch lines.

Sayyid Qishta, whose name means "the hippopotamus" in colloquial Egyptian and who apparently was dubbed with this nickname because of his appearance, made at least forty-three records of his monologues and comedic songs with over half a dozen different record companies.[54] At the height of his popularity, Qishta appeared on the cover of Zonophone's 1908 catalogue, along with Munira al-Mahdiyya, who was one of the most famous Egyptian singers at the time.[55] Qishta's recorded sketches and songs had typical farcical names, for example, "*Sayyid Qishta fi al-Khamara*" (The Hippopotamus at the tavern), "*Tuhur Ibn al-Haj Sayyid*" (The circumcision of the son of al-Haj Sayyid), and "*Nuzhit Qishta fi Bariz*" (Sayyid Qishta's vacation in Paris). In typical vaudeville fashion, most of these sketches used physical humor and made fun of elite culture, especially Westernized culture, and championed urban middle-class values.[56]

As with most forms of colloquial mass culture, humor in these sketches was usually achieved with linguistic subterfuge, where, for example, foreigners or those who were deemed outsiders incorrectly pronounced colloquial Egyptian, creating the expected comedic effect. Many of these sketches featured European, and especially Greek characters, who were always portrayed with distinctively stereotyped *khawaga* (foreign) accents. The Nubians and Sudanese were arguably the most maligned "outsider" group; they were mercilessly stereotyped for cheap laughs by most forms of Egyptian mass culture. Fitting this mold were Qishta's sketches "*al-Babari wa al-Haj Sayyidu*" (The Nubian and Haj Sayyid) and "*Hikayit al-'Abid al-Talata*" (The story of the three black slaves). Four of the twelve recorded comedic sketches of Ahmad Fahim al-Far available in the Egyptian National Library collection stereotypically satirize Nubians and sub-Saharan Africans.[57]

The Egyptian-Turkish aristocracy, also a favorite target of the comedic sketch artists, was typically satirized as being cruel and coldly unaware of Egyptian daily life. The spoken Arabic pronunciation of these Turkish characters was full of Turkish words and exaggerated mispronunciations of colloquial Egyptian, and the characters were portrayed as inherently alien and out of touch with everyday Egyptian reality.[58] This anti-elitism also had an anticlerical component to it, as religious figures such as sheikhs and *fiqi*s (Qur'anic reciters) were satirized for speaking in Fusha and not the language of the masses. Qishta's "*'Afiyat al-Fiqi*" (Verbal duel of the *fiqi*) mockingly portrays the inevitable misunderstandings that take place when a Fusha-speaking cleric is speaking with an *ibn al-balad*. In "*'Afiyat al-Nahu*" ([Fusha] grammar verbal duel), also by Sayyid Qishta, the incomprehensibility of Fusha's grammar rules are mocked with numerous double entendres.[59]

Thus, in addition to the representation of foreigners and other "outsiders," religious figures and intellectuals who unnecessarily made use of spoken Fusha were viewed as anachronistically detached from everyday Egyptian life. Only Cairene Egyptian-Arabic was portrayed as understandable (to all) and hence familiar and normal. According to the discourse of Egypt's new vernacular mass culture, the primary prerequisite of Egyptian identity or Egyptianness was (and to a great extent still is) to speak in a flawless colloquial Cairene accent. This message of equating Cairene linguistic facility with Egyptian national authenticity was not only repeatedly represented on the comedic stage but also, as we shall soon see, in all forms of Egyptian mass culture.

The developing colloquial theater, and especially the comedic sketch phenomenon, was an important and extremely popular form of entertainment in turn-of-the-century Egyptian society. The effectiveness and reach of the sketch comedies were multiplied dramatically with the introduction of the gramophone and the recording of dozens of comedic records, which reached thousands of listeners. These new sound media allowed for music, sounds, and the human voice to be captured, duplicated, and heard by countless listeners. For the first time, the preserved human voice could be replayed on demand, functioning as an aural register of articulated words. More important perhaps, wordless vocalizations that captured the full range of human emotions, from sighs and grunts to weeping and laughter, were also deployed on demand, forging an emotive bond with thousands of potential listeners. Indeed, the recorded human voice can be a powerfully embodied aural register of identity. As we have seen, often these recorded vocal performances were loaded with notions of race, ethnicity, and national identities. Or as Jacob Smith eloquently elaborates, "The voice can function as an index of the body, a conveyor of language, a social bond, a musical instrument of sublime flexibility, a gauge of emotion, central component of the art of acting, and a register of everyday identity."[60]

## THE GRAMOPHONE ERA AND
## THE ADVENT OF THE *TAQTUQA*, 1903–1910

Never before, had performers been separated in time and space from a face-to-face audience. New sound technologies such as the phonograph also preserved nuances of performance such as the grain of the voice and wordless vocal expressions of intense emotion that would have eluded written scripts or musical scores.

—Jacob Smith, *Vocal Tracks*

Recorded music was already known in Egypt in the 1890s, as advertisements for purchasing gramophones directly from Europe appeared periodically in the Arabic press; however, the cost was still prohibitive for widespread middle-class consumption. At the beginning of the twentieth century, the cost of a new machine began to decrease steadily, thereby giving rise to a large demand for Arabic recordings.[61] By 1903, media capitalists and agents of multinational recording companies began expanding into the Egyptian market, and gramophones gradually became important instruments in forming an increasingly national musical identity.[62] The British Gramophone company and its subsidiary Zonophone were the first record companies to make large-scale recordings in Egypt in 1903, followed in 1905 by Odeon and Baidaphon (Baydafun), which in 1907 became the first Middle Eastern recording company to enter the Egyptian market.[63] Before World War I these three companies competed with each other to sign famous comedians and singers to their labels (see Chapter 5).[64]

Although the comedic monologues and dialogues that were recorded by the developing Egyptian music industry were popular, it was the colloquial Egyptian song that elevated the commercial record industry into the most important player in shaping early twentieth-century Egyptian mass culture. More than ever before, Egyptians of all walks of life were repeatedly exposed to the same music and the same songs by ever more popular national stars. In addition, this new recording medium had a role in shaping the evolution of Egyptian music into shorter and simpler colloquial songs that better suited the length limitations of the recording discs as well as the musical tastes of an increasingly middle-class consumer. The most popular and revolutionary of the colloquial songs was the *taqtuqa* (pronounced *ta'tu'a* in *'ammiyya*), which because of its popularity and simplicity became the song of choice for the Egyptian record industry. A *taqtuqa* was a short (2 to 5 minute), lighthearted, colloquial Egyptian pop song. Until World War I, *taqatiq* (plural) were sung primarily by women.[65] According to Frédéric Lagrange, before 1913, 83% of all the *taqatiq* recorded by Odeon were sung by women, dropping to 65% by 1929.[66] This demand for *taqatiq* required record companies to compete to sign female singers, thereby dramatically increasing the popularity, public exposure, and respectability of female artists throughout early twentieth-century Egypt. Egyptian female singers such as Tawhida al-Suwaysiyya (from Suez) and Bahiyya al-Luwati (Bahiyya the General) were already singing to the Egyptian masses in coffeehouses and cabarets.[67] By making records, however, such women were heard in thousands of homes, coffee shops, and businesses throughout Egypt, achieving for the first time true national exposure; this process created a number of renowned female singing stars. Before 1907, Gramophone signed Nafusa al-Bimbashiyya (Nafusa the Colonel) and Fatma al-Baqaliyya (Fatma the Grocer); Odeon signed 'Asma al-Kumsariyya ('Asma the Tram/Train Conductor), and Bahiyya al-Mahalawiyya (i.e., from the town of al-Mahala al-Kubra);

and Baidaphon signed Badriyya Sa'di. Later, Baidaphon lured Munira al-Mahdiyya away from Gramophone, and in the 1910s and 1920s she would become the most famous singer in Egypt (see Chapter 5).

The popularity of *taqatiq* soared even higher during and after World War I. As we will see in Chapter 5, the expansion of the comedic musical theater, coupled with the growing recording industry, created national superstars, such as Munira al-Mahdiyya and Sayyid Darwish, who would later have an unparalleled influence over millions of Egyptian listeners. By the 1920s, the laws of supply and demand fostered an elaborate music industry composed of writers, musicians, and singers to cater to this growing demand for new hits.[68] This new mass entertainment industry increased the democratization of Egyptian music by exposing more and more Egyptians to the same musical "recording culture," creating in the process a national community of listeners. The growth of this recording culture, complemented in many ways by the growth of a parallel print culture, created for the first time a nationally consumed mass culture.

### THE COLLOQUIAL PRESS:
### THE RAPID GROWTH OF AN INDUSTRY

There is no more striking manifestation of the New Spirit than the rapid growth of the Arabic daily press. In the afternoons the various native newspapers as they appear are bought up rapidly; the barefooted newspaper boys in their blue or white robes and grubby turbans do a bustling trade. The newspaper habit has taken a firm hold, and there can be no doubt that it does some good, very likely, but also a great deal of harm.                    —H. Hamilton Fyfe, *The New Spirit in Egypt*

The mass-cultural production of the comedic theater and the developing music and recording industry were complemented, supported, and in some cases driven by the Egyptian press. The press advertised for, critiqued, and sustained both of these mass industries, creating a lasting symbiotic relationship among the three media. Satirical periodicals were especially connected to colloquial theater and music, as many of their editors were *zajjalun* by training and were often commissioned by producers and directors to write colloquial song lyrics and plays. Thus it is not surprising that the colloquial press at the least matched the growth of its sister media. Indeed, from the inception of Sannu''s *Abu-Naddara* newspaper in 1877 until 1930 at least 168 new satirical periodicals were specializing in the comedic use of colloquial Egyptian (see Table 5). This figure is misleading, however, because for political or financial reasons many of these magazines and newspapers did not last more than a few issues, and sometimes a newspaper that changed only its name was counted as a new periodical.

TABLE 5. *Percentage of new colloquial periodicals,*
*1880s–1940s*

| Years | New colloquial periodicals | Total new periodicals | Percentage of colloquial periodicals |
|---|---|---|---|
| 1880–1889 | 6 | 49 | 12.2 |
| 1890–1899 | 39 | 163 | 24.0 |
| 1900–1909 | 62 | 278 | 22.3 |
| 1910–1919 | 10 | 80 | 12.5 |
| 1920–1929 | 45 | 442 | 10.2 |
| 1930–1939 | 8 | 382 | 2.1 |
| 1940–1949 | 3 | 187 | 1.6 |
| Total | 173 | 1,581 | 10.9 |

SOURCE: *Dar al-Kutub al-Misriyya.* The number of periodicals is based solely on the periodical collection available at Dar al-Kutub. The actual number of periodicals is likely to be higher. The decline in the number of periodicals from 1910 to 1919 is due to the reinforcement of the press law of 1881 in 1909 and stringent British censorship during World War I.

For example, the first issue of a satirical cartoon-filled newspaper called *Ha-ha-ha* appeared on March 8, 1907, whereas the second issue of the same magazine appeared a week later but with the new name of *Khayal al-Zil* (The shadow theater). *Khayal al-Zil* consisted of only eight pages, half of which were filled with cartoons. The editor, Ahmad Hafiz 'Awad, was not afraid of controversy and aggressively lampooned Cromer and several Egyptian ministers, although he saved his most aggressive attacks for Faris Nimr, the editor of the pro-British *Muqattam* newspaper. Perhaps because of its controversial nature, *Khayal al-Zil* was shut down a year later (1908) and remained in hibernation for sixteen years until reappearing with the same editor on June 12, 1924.[69]

Despite this apparent volatility, the popularity and mass appeal of these types of periodicals were enormous, because they presented to the Egyptian masses an alternative (unofficial) and more accessible form of cultural expression. The following quote from the memoirs of Muhammad Lutfi Jum'a demonstrates the importance of satirical periodicals, not just as an instrument of entertainment but as a source of "serious" news.

I learned to read newspapers and pay attention to internal politics through reading the satirical magazines [*al-Magalat al-hazaliyya*] like 'Abdallah Nadim's *al-'Ustadh* and *Abu-Naddara Zarqa'*, the magazine belonging to Sannu', the Egyptian Jewish nationalist, and *Humarit Muniyati.* These periodicals were much more candid than newspapers like *al-Mu'ayyid* and *al-Ahram.*[70]

In addition, and perhaps more important, by satirizing and laughing at the injustices of the occupation and elite exploitation, the satirical press provided a much needed forum for everyday resistance for many Egyptians.

The two decades from 1890 to 1910 were the beginning of the golden age of colloquial and satirical journalism in Egypt, which lasted for almost half a century. During that first twenty-year period, there were more than 100 new satirical periodicals, which corresponded to roughly 20% of all new periodicals.[71] The number of colloquial periodicals forming at the turn of the twentieth century indicated not only the amount of disaffection caused by the tremendous changes taking place in Egyptian society but also the need for a more popular and accessible forum to express these frustrations and perhaps harness it politically. The competition among the different periodicals was fierce, leading to a slippery slope of controversial yellow journalism in an effort to attract more readers. Personal attacks on prominent Egyptian and British leaders were common, driving up newspaper sales. This early "journalistic" boom period was followed by a decade (1910–1920) of relative decline for all Egyptian journalism. Partly in reaction to the perceived transgressions of the colloquial press, in 1909 the restrictive 1881 press law was reapplied to the Egyptian press, which caused many of the controversial periodicals to shut down and temporarily discouraged new newspapers from opening. This general decline intensified during World War I because of repressive British wartime censorship (see Chapter 5).

In the 1920s the Egyptian press rebounded again with more than 442 new periodicals, averaging an astonishing new periodical every eight days. The colloquial press also made some gains with forty-five new periodicals, although comparatively the ratio of colloquial to Fusha newspapers was halved from the highs of the 1890s and 1900s. This relative decline in the number of colloquial newspapers continued sharply in the following decades, until they disappeared completely by the 1950s (see Table 5). This was partly because of the endless assaults by intellectual and religious orthodoxy on the "corrupting" influence of low-class colloquial discourse, although the most important reason was the introduction of new technologies better suited for colloquial expression. Colloquial Egyptian was especially deemed a danger to orthodoxy when it was written or printed. The perceived permanency of print seemed to threaten the written language of the Qur'an. Egyptian radio, movies, and television, which almost exclusively relied on colloquial Egyptian, filled the need for colloquial cultural expression and did not reap the ire of the conservatives, primarily because they did not disseminate colloquial Egyptian in a written form.

Most satirical newspapers had a similar organizational structure. The main component of most colloquial newspapers was a colloquial poetry section, which often functioned as a forum for the exchange of colloquial poetry, with many readers sending in their own writings for publication. Usually there was a major section written in Fusha, and it often contained "serious" editorial pieces. Many newspapers featured regular theatrical pieces or dialogues written fully in colloquial Egyptian, typically with educational, morally driven civic themes. Some newspapers featured political cartoons, almost always with colloquial Egyptian captions. The letters to the editors in many of these satirical periodicals were usually lively with debate, with some readers sending in the latest joke, and at times readers sent their letters and comments in *zajal* form. These virtual discussion forums played themselves out in print in most literary and satirical periodicals; some of these discussions, along with the latest political rumors, were played out and debated face to face in coffee shops and other popular public meeting areas.

### REPEATING THEMES IN THE SATIRICAL PRESS

The colloquial press implicitly criticized the West either by directly blaming it for domestic concerns or by "othering" Westerners and excessively Westernized Egyptians and contrasting them to "authentic" Egyptians. One of the most common topics addressed by the colloquial press was the concern over an increasingly undiversified Egyptian economy and the loss of traditional Egyptian jobs. These concerns were often tackled in *azjal* and in colloquial dialogues. Typically the blame was directed at the foreign communities in Egypt, although sometimes the Egyptians themselves were blamed for not "buying Egyptian" and supporting the Egyptian economy. Another commonly repeated theme was the portrayal of Egyptian "traditional morality" as being continually compromised by alien Western values. Almost anything ailing Egyptian society, from excessive gambling to drug use, public drunkenness, and prostitution, was blamed entirely on European influence. These often gendered critiques attempted to fashion an implicit code of moral behavior for "modern" Egyptian men and women. More important, the colloquial press persistently portrayed colloquial Cairene as the only "authentic" Egyptian dialect and contrasted it with other Arabic dialects and with foreign pronunciations of Arabic. It typically portrayed an Egyptian culture continually besieged by Western culture.

### The Economy and National Solidarity

The satirical press's portrayal of a national mood of economic and cultural anxiety reflected the rapid changes taking place in Egypt at the time. Nadim's *al-'Ustadh*, for instance, confronted the loss of traditional

Egyptian values, attributing it to the "corrupting" influences of the West. Nadim was troubled by everything from the Europeanization of clothing styles and the encroachment of Western culture to the apparent decrease in economic opportunity for the average Egyptian. He was concerned particularly with the loss of local jobs and the relative decline in Egyptian manufacturing brought about by the increasing importation of European ready-made goods. In a colloquial dialogue titled "*al-Mu'alim Hanafi wa Nadim*," al-Mu'alim Hanafi (Master Hanafi)[72] approaches Nadim and begins to complain about the worsening economic conditions, where-upon Nadim angrily responds, "What can the people do, now that all the goods are imported? Cooked canned meat, dried milk, tailored garments, even cotton and woolen textiles used to make turbans and caftans are manufactured and imported from Europe. What are we supposed to do about this calamity?" By reenacting the worsening economic conditions and setting the blame entirely on the British and European residents of Egypt, Nadim is implicitly asking for a reaction from the masses. The sarcastic element in Nadim's dialogue is evident when he asks Hanafi, "So, we don't have any craftsman?" To this Hanafi sarcastically responds, "Oh, not at all. Thank God we still have plenty of garbage men, donkey drivers, porters, servants, shoe shiners, doormen [*bawwabin*], falafel and bean [*ful*] sellers, etc."[73]

Sannu' also dealt with economic issues, often depicting the increased hardships of the overtaxed and exploited Egyptian fellah. Because he was publishing his journal from Paris, Sannu' was much more direct in his attacks on the British and the khedives.[74] The characters in Sannu''s dialogues often included either Isma'il, Tawfiq, or Lord Cromer engaged in different fictional scenarios with Sannu' (as Abu-Naddara) and the Egyptian fellah. Invariably, the fellah, with Sannu''s help, would end up outwitting the British "villains" and their supporting casts.[75]

Some enterprising Egyptian business owners advertised in the satirical press to urge readers to buy their Egyptian-made products. For example, an advertisement in the form of a short article titled "Toward Solving the Egyptian Problem," in *al-Kashkul al-Musawwar* (The illustrated note-book), starts out by advising its readers that "economic independence is the true foundation of political independence . . . and the only way to do this is through buying Egyptian-made goods. . . . So you should ask yourself: Are you among those who passionately yearn for the indepen-dence of this great country?" After this patriotic call to action, the article continues: "Why not buy your tarbush [fez] from the store of Khalil Ali 'Uthman in Azbakiyya, right next to al-Luvr [the Louvre] coffee shop? And why not buy the healthy cigarettes of this fine establishment, which are pure tobacco, not cheated and are 100% Egyptian."[76] In the first quarter of the twentieth century, these types of nationalist advertisements were quite common on the pages of the Egyptian press. Petty merchants, clothing manufacturers, cigarette makers, and even bakers advertised the fact that their goods and products were Egyptian-made.[77]

### Women, Men, and "Preserving" National Morality

The perceived collapse of "moral" order in Egypt as a result of increased European cultural influence was discussed in most satirical periodicals. It is impossible to empirically measure the decline in "morality" in any society, but some contemporary observers note that public drunkenness and gambling by Egyptian men increased noticeably. Wilfrid S. Blunt, an Englishman who supported the nascent Egyptian national movement, recorded this phenomenon in his diaries. In his February 20, 1890, diary entry, Blunt observed that heavy drinking was "beginning to show itself markedly in Egypt as a consequence of the establishment of English rule." He then described the increase in the number of "Greek drink sellers" who set up shop in every train station along a small railway line that connected several villages with Cairo (near his country house in Shaykh Obeid). Blunt felt so strongly about this issue that he specifically met with Lord Cromer on March 25 and April 6, 1890, to discuss it. At the April 6 meeting Blunt gave Cromer a petition signed by seventy-three notables from neighboring villages calling for the closing of these "drink shops."[78]

Concern over the alleged increase in gambling and public drinking filled the pages of the Egyptian press and was a favorite subject of the satirical periodicals. A *zajal* in *al-'Arghul* (The flute), titled "*Zajal al-'Arghul fi al-Sarmaha*" (Zajal al-'Arghul on frolicking about), addressed this issue directly and placed the blame for this apparent decline in morality squarely on the shoulders of Europeans.[79]

> After selling the cotton—taking the country's wealth in his pockets
> He arrives in Cairo riding a donkey
> . . .
> He drinks alcohol, smokes hashish and loses all awareness
> After "enjoying-himself" and gambling away all his money in one night
> The Jackass [*al-bihim*][80] is finally aware of what he has done
> . . .
> What if instead he took a walk to enjoy the fresh air
> Drinking a coffee, smoking a cigarette and then returning home
> Walking politely/discreetly as you would in plain daylight
> Then "Elias" would not have taken away all his money[81]

In short, one of the messages constantly repeated on the pages of the satirical press was that Egypt's wealth went directly from its fertile fields into the pockets of non-Egyptians, who cunningly exploited the naïveté of Egyptian men.[82] Some satirical periodicals, especially those professing to be "morally instructional" (*tahdhibiyya*), offered some possible solutions.

Nadim's remedy for curing Egyptian males of their destructive gambling and alcohol habits was to enlist the aid of their wives. This approach not only encouraged Egyptian women to rein in their wasteful and morally corrupt husbands but also tried to shame Egyptian males into taking care of their domestic responsibilities. Nadim's eight-page "Hanifa and Latifa" colloquial dialogue in the September 27, 1892, issue of *al-'Ustadh* features two housewives who are tired of their morally irresponsible husbands and take turns complaining to each other. For instance, in a "low" Cairene pronunciation, Latifa declares:

You cry to me and I complain to you, but by the Prophet, if I told you what our dog [i.e., her husband] does to us, you would not believe it. When he gets paid his salary, I can barely get money from him to pay even the rent, and I have to beg him to get two pounds of his twenty-pound salary. . . . He has no shame for leaving his children with barely any clothes on their backs and spends five or six days at a time outside the house in the company of other women . . . while the children and I can barely feed ourselves.[83]

In the next issue, another dialogue, titled "Latifa and Damiyana," continues with the same storyline, but this time the ladies and their friends decide to hold a meeting to discuss their husbands' problems and attempt to devise a solution. To demonstrate that this was a national "crisis" and to preach Egyptian national unity, Nadim created religiously diverse characters to narrate his morality tale. The same Latifa (a Muslim) from the dialogue met with Damiyana (a Coptic Christian), Rif'a (an Egyptian Jew), and a few other concerned wives. To further reinforce Nadim's call for national unity, the three women, all speaking in colloquial Cairene, stressed the universality of this problem across religious lines through deliberately emphasizing the fact that such behavior is discouraged in Islam, Christianity, and Judaism. In the first part of the dialogue, the characters complain about the details of their husbands' indiscretions, whether alcoholism, gambling, drug abuse, or infidelity, and together they decide to regularly meet and attempt to deal with their collective problems, or as Latifa, the main protagonist, declares, "So we decided to meet at 'Umm Shafiq's house and invite all of our dear female friends to discuss a way to stop our men from drinking alcohol and gambling and force them to pay attention to the needs of their households." And in a surprising nineteenth-century gender reversal, Latifa continues, "Our purpose is to preserve the honor and wealth of our men and keep them away from these harmful pursuits." Thus the meeting is held and the solution is declared by Nagiyya, who explains to all the women who attend, "Women play an enormous role in keeping their men away from such destructive behavior." She then stresses to her audience that "any woman can surely set her own husband straight, although to be entirely successful, her sisters have to support her so they can also cure their own husbands from impropriety. Because if one of his friends is still on this destructive path, he might again lead your husband astray [*yi laghbat 'a'luh*], but if we all work together, then all of them will be set on the correct path."[84]

This positive portrayal of Egyptian women as the moral compass and educator of the nuclear family contrasts with the following 1895 *zajal* that appeared in *al-'Arghul*; the poem criticizes what the editor perceives as increasingly "loose" behavior by some Egyptian women.

> The lady is walking with the veil [*il-bur'u'*]
> Though her eyes wander everywhere [*'iyunha makhyula*]
> And on the road she's walking playfully [*tidala'*]
> She really knows all the ins and outs [*ti'raf al-sim wil-fula*]
> The woman is walking in the quarter [*al-haara*]
> Continuously teasing and calling out to men [*ti'akis riggala*]
> These are the times, but oh, what a great loss [*'akhir zaman ah ya khusara*][85]

In this manner both Egyptian men and women were chastised for "improper" behavior by the satirical press, always with the insinuation that these "moral" problems were a result of blind imitation of the West or direct exploitation by corrupting Westerners. Or, as another *zajal* in *al-'Arghul* advised its readers, "Leave all this imitation of the West and live the life of your country, or else this blind mimicry will surely lead to endless troubles."[86]

## CULTURAL AND LINGUISTIC SATIRE AND
## THE LANGUAGE OF "TRUE" EGYPTIANS

Identical to what we have seen with the comedic theatrical sketches, a great deal of the comedy in the satirical press was derived from the "language play" of colloquial Egyptian dialogues, which often contrasted the "normal" sounding Cairene dialect with the mispronunciation and accents of foreigners or of those deemed cultural outsiders. Unlike Fusha, which was considered too serious for effective satire, colloquial Egyptian provided the cultural and linguistic flexibility necessary for mimicking the various accents and pronunciations of European and other non-Egyptian characters. Aside from achieving the intended comedic effect, contrasting the familiar Cairene Egyptian pronunciation with the alien pronunciations of the "other" created a sort of national consensus, reinforcing the notion that Cairene Egyptian Arabic was the only authentic national Egyptian dialect.

The plasticity of colloquial Egyptian was masterfully illustrated by 'Abdallah Nadim, who accurately portrayed the slurred speech of drunken Egyptian men, the pronunciation and idioms of uneducated Egyptian housewives, and the linguistic mannerisms of the fellah.[87] One of Nadim's best characterizations was his portrayal of the Westernized pronunciation of Arabic by European-educated Egyptian men.[88] One of these early sketches by Nadim was printed in the June 6, 1881, issue of *al-Tankit wa al-Tabkit*. In the sketch "*'Arabi Tafarnag*" (An Arab à la Franca), Nadim introduces us to Mi'ayt, Ma'ika, and their son Zi'ayt.[89] Upon Zi'ayt's return from his European education, his father Mi'ayt happily embraces him, causing Zi'ayt to forcefully push him away. The following conversation ensues:

ZI'AYT: O God! You Muslims still have this very ugly habit of hugging and kissing.[90]
MI'AYT: But son, how are we supposed to greet each other?
ZI'AYT: You say *bonne arrivée* and shake hands once, and that is it.
MI'AYT: But son, I have never denied that I am a fellah.
ZI'AYT: Fellah or not, you Egyptians are like farm animals [*bahayim*].
MI'AYT: Thank you, Zi'ayt, you are so kind. Come on, let us go.

Both men went home, where Zi'ayt's mother had prepared baked meat with onions. Upon seeing the cooking pot Zi'ayt yelled:

ZI'AYT: Why did you put in so much of that . . . that . . . *comment ça s'appelle*?
MA'IKA [the mother]: That . . . that what, Zi'ayt?
ZI'AYT: That thing . . . called?
MA'IKA: Called what? Pepper?
ZI'AYT: *Non, non.* The thing you plant!
MA'IKA: Garlic! I swear son, there is not any garlic in it.
ZI'AYT: No, I mean that thing that brings you to tears, they call it *des onions*.
MA'IKA: I swear, son, I put no *des onions* in there. This is just meat with *basal* [onions].
ZI'AYT: *C'est ça! Basal! Basal!*
MA'IKA: What happened to you, Zi'ayt, you forgot *basal*? You used to always eat it.[91]

Throughout this dialogue, Nadim attempts to discourage young educated Egyptians from what he perceived as the blind imitations of the customs and traditions of Europe at the expense of traditional Egyptian culture.[92] This sketch became a timeless classic; it was reprinted twenty-six years later in the May 1, 1907, issue of *Majalat Sarkis*, retaining its relevance and its humor a full generation after the printing of the original.[93]

### STINGING POLITICAL ATTACKS AND
### COUNTERHEGEMONIC SATIRE

The lower class journals indulge in scurrilous abuse of the highest dignitaries in the country, both in their public and private lives, which, apart from the annoyances it causes, must tend to undermine all respect for authority.

—Eldon Gorst, Parliamentary Papers, 1908

Not all of the colloquial press's satirical commentary was as "subtle" as some of the mentioned economic and moral commentary. As we saw with Sannuʿ earlier in the chapter, the satirical press in Egypt often directly satirized important political figures in Egypt, be they British or Egyptian. *Al-Babaghlu al-Misri* (The Egyptian parrot), one of the many Egyptian satirical periodicals appearing at the turn of the twentieth century, preferred this less restrained, more direct approach. The editor, ʿAbd-al-Majid Kamil, especially courted controversy by specializing in plainspoken anti-British and anti-elite discourse. In the first issue of his magazine, dated January 8, 1904, Kamil placed a large cartoon on the front cover that filled up half the page. With the pyramids in the background, the sketch depicted a monkey dressed as an Englishman (most likely representing Lord Cromer), with a whip in hand, training several circus animals (representing the Egyptian people). The dogs and cows, being whipped by the "British monkey," are wearing a variety of fezzes and turbans. The rhyming colloquial Egyptian commentary below the picture declares: "Here is a *tarbush* [fez] that is mute, and here is a turban [*ʿimma*] without any action [*himma*], and here is the Pasha with his useless soldiery." The animals wearing the *tarabish* represent the urban *ʾafandiyya* class, whereas those wearing the turbans are the religious sheikhs and other elements of the traditional elite. The text proceeds: "The respectful monkey [*ginab al-ʾird*] then declared: Oh what is this noise my little children . . . for this country is my country, and those people [*ʿibad*] are my people [*ʿibadi*], and these dogs are my dogs, and they fear me [*ginabi*], since the days of ʿUrabi." The narrator then advises, "Stand up, oh *ibn al-hara* [son of the urban quarter], and see what is going on around you."[94]

The obvious call to action by Kamil attempted to shame Egyptians into resisting the British. The remainder of the first issue continued with the same message, although instead of using colloquial prose, as in the first segment, Kamil used a simplified Modern Standard Arabic (half colloquial Egyptian and half Fusha) in a piece titled "*al-Qadi ʿUmar*" (Judge ʿUmar). This section described the observations of a "fictional" judge on ongoing current events. Judge ʿUmar proceeded to pointedly criticize the Egyptian government, the sociopolitical status quo in Egypt, and especially the Egyptian elite, whom he viewed as traitors and/or collaborators with the British. 'Umar begins his commentary by announcing that he has traveled widely, yet he has not seen a government that is "as cowardly or as weak as our government." He then makes known that "the more prominent of our elite [*al-Nuzar*] don't utter a sound unless dictated by the Lord [Cromer] . . . and the others don't care about anything except for receiving their salaries and riding in their cars and attending balls." 'Umar spares no one, declaring at the end of his diatribe that "the religious scholars [*al-Shar'iyun*] are going against the book and the *sunna* and are visiting the Lord [Cromer] and European capitals [here he means Muhammad 'Abduh] and no longer go to the *Haj*. . . . And as for *Majlis al-Shura* [the Shura Council] and *al-Gam'iyya al-'Ummumiyya* [the General Assembly], most are huge morons [*aglaf Kubar*]. What do you expect from people who are no different than jackasses?"[95]

Queen Victoria was also not spared in these anti-British satirical attacks. The Egyptian chronicler Mikha'il Sharubim describes how the editors of the satirical press "darkened the pages of their newspapers with attacks on the Queen of the English, making fun of her old age, infirmity, and immobility, in the most low class and vulgar language."[96] More specifically, Sharubim continues, "The owner of the *al-Waqt* [*The Times*], which is one of these lowlife newspapers, printed a very shameful [*mu'iba jiddan*] cartoon of the Queen of England; this was followed by a rude and tasteless description of the Queen in the *Munir* newspaper. The masses [*al-'amma*] spread the words of these two papers, singing some of them publicly and often improvising even more distasteful lyrics to these chants."[97]

This firsthand account by Sharubim highlights the power of these satirical papers and especially their colloquial prose. Not only were printed colloquial Egyptian poems and jingles, especially when they were controversial, read out loud, but also some of them were memorized and chanted in the streets, passing from mouth to mouth and spreading well beyond the newspaper readership. As Sharubim confirms, the chanting crowds often added lyrics of their own.[98] Thus, being in print was not necessarily the end of the life cycle of some of these texts, because not only were many of the popular satirical ditties orally retransmitted, but some were also improvisationally revised to better express the contemporary politicocultural environment. These "rewritings" by some of the readers and listeners testify to a more complex relation between printed texts, their oral dissemination, and, in this case, their instantaneous improvisational "oral" revision and redissemination—moving well beyond the limits of the initial printed text. It is conceivable, for example, that some of the individuals who were part of this oral/aural chain of transmission never had access to the original printed *zajal* but instead aurally consumed one of the evolving versions of this *zajal* and after perhaps revising it yet another time, proceeded to orally rebroadcast it themselves.

## MUHAMMAD ʿABDUH AND THE SATIRICAL PRESS, 1902–1904

Queen Victoria, Lord Cromer, and other British officials were not the only targets of the satirical press. Prominent native Egyptians, especially those who were labeled collaborators, received their share of journalistic attacks. Despite his esteemed position as grand mufti of Egypt (*Mufti al-Diyyar al-Misriyya*), the reformist Sheikh Muhammad ʿAbduh was frequently attacked as a result of his liberal policies and his perceived close relationship with the British.[99] In traditional Azhari circles, he was early on accused (along with his mentor Jamal al-Din al-Afghani) of not being a true Muslim. Some even accused him of being an atheist and a collaborator with the British. One of these explicit attacks on ʿAbduh lasted for a couple of years and spanned several satirical newspapers.[100]

According to Mikhaʾil Sharubim, on one of Muhammad ʿAbduh's trips to England he visited one of his "intellectual Orientalist friends" and posed for a photograph with an English man, his wife, and two other ladies. When Muhammad Tawfiq, the owner of *Humarit Munyati*, found out about this picture, he acquired a copy of it and published it in his satirical newspaper.[101] However, the picture that appeared in the March 1, 1902, issue of *Humarit Munyati* is of such poor quality that it is impossible to determine whether it has been doctored or not. Regardless of the published photo's authenticity, the damage was already done. Below the picture, Tawfiq wrote an elaborate attack on the sheikh's religiosity, integrity, and patriotism. In addition to the commentary, the paper published poems and *azjal* vigorously lampooning ʿAbduh, which according to Sharubim was quickly exploited by ʿAbduh's political enemies.

He [Muhammad Tawfiq] maliciously placed this photograph in his magazine [*Humarit Munyati*] and filled the pages of his periodical with the most awful and most hateful speech, accusing him [ʿAbduh] of every moral failing and described him in the most vulgar manner. He attacked him with two poems, the likes of which no one has uttered before or since. The enemies of the Sheikh proceeded to read those poems to every passerby from the masses and low class inhabitants of the Al-Azhar district [*al-ʿama wa zaʿanif al-Azhar*]. They bought this paper in great number until its price reached five piasters. They even placed copies of the paper near ʿAbduh's sitting area at the Azhar mosque and on his dining table.[102]

As a result of these personal attacks, 'Abduh brought this issue before Khedive 'Abbas Hilmi II and pleaded his case with several ministers, prompting the public prosecutor to summon the owner of *Humarit Munyati*, accusing him of "threatening Islam by quoting Qur'anic verses in a corrupt and vulgar newspaper." According to Sharubim, however, Muhammad Tawfiq "was not the least bit shaken during his trial and did not hold back his typical satirical and comedic remarks, amusing the judges and agitating the prosecutors."[103] However, this was only the beginning, as the baton was passed to other satirical newspapers, which continued on the same theme. *Al-'Arnab* (The rabbit) also printed a "vulgar drawing of the Sheikh which shocked the readers . . . and resulted in the prosecution and imprisonment of its editor, Husayn Tawfiq, for four months."[104] Also playing off the photograph that was printed in *Humarit Munyati*, 'Abd-al-Magid Kamil, the editor of *al-Babaghlu al-Misri*, printed a large cartoon of Muhammad 'Abduh. The cartoon, which took up most of page 4, depicted 'Abduh with a glass of wine and standing close to a scantily dressed (most of her breasts showing) European woman. To add to the shock value of this scene, the cartoonist placed a dog, considered highly unclean in Islamic tradition, standing on the leg of the Egyptian grand mufti.[105]

A colloquial Egyptian article, "Mister Muhammad 'Abduh: The Grand Mufti of Egypt" (*al-Mister Muhammad 'Abduh: Mufti al-Diyar al-Misriyya*), followed the cartoon. Although giving the mufti of Egypt the title of "Mister" was insulting enough, Kamil escalated the attack: "In the last few days the newspapers have been wildly writing about the glories of Mister [*al-'ustadh al-mister*] Muhammad 'Abduh, the Grand Mufti of Egypt; oh how joyful we are of the Sheikh [*ya farhitna bi-si-al-shaykh*] because of the fatwa his highness [*ginabu*] made, which sanctioned [*hallalat*] what God almighty has forbidden." Here Kamil alludes to the fatwa made by 'Abduh allowing the accumulation of interest by Muslims. Kamil then continues: "Although I must say that there is no real need for any blame [*'itab*], since it has been shown to us more than once that the honorable Sheikh [*ginab al-shaykh*], may God take him, has little knowledge of religious matters [*malush tuql 'aldin*]. And we know that though he is a Muslim on the outside, and his *madhab* is Maliki [*maliki al-madhab*], he is in reality a Maltese in his drinking habits [*malti al-mashrab*]. For it is said that faith is in the heart and not on the tongue [*bil-lisan*]." The article continues its sarcastic tone by describing 'Abduh's "yearly hajj to the European capitals." Kamil then asks the readers why the "British government has not yet knighted 'Abduh with a title of 'sir' or 'mister' at the very least?" and even suggests that 'Abduh seal his marriage to the "*madhhab* of Darwin" by signing a contract at the mixed courts.[106]

The iconoclastic vigor with which some satirical periodicals pounced on their political enemies had a perceivable effect on the Egyptian streets. By undermining "all respect for authority" (as Eldon Gorst described in his 1908 annual report to the British Parliament), these attacks created a counterhegemonic atmosphere, legitimizing acts of public resistance toward the British colonial authority and those who, like 'Abduh, were scapegoated as collaborators. One of the most common acts of resistance was the recitation of anti-British *azjal* in the streets and in popular coffee shops. For instance, as I have noted with the chants directed at Cromer and Queen Victoria, it was not uncommon for Egyptian children to yell out insulting chants or slogans directed at British troops and British public figures. Often these chants and *azjal* were first disseminated on the pages of the satirical press.[107]

### VULGARIZING AND SUPPRESSING
### THE COLLOQUIAL PRESS

There are ninety-seven political newspapers that closed down [died] in the last five years [1897–1902]. We would have liked to name them all but for the lack of space. But we can say that out of these newspapers, nine were prosecuted for making vulgar insults, personal attacks, and fraud. Among them, two newspapers insulted her deceased majesty, the queen of England; one periodical vulgarly attacked his highness the khedive; the rest insulted members of the aristocracy [*al-'Umara'*] and the elite of society [*al-'Uzama'*].
—Muhammad 'Umar, *Hadir al-Misriyyin Aw Sirr Ta'akhkhurihum*

The iconoclastic counterhegemonic nature of the colloquial satirical press and its mass appeal made some of the Egyptian elite uneasy, and from the beginning there were immediate condemnations and complaints against it. Elite protests were typically focused on either the printing of colloquial Egyptian or the "vulgarity" of such newspapers. Sometimes the mere printing of colloquial "street language" was deemed vulgar by many cultural or religious conservatives. One of the earliest critiques of the colloquial press was made by none other than Muhammad 'Abduh. In an 1879 *al-Tijara* article, 'Abduh wrote a scathing attack against Sannu''s *Abu-Naddara Zarqa'*, accusing him of "not leaving out any obscenities or vulgarities from his newspaper" and coming up with "expressions that are even beyond the scope of the lower classes and the most vulgar of people." 'Abduh finished his article by accusing Sannu' of "making a living out of hurling insults and the tearing of the veil of decency [*tamziq hijab al-'insaniyya*]."[108]

Many Egyptian intellectuals were on their guard regarding the preservation of classical Arabic, and despite the popularity and the obvious advantages of vernacular language use in the press, a tremendous amount of hostility was directed at colloquial journalism. The British presence in Egypt and the increase in the number of European words used in everyday conversational Arabic increased the overall anxiety of many intellectuals and religious authorities. Because of those fears and pressure from conservatives, 'Abdallah Nadim considered removing the vernacular segments of *al-'Ustadh*. In one of his dialogue sketches, "A Contractual Agreement," Nadim declares to several of his vernacular-speaking fictional characters, "I am afraid that in writing our language in colloquial, we would be assaulting classical Arabic by means of two armies, the army of European intrusion and the vernacular army. I have called you here to announce that starting today I will speak to you in simple and easy to understand classical Arabic instead of colloquial Egyptian."[109] However, this announcement sparked an immediate response; the following week Nadim received a long letter from one of his readers urging him to reconsider his position.[110] In this letter the reader affirms, "When your paper appeared with its colloquial sections, addressing housewives and uneducated young men through the use of everyday language, it became extremely popular among the masses. Even those who are illiterate bought your paper and gave it to others who could read it aloud for them. In this way all can benefit, men or women, young or old, ignorant or wise."[111]

Partly because of this type of reaction from many of his readers, Nadim reconsidered his earlier decision and continued to print his popular vernacular dialogues. However, just two months after Nadim's decision to continue writing in colloquial Egyptian, the situation spiraled out of control, as William Willcocks (1852–1932), who was then an irrigation inspector in the Delta, gave a public speech in Azbakiyya advocating the abolition of Fusha and the official adoption of 'ammiyya as the language of all scientific and official discourse. According to Willcocks, the inflexibility of Fusha hinders innovation and only through the adoption of colloquial Egyptian would the Egyptian people regain their lost inventiveness. Coming from an Englishman, this message had the opposite of its intended effect and mobilized the Egyptian press against Willcocks for assaulting the sanctity of the language of the Qur'an.[112] Perhaps feeling defensive for writing in 'ammiyya, Nadim wrote a ten-page response countering Willcocks's claims, and for the next six issues Nadim refrained from writing in colloquial Egyptian.[113] The "Willcocks incident," however, did not discourage the overall trend of increasing colloquial press production. The next two decades after the 1893 Willcocks speech sustained the largest increase in new satirical periodicals (see Table 5). This infuriated a conservative faction of the Egyptian intelligentsia, who continued to attack printed colloquial production, accusing it of increasing vulgarity and ignorance and contributing to what was perceived as the destruction of the language of the Qur'an. Muhammad 'Umar talked at length about this perceived threat.

If those people cared about retaining their language, then they wouldn't have carelessly lost command of it, or if they regularly read and studied from properly written language books, instead of comedic and satirical books, then their language skills would have improved. However, as you all know, they only read low-class vulgar books and colloquial newspapers. . . . Unfortunately, most of the editors of these vulgar newspapers, which cause the destruction of the language of religion [*lughat al-din*], the language of the Qur'an and *hadith*, are Muslims. They unknowingly perhaps destroy their own glorious legacy with their very own hands and tongues [*alsinatihum*]. Most of the readers of these newspapers are Muslims, who often read them to their children. They are published in their neighborhoods and mostly sold among them. Typically a father would call his son over and insist that he read the periodical out loud and upon listening to it, the father would declare: "God bless this journal, for it speaks the truth in a form that is understood by the elite and the masses [*al-khasa wa al-'amma*]." . . . As for the newspapers written in Fusha [*al-jara'id al-fassiha*], they never read them unless they contain some information or news that personally concerns them.[114]

The incessant attacks on the colloquial press increased after Muhammad 'Umar wrote his book in 1902.[115] In the five-year period from 1897 to 1902 only nine satirical newspapers were prosecuted by the Egyptian courts, typically for making libelous attacks and insulting major political figures, such as 'Abduh, the khedive, and Cromer.[116] In the following years, however, the number of successful libel cases against the press dramatically increased as the press continued its hounding of political elites. In 1903 alone there were twelve editors and writers belonging to seven different satirical newspapers who were convicted of libel by the Egyptian courts (see Table 6).[117]

In the following year, the arrests continued with fourteen prosecutions brought before the Egyptian courts, almost all for libel. According to Cromer's annual report to the British Parliament, "In almost all the cases convictions were secured," with the sentences varying from "six months imprisonment to a fine of 1 LE [Livre Egyptien]."[118] These arrests and fines, however, did not make much of a dent in the popularity of the satirical press, and the barrage of satirical attacks continued. Ironically, the principal reason for the ineffectiveness of this crackdown on the press was Lord Cromer's policy of noninterference with the local press.

TABLE 6. *Newspaper editors convicted of libel in 1903*

| Name | Newspaper |
| --- | --- |
| George Ishak | *al-Saham* (The archer) |
| Bayumi Ibrahim | *al-Tamthil* (Acting) |
| Muhammad Farah | *al-Juhayna* |
| Ahmad Abbas | *al-Khala'a* (Loose behavior) |
| Raghib Hassan | *al-Khala'a* |
| Abd al-Ra'uf Hilmi | *al-Khala'a* |
| Abd al-Majid Kamil | *al-Babaghlu al-Misri* (The Egyptian parrot) |
| Husayn Tawfiq | *al-'Arnab* (The rabbit) |
| Muhammad Tawfiq | *al-Hammara* (The donkey drivers) |
| Ahmad Mutawali 'Azmi | *al-Funughraf* (The phonograph) |
| Muhammad 'Abbas | *al-Khala'a* |
| Raghib Hassan | *al-Khala'a* |

SOURCE: United Kingdom, Parliamentary Papers, *Reports*, 1904, 32–33.

Despite the attacks on the satirical press by the Egyptian cultural conservatives and the direct lampooning of Cromer himself, the council-general was a staunch defender of the freedom of the press and did not allow any major censorship policy during his tenure. To be sure, Cromer had some realpolitik reasons that explained his insistence on a free Egyptian press. He acknowledged in his parliamentary report that the "purely practical arguments against the adoption of repressive measures were twofold." First, he argued that the strong British military presence in Egypt guaranteed that "inflammatory writing would not lead to any serious disturbance of public order." Second, Cromer asserted that "it would have been useless, even had it been desirable, to pass any special law affecting the native press unless the same measure had been applied to European newspapers, for any native newspaper editor who felt himself threatened could easily have transferred his rights, either really or nominally, to some European."[119] In addition, the satirical press provided an important safety valve for relieving the frustrations of the Egyptian masses, something the politically astute Cromer must have known.[120]

Print culture was never solely the playground of the elite; in Egypt, the urban middle class and increasingly the growing student and working classes participated in reading, listening, and responding to the discourses of the Arabic press and especially the more accessible colloquial journals. The sensationalism and packaging of the satirical presses' articles, theatrical sketches, and cartoons, especially when they involved a controversial attack or scandal of a public figure, greatly expanded the listening and reading audiences and consequently created a mass-mediated public forum with a shared national experience irrespective of class and literacy boundaries. The humor, satire, and cartoons in many of these journals played an important role in the dissemination of their social and political messages. Their novelty, entertainment value, and accessibility to a greater number of Egyptians greatly contributed to their popularity and hence their cultural reach and influence. In addition, some of the repeating satirical press themes elevated local concerns about the economy and moral propriety into national concerns, becoming an integral part of nationalistic rhetoric.

Although the satirical press was undoubtedly consumed directly or indirectly by Egyptians from across the socioeconomic spectrum, many of the attacks on these periodicals were infused with a class-based bias. In his account of turn-of-the-twentieth-century Egypt, Mikha'il Sharubim spends a great deal of time describing what he perceives as the corrupting influences of the "vulgar" and "lower class" colloquial newspapers. Sharubim, who came from a privileged background, paints the owners and editors of the satirical press as "a new class of ill-mannered people, who have taken up the lowest of professions and the most harmful to people's souls." Continuing his diatribe, he adds that "these satirical newspapers are written in the language of the masses [al-'amma], and the accents of the rabble [al-sawqa]." Sharubim then declares that the very names of these newspapers reveal "the depths of their moral depravity," and he proceeds to list some of the worst offenders, which include *al-'Arnab* (The rabbit), *al-Masamir* (The nails), *al-'Arghul* (The reed flute), *Humarit Munyati* (The idiocy of my desire), and *al-Ligam* (The horse rein). Sharubim then concludes that "the sole purpose of these papers is insulting people, exposing their imperfections, and desecrating the memory of the living and the dead with truths and untruths."[121]

This classist antipopulist language deployed by Sharubim and others against the satirical press mirrored the language used to describe Mustafa Kamil's Watani Party, which was feared for its active mobilization of the Egyptian street. This is not surprising, because most of the consumers of these satirical periodicals were likely supporters of Kamil and his party. Sharubim, for example, disapprovingly describes how because "the masses have continued to increase their hallucinatory love of this [Watani] party and its leader [Mustafa Kamil]," one frequently heard in the urban streets the chanting of words such as "evacuation [of the British from Egypt], constitution, and freedom [al-jala' wa al-dustur wa al-huriyya]." These words and phrases were to Sharubim's horror chanted and spoken by "carpenters, plumbers, ironsmiths, grain, cooking oil, and sugarcane sellers, and their ilk." According to Sharubim, "The rabble gather in their usual meeting places—coffee shops and barber shops—and repeat these words and falsely and inaccurately explain their meaning with an admixture of ignorance and arrogance."[122]

### THE NEW MASS CULTURE, MUSTAFA KAMIL,
### AND DINSHAWAY AS A NATIONAL MYTH

Sir Edward Grey loudly declared in the House of Commons that Lord Cromer did not treat the Egyptians as an inferior people. . . . However, is not Dinshaway alone sufficient in proving for all time and for all future generations that the English have mercilessly inflicted on the Egyptians an unforgettably ruthless humiliation concerning which no two impartial people could dispute?

—Mustafa Kamil, *What the National Party Wants*

On June 11, 1906, a group of British officers set out on a pigeon-hunting excursion near the village of Dinshaway. Some of their shots accidentally caused one of the barns to catch fire. In retaliation, angry villagers attacked the officers with wooden staves, and in the ensuing struggle a female villager was wounded by another stray shot and was presumed dead. After the irate villagers violently beat and disarmed the officers, Captain Seymour Clarke Bull, who suffered a severe blow to the head, fled the scene and ran almost 8 kilometers back to base camp. However, he collapsed and died just a few hundred meters from his destination, the result of a combination of injuries and heatstroke. When a fellah named Sayyid Ahmad Sa'id (who was uninvolved in the earlier skirmish) saw the dying Captain Bull and attempted to help him, he was caught and beaten to death by British troops who mistook him for the murderer.[123]

The Dinshaway incident might have been politically contained had the British not retaliated so harshly. A special tribunal was quickly set up—led by future prime minister Butrus Ghali Pasha—and on June 27, the court passed sentences on twenty-one of the fifty-two accused villagers. Four were sentenced to death by hanging, two to life imprisonment, one to fifteen years' imprisonment, six to seven years' imprisonment, three to one year's imprisonment and fifty lashes, and five to fifty lashes. By orders of the court, the sentences were carried out in public, and the remaining villagers were forced to watch.[124] The severity of these sentences infuriated the Egyptian masses and gave ample ammunition to the nationalists. Mustafa Kamil, who was by now a seasoned political agitator, did not miss this opportunity and was by far the most vocal propagandist of Dinshaway.

Kamil was also aware that to maximize the political capital of this event, arousing the Egyptian masses would not be enough, and so he quickly set out to internationalize the incident.[125] On July 11, 1906, Kamil wrote a lengthy article for *Le Figaro* publicizing and condemning what happened at Dinshaway.[126] On July 15, Kamil left Paris for London, where he held many interviews with the British press, and on July 26 he made a speech explaining the views and demands of the Egyptian nationalist movement at a dinner held in his honor at the Carlton Hotel in London. The climax of his trip was a meeting with the liberal British prime minister, Sir Campbell Bannerman, who asked Kamil to supply him with a list of capable Egyptians who could participate in an Egyptian ministry.[127] The results of this meeting were immediate, and from Kamil's list the British government assigned Sa'd Zaghlul as minister of education. This would be the first step in the inclusion of more Egyptians in key government positions. In addition, Dinshaway and Kamil's vigorous European propaganda campaign led directly to the resignation of Lord Cromer from his position as British proconsul in Egypt.[128] Partly because of these events, Cromer detested Kamil and consequently left out any direct mention of him in both of his books on Egypt. When he did refer to him in one of his books, he never mentioned his name, calling him either the "foolish youth" or the "Gallicised Egyptian."[129]

Aside from the immediate political benefits that accrued to the nationalists, Dinshaway, with the help of the newly emerging mass culture, was quickly and effectively reified into a functional national myth. As was to be expected, the Egyptian newspapers, especially Mustafa Kamil's *al-Liwa*, were the first to take the offensive.[130] What was surprising, however, was the almost instantaneous reaction by other national mass media. On July 2, 1906, just five days after the court ruling on Dinshaway, Hafiz Ibrahim, the well-known Egyptian poet, wrote a long poem memorializing the events while harshly criticizing the British for the purposeful "hunting of men in pursuit of their sport" and for carrying out "inhuman persecutions." The Fusha poem was printed widely in the Egyptian press and was even translated into English and printed the following month in *Majalat Sarkis*.[131] Other poets, including Isma'il Sabri and Ahmad Shawqi, followed Ibrahim's lead and published their own poems to memorialize Dinshaway.[132]

Dinshaway was also almost immediately commemorated in rural colloquial Egyptian *mawawil* (ballads; sing. *mawwal*) that were sung widely in the countryside. Many of these works were probably not composed by a single writer, reflecting a more genuine grassroots response to the events. In a *mawwal* attributed to Sheikh Mustafa 'Ajaj, the Dinshaway incident was viewed strictly as a gendered honor crime, where revenge was the only means to restore the violation of national "honor" that took place when male British soldiers injured an Egyptian woman in her "father's barn." The ballad mentioned Cromer by name and concluded that he is just a "dimwitted Englishman who deserves a beating with a shoe" (*ghabi 'ingilizi yastahil al-darb bil-na'l*).[133]

Barely two weeks after the Dinshaway court ruling, a play titled *Hadithit Dinshaway* (The Dinshaway incident), already in the planning, was advertised for an August 19 opening date. The play, which was supposed to be performed in one of the theaters near the Azbakiyya gardens, was quickly banned by the Egyptian interior ministry. Mustafa Kamil's *al-Liwa* newspaper attempted to justify the banning by stating that it was "so the people would not be further saddened by a reenactment of one of the worst displays of cruelty and unrestrained power."[134] In an attempt to bypass the government's banning of his play, Hassan Ramzi changed the name to *Sayd al-Hamam* (The pigeon hunt) and was able to perform his play for a few nights before the government shut it down in August 1906. After the second banning, the unrelenting Ramzi immediately published the script of his play and offered it for sale.[135] Two years later Ramzi made yet another unsuccessful attempt to stage his play, and in response he wrote an article in *al-Ahram* attacking government censorship.[136]

Dinshaway was also memorialized in the form of an early novel by Mahmud Tahir Haqqi, titled *'Adhra' Dinshaway* (The Dinshaway virgin).[137] *'Adhra' Dinshaway* was first published in serialized form in *al-Minbar* newspaper in July 15, 1906, and was published in its entirety in book form in July 1909. According to Yahya Haqqi, the novel sold "thousands of copies and went through several editions in an extremely short time."[138] What added to the popularity of the novel was the use of colloquial Egyptian Arabic for the dialogue of the Egyptian fellahin, which, as Haqqi admits in his preface, caused it to be criticized by the literary conservatives.[139] The depiction of colloquial-Egyptian-speaking peasants not only contributed to the realism of the events but also made the readers even more sympathetic to the plight of the villagers, especially when contrasting their familiar pronunciations with the distant Fusha spoken by the British characters and the villainous Egyptian prosecutor.[140]

*'Adhra' Dinshaway* unabashedly ends with an emotion-filled lyrical verse exclaiming: "Dinshaway! Dinshaway! Oh . . . grief-stricken village, do not think for one moment that Egyptians will forget your anguish and the hardships you endured. . . . Dinshaway! Dinshaway! Let your name ring eternally . . . and do not forget to recount to all future generations what took place here. . . . Let them know the price of twentieth-century modernity under British rule."[141] Although Haqqi's short, eighty-page historical fiction lacks literary sophistication and reads more like a documentary of the events in Dinshaway than a true novel, it served its purpose of nationally memorializing the Dinshaway incident.

Just in the first few years immediately after Dinshaway, poetry, *azjal*, theatrical plays, newspaper editorials, speeches, and novels were produced that mourned and commemorated the event. This multifarious and systemic reaction to the Dinshaway incident clearly demonstrates the effectiveness and responsiveness of Egypt's newly formed mass culture and the degree with which it transformed Egypt's collective national memory.[142] Indeed, all the diverse branches of Egyptian mass culture—functioning as an integrated media system—memorialized these events, creating for the first time a truly national myth.[143]

## CONCLUSION

From the beginnings of "modern" Egyptian mass culture, there was immediate synergy among the different media. Technological innovations in the entertainment industry coupled with the increasing demands of consumers forced the rapid commercialization of Egyptian entertainment. For instance, *azjal* were mass-produced at the turn of the century, partly to fill the demands of the burgeoning satirical and literary periodicals. The increasing demand for colloquial entertainment forced enterprising colloquial poets and writers to start their own satirical periodicals. By the early twentieth century, the lyrics of vernacular songs, especially *taqatiq*, were directly adapted from printed *azjal*, and colloquial poets were commissioned to write exclusively for particular singers or record companies. Finally, many of the songs that were initially written for musical and comedic plays were later recycled and performed by street performers at coffee shops and weddings, and some were eventually resung by Egyptians in their everyday lives.

The growth of the Egyptian comedic and musical theater, along with the parallel development of an expanding satirical and illustrated press and an influential recording industry, marked the beginning of popular entertainment as a big business, dependent on the organizational efforts of a large number of middle-class urban workers who specialized in a variety of entertainment-related fields. This institutionalization of Egyptian popular entertainment, with Cairo and to a lesser extent Alexandria as its hub, would be the central component in defining how Egyptians perceived their identity in the first quarter of the twentieth century.

## CHAPTER FIVE

# Media Capitalism

## *From Mass Culture to Mass Practice, 1907–1919*

> It is likely that the most effective forms of communication at this
> time were—as they are today—those which appealed simultaneously
> to the eye and to the ear and combined verbal with non-verbal
> messages, musical as well as visual, from the drums and trumpets of
> military parades to the violins accompanying indoor performances.
> In early modern Europe these forms included rituals, spectacles,
> plays, ballets and operas.
> —Asa Briggs and Peter Burke, *A Social History of the Media*

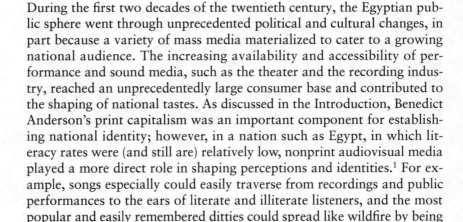

During the first two decades of the twentieth century, the Egyptian public sphere went through unprecedented political and cultural changes, in
part because a variety of mass media materialized to cater to a growing
national audience. The increasing availability and accessibility of performance and sound media, such as the theater and the recording industry, reached an unprecedentedly large consumer base and contributed to
the shaping of national tastes. As discussed in the Introduction, Benedict
Anderson's print capitalism was an important component for establishing national identity; however, in a nation such as Egypt, in which literacy rates were (and still are) relatively low, nonprint audiovisual media
played a more direct role in shaping perceptions and identities.[1] For example, songs especially could easily traverse from recordings and public
performances to the ears of literate and illiterate listeners, and the most
popular and easily remembered ditties could spread like wildfire by being
sung and resung by those very listeners, who in turn could propagate
those songs to an even wider audience.

For this reason, I consider the term *media capitalism* more appropriate for examining the cultural processes taking place, because it is broad

enough to incorporate all forms of mass media, including print, performance, recording, broadcast, and eventually Internet and satellite media. The broader scope of media capitalism is also less visual-centric than Anderson's print capitalism—better integrating the oral and aural along with the visual. As new sound and audiovisual media were being introduced, cultural consumers listened and watched as well as read. In other words, media capitalism is more realistically engaged with the wider range of sensory culture. Certainly in the Egyptian case, and I suspect in other cases as well, a synergetic combination of all available media, from print to music recording, simultaneously shaped the "modern" identities of cultural consumers. As Asa Briggs and Peter Burke suggest, "To think in terms of a media system means emphasizing the division of labour between the different means of communication available in a given place and at a given time without forgetting that old and new media can and do coexist and that different media may compete with or echo one another as well as complement one another."[2]

The print industry, for example, was intimately linked with the theater, music, and recording industries. Plays, music concerts, dance performances, and gramophone records were advertised, critiqued, and discussed in the press. Pictures, news, rumors, and juicy gossip surrounding all the rising stars of these new media were thoroughly discussed in the pages of newspapers and tabloids. In turn, this wider public interest increased the number of records, newspapers, and tickets sold. Also, as we examined in earlier chapters, all the differing forms of colloquial mass culture, from print to the audiovisual variety, were essentially produced by the same colloquial writers, who were valued and sought after for their mastery of colloquial Egyptian. In addition to writing songs and plays for the theater and record companies, lyricists and playwrights such as Bayram al-Tunsi, Yunis al-Qadi, and Badi' Khayri also wrote *azjal* in colloquial newspapers, which they often edited (or owned). Typically, the songs that were successful on the theatrical or musical stage were resold by composers and lyricists to record companies, which were always on the lookout for commercial hits. Almost all the singers who sang in vaudeville and burlesque theater productions were already recording most of their songs. Indeed, because of this elaborate interconnectedness, a comprehensive picture of these important culture-shaping media can be achieved only when they are examined together as a media system.

Before examining the impact of Egyptian mass culture, in this chapter I first cover the explosion of urban mass politics from 1907 until the beginning of World War I. The political capital gained by Mustafa Kamil and his Watani Party after the Dinshaway incident was quickly translated into mass action, as public demonstrations became common practice in Egyptian cities. I then cover the World War I period strictly from a popular culture perspective. During the war, Egyptians experienced many political and economic hardships and, because of the wartime application of martial law, anti-British resistance took on more nuanced forms. Jokes were certainly an important part of this passive defiance. Vaudeville, burlesque comedy plays, and recorded satirical *taqatiq* (colloquial songs; sing. *taqtuqa*), which were all well suited as muted forms of discourse, became extremely popular at this time, providing both a form of resistance and, as we shall see, dynamic public forums where identities could be discussed and negotiated. Near the end of the chapter I ponder the inevitable class and cultural tensions that occurred when these new media were introduced. The conservative cultural elite, the traditional backers of Fusha, were incensed that colloquial Egyptian had become the language of choice for music and performance media. This view contrasted with the interests of the owners and workers of the growing mass media industries, who were primarily interested in profit and consequently catered to the overwhelming demands of the Egyptian cultural consumers, who almost always favored colloquial productions.

## THE WATANI PARTY AND MASS MOBILIZATION

We went to observe the big demonstration that was announced in the newspapers and we reached Bab al-Khalq [one of Cairo's medieval gates]. We rented a carriage and decorated it with flags and two banners on which we wrote "Long live independence and long live the constitution" [*yahiyya al-'istiqlal wa al-dustur*]. All of the Egyptian store owners and the masses [*al-'amma*] helped us in every way upon finding out that we were nationalists and doing our part to save Egypt from the foreign enemy. We went around the streets with our carriage and chanted with the people in the streets: "Long live Egypt . . . long live our nation . . . long live our independence . . . long live the constitution." A large number of people gathered around us in 'Abdin Square . . . and they followed us into the Azbakiyya Garden.
—Muhammad Lutfi Jum'a, *Shahid 'Ala al-'Asr*

Perhaps the best measure of successful discourse is its potential to motivate public action. The successful manipulation of mass culture by the nationalists, as demonstrated in Chapter 4 by the retelling of the Dinshaway story, potentially transformed the Egyptian masses into an easily mobilized force that equally threatened the British, the khedive, and some of the conservative Egyptian elite. As the epigraph indicates, the emerging mass media could easily rally people into political action. Public demonstrations and other political actions, such as public speeches or even strikes, were announced in the press and often through the "shouting and hollering" of roaming newspaper boys.[3] As Mikha'il Sharubim disapprovingly describes, "Newspaper sellers of *al-Liwa* and other Watani papers are spreading the word about a political speech to be given by the leader of the Watani Party [Muhammad Farid] in the theater of Dar al-Tamthil al-'Arabi. They went on shouting and hollering annoyingly, for two full days, while waving around their newspapers and the cloth of their turbans."[4] In this classic example of the interaction between speech and print, newspaper boys used oral communication to advertise and sell their printed periodicals, which in turn promoted a public gathering where a presumably written speech was read aloud to a mass audience (see Figure 5).[5] This increase in potential political activism by the urban population transformed the Egyptian masses, for the first time perhaps, into a viably powerful political actor, which was one of the primary causes for a realignment of the differing power groups in the Egyptian political landscape.

FIGURE 5. *Newspaper boy selling "seditious" periodicals.*
*From Sladen,* Oriental Cairo, *64.*

For most of Cromer's tenure, the nationalists, primarily consisting of the petit-bourgeois *'afandiyya* class, were aligned with the khedive ('Abbas Hilmi II), who attempted to counterbalance the power of the British authority. In turn, the British, especially under Cromer, made tacit alliances with many of the Egyptian economic and intellectual elite.[6] The steady growth of the Egyptian urban masses as a political force equally threatened the khedive and the British; with the replacement of Cromer by the more diplomatic Eldon Gorst, a rapprochement between the British and the khedive changed the political equation and forced the nationalists to rely on the urban masses even more.

This political realignment was reflected rather pointedly in the 1907 official organization of political parties, which represented the differing political power bases at the time. Although Mustafa Kamil had been for more than a decade the leading nationalist leader in the country, he did not officially organize his movement into a political party until late in 1907. The principles of the new Watani Party were first publicly articulated by Kamil in front of 7,000 people at an October 22, 1907, speech at the Zizinia Theater in Alexandria.[7] The 'Umma (Nation) Party, mostly led by wealthy pashas, represented the interests of the educated landowning elite and was developed in part as a reaction to the more radical nationalists who followed the charismatic Mustafa Kamil.[8] The 'Umma Party was officially established on September 21, 1907, and favored a more gradual road to independence; it advocated the need for consulting with and benefiting from British tutelage whenever possible. Inherent in this policy was an aversion to any change in the stability of the status quo and a general distrust of the masses, who were deemed not ready for political independence.[9] Rounding out the new parties was 'Ali Yusif's Constitutional Reform Party, which was mainly funded by the khedive to support his policies and, as such, was viewed with suspicion by most Egyptians.[10]

With the support of the urban masses, the Watani Party was by far the most powerful of the three. In his well-attended public speeches, Kamil repeatedly attacked the other two parties for not being true to Egyptian nationalism and for not demanding the immediate withdrawal of the British.[11] The activism of Mustafa Kamil (1874–1908) and the populist message of the Watani Party began the process of defining and popularizing urban Egyptian nationalism. After Kamil's premature death in 1908, there was more of an "urgent need," as described by Zachary Lockman, for "tapping into and mobilizing new domestic constituencies in order to build a more broadly based independence movement."[12] A rapprochement was also gradually reached between the Watani and 'Umma parties in an attempt to counter the developing close relationship between Eldon Gorst and 'Abbas Hilmi II.[13]

## THE DEATH OF MUSTAFA KAMIL AND
## THE RADICALIZATION OF EGYPTIAN POLITICS

Mustafa Pasha Kamel, the leader of the Egyptian Nationalist party, died on the 10th instant [February 10, 1908]. The funeral, which took place on the following afternoon, gave rise to a remarkable display of the regard felt for him by sections of his compatriots. The cortège was accompanied by the Grand Cadi [Qadi], the Sheikh of the El Azher [al-'Azhar] University, and a number of Notables, some of whom had previously held high posts under the Government. The procession was headed by students of all the secondary and higher schools and colleges in Cairo, who had absented themselves from their studies *en masse*, and who marched in good order in ranks of four. After the Notables came a great crowd composed of people of the lower middle class, minor government *employés*, and small shop-keepers. Some idea can be formed of the magnitude of this crowd by the fact that it took fifty minutes to pass by a certain spot. . . . At the cemetery a poem in praise of the deceased was recited, which produced considerable emotion among the bystanders. The crowd then dispersed without the slightest disturbance having taken place. Their orderly conduct throughout the whole proceedings was remarkable, and perfect order was maintained without the least difficulty.
— Sir Eldon Gorst to Sir Edward Grey, February 16, 1908

Mustafa Kamil's funeral demonstrates like no other event the extent of the demographic power and organizational ability of the Watani Party and the influence of the emerging mass media. This mass ritual, perhaps Egypt's first national funeral, was covered extensively by all Egyptian newspapers. Most of these periodicals described the tens of thousands of Egyptians walking in the procession, illustrating an entire nation in mourning, a snapshot of a national symbol in the making. To the consternation of the British and the khedive, the influence of Kamil did not end after his death; in fact, Kamil's historical memory was carefully cultivated and shrewdly used by his successors to mobilize the masses for years to come. Almost immediately after Kamil's death, anthologies of his writings, speeches, and ideas were printed and disseminated all over Egypt. As other nationalist leaders soon realized, merely invoking Kamil's memory, displaying his picture, or mentioning his name carried useful emotional capital, which they readily exploited.[14]

Muhammad Farid, who was selected to lead the Watani Party after Kamil's death, continually made sure to honor, as well as politically benefit from, Kamil's memory. As a contemporary observer noticed, for one of Farid's public speeches a makeshift memorial, including a large shrine honoring Mustafa Kamil, was strategically placed to evoke maximum emotional effect from the gathering audience.

On Saturday April 18 [1908] at 5:00 o'clock, people raced to listen to the speech and a great mass of people showed up, almost trampling each other. The number of those who were outside attempting to get in was much greater than those who were able to enter the premises. Tempers were flaring because of the general disorder caused by the presence of a large number of vulgar rabble, common peddlers, and the overall dregs of society, mostly from Bulaq. At the center of the stage they placed a large picture of the deceased Mustafa Kamil on top of a table covered with flowers. Sitting behind this table was Muhammad Farid, who upon standing up to give the speech, was drowned out with applause and chants of "Long live Muhammad Farid" and "Long live the Watani Party."[15]

In his speech Farid emphasized the need for the Watani Party to continue its struggle after the death of Kamil, and he accused the 'Umma Party of collaborating with the British. To the delight of the gathering crowd, Farid ended his speech by shouting, "Long live Egypt! Long live the constitution [*dustur*]!" The crowd, as Mikha'il Sharubim disapprovingly described, shouted the same slogans loudly while "clapping, whistling, and pounding their feet uncontrollably for almost an hour." Sharubim described the entire gathering as disorganized and primarily lower class, snobbishly recounting that "most of those who attended this gathering were a mix of rabble, craftsmen, and artisans of the lower professions, like metalsmiths, carpenters, barbers, and tailors who inhabit Bulaq and other such areas of Cairo. Whenever they heard the speaker mention the British, they got excited and rose up chanting anti-British slogans about how the British are the enemy and that they should get out of Egypt."[16] Sharubim's obvious disdain for the urban masses was reflective of the general attitude shared by many of the Egyptian elite. This general condescension toward the masses was also, as we have seen in earlier chapters, directed toward colloquial cultural production, which was deemed as vulgar as its readers and audiences.[17]

In the years after the death of Mustafa Kamil the radicalization of Egyptian politics increased dramatically, as Sharubim described: "In those days, speech makers and loud agitators increased in number to an unprecedented level. For every day there was some speaker or other who supported some sort of issue . . . to the extent that the sane among us began to wonder at the effects of this (rebellious) spirit among the nation and began to speculate on the long-term effect of these disturbances."[18] The Watani Party lacked effective centralized leadership, which contributed in part to the radicalization of some of its splinter groups. Muhammad Farid, who assumed the mantle of leadership after Kamil's death, lacked the leadership skills of Kamil and to a certain degree fell under the ideological influence of Sheikh 'Abd al-'Aziz Jawish. Jawish, a religious conservative who was appointed by Farid as the editor of *al-Liwa*, perpetually courted controversy. A British intelligence report referred to him as "the notorious Sheikh 'Abdel Aziz Shawish," whose hand, the report continues, "can be discerned in almost every occurrence during the past few years which has disturbed the public peace or embarrassed the authorities."[19] The frequency of these public disturbances led to sustained efforts by the British and the Egyptian authorities to regulate and censor new media expression.

## MASS POLITICS AND THE REVIVAL OF THE 1881 PRESS LAW

In recent years the virulence of a certain section of the vernacular press in Egypt has greatly increased, and false news and misleading comments on the actions and motives of the government are spread broad-cast, adding greatly to the difficulties of administrating the country. Many of the articles published in these newspapers are calculated to arouse the passions of the mass of the people, who are, and must remain for years to come, far too ignorant to appreciate the absurdities and the falseness of the diatribes which are read out to them daily in the villages.
—*Reports by His Majesty's Agent and Consul-General*

This quote from a British intelligence report[20] not only demonstrates the importance and increasing influence of the colloquial Egyptian press but also the mounting fears of the British and some of the Egyptian elite over the effectiveness of such a medium in communicating counterhegemonic ideas and rousing ordinary Egyptians. This was especially true after the death of Mustafa Kamil, with the weaker Muhammad Farid unable to keep in check Sheikh 'Abd al-'Aziz Jawish and the militant branch of the Watani Party. Thus, when political discourse regularly began to motivate mass political mobilization, the British, in conjunction with the Egyptian ruling elite, began entertaining the idea of reviving the press censorship law.[21] According to the memoirs of 'Ahmad Shafiq Pasha (1860–1940), president of the Khedival Council (*diwan*) at the time, 'Abbas Hilmi II warmed up to the idea of increasing press censorship in part because of some pressure from Eldon Gorst and mounting attacks by the nationalist press, which "accused him of betraying his nation to the British." After some consultation with his advisers, the khedive asked Butrus Ghali, the newly appointed and increasingly unpopular prime minister, to reenforce the 1881 press law.[22]

The revived law went into effect on March 27, 1909, and contained several detailed stipulations aimed at suppressing and controlling the press: (1) The names and addresses of the owners of all printing presses that were publishing newspapers in Egypt had to be "printed on every issue of every newspaper"; (2) all newspapers were required to "send five copies of every issue by mail to the Department of Publications of the

Egyptian Interior Ministry [Nuzarit al-Dakhiliyya]"; (3) "any changes in the ownership or editorship of any newspaper that deal[t] with political, administrative, or religious issues" had to be "immediately report[ed] to the Department of Publications"; (4) newspapers that were categorized as having "the above mentioned subject-matter must acquire a license from the government in advance"; and (5) printing press owners also had to make "an official request with the Department of Publications in order to acquire a printing license" if they planned on printing a newspaper. The March 27 declaration also provided a list of thirty-one Arabic periodicals and twenty-four foreign newspapers and magazines that the authorities deemed "acceptable periodicals" and thus exempt from acquiring a press license. Or as Gorst described it, "The higher-class Arabic newspapers and the local European press will be in no way affected."[23] The owners of the rest of the regularly published periodicals (i.e., those deemed unacceptable or "lower class") were given until April 15 to license their newspapers with the Ministry of the Interior.[24]

The result of this attack on press freedom was an immediate backlash by the urban masses, which "extended to manual workers and craftsmen like metalsmiths, carpenters, barbers, plumbers, other blue-collar workers and even 'Azhari sheikhs."[25] Political demonstrations were organized and preannounced by the press. Several of them were held in Cairo, and some led to violent confrontations with the police. One of the demonstrations began on Wednesday, March 31, 1909, at 4 o'clock in the afternoon. The demonstrators met in Gizira (Zamalek) and, after listening to a few speeches, marched across the Qasr-al-Nil Bridge to 'Abdin Square, eventually ending up in Opera Square in Azbakiyya.[26]

According to a contemporary observer, throughout the march the protesters continuously shouted slogans such as "Long live the press! Down with the publication law! Long live the nation [*al-Watan*]! Long live the homeland [*al-'umma*]! Down with despotism ['*istibdad*]!" The demonstrators singled out the khedive and Butrus Ghali for most of their shouts and insults. Because of his role as the president of the special Dinshaway tribunal, Butrus Ghali was especially unpopular. Dozens of arrests were made, and many of the demonstrators were imprisoned, which prompted the Watani Party newspapers to "insult the judges and accuse Prime Minister Butrus Ghali of being an unjust, thoughtless tyrant."[27] By April 1909 the public demonstrations were so widespread that serious discussions took place between Gorst and the khedive over the creation of laws to discourage large public meetings. The significance of these demonstrations lay not only in the concern of the public over the freedom of the press but also in the apparently active relationship between the press and the urban Egyptian middle classes. Concerned newspaper editors announced and planned these demonstrations in their respective newspapers, and the readers (and listeners) responded with instant mobilization and action.[28]

## COPTIC-MUSLIM STRIFE AND
## THE ASSASSINATION OF BUTRUS GHALI

The press law was tested and put into practice almost immediately after its implementation with the prosecution of 'Abd al-'Aziz Jawish for a June 28, 1909, article in *al-Liwa* commemorating the Dinshaway incident. In his article, "Reminiscences of Dinshaway," Jawish went on the offensive, particularly attacking Butrus Ghali for his role in the trial.

Hail to those innocent souls which Boutros Ghali Pasha, President of the special tribunal, tore from their bodies as silk is torn from thorns! He took these souls in his hand and offered them as a holocaust to the cruel and oppressive tyrant whose only aim is to destroy us. . . . He [Boutros] belongs to a party among the Egyptians which fears the English more than God—people who only seek fortune and promotion, even though their country is oppressed and their own dignity "sacrificed."[29]

During his trial, Jawish took advantage of the extensive press coverage and used his defense to continue the offensive against the British and Ghali. In their reports back to the Foreign Office, the British authorities were dismayed by the theatrics of Jawish, who considered it "incumbent upon himself to sob bitterly whenever his counsel uttered the word 'Denshawai' [Dinshaway]."[30] For this first offense, Jawish was only fined, although within a few weeks he was brought to trial again for writing several articles praising the Indian nationalist Madan Lal Dhingra (1887–1909) for assassinating Sir William Hutt Curzon Wyllie, the political aide-de-camp to the secretary of state for India.[31] The British cited Jawish's article in the August 17, 1909, issue of *al-Liwa* as particularly inflammatory. The article, *"al-Yawm Yuqtal Dhingra"* (Today Dhingra will be killed), was an unapologetic panegyric to Dhingra, who was to be executed that day. The murder was deemed dangerous by the British authority for its potential to incite copycat assassinations.[32] This time, along with another fine, Jawish was sentenced to prison, prompting yet more demonstrations at the Azbakiyya Gardens.[33]

Although the reapplication of the press law was theoretically supposed to decrease the number of "libelous" claims and accusations, it did not stop a growing trend of attacks and counterattacks by radical Muslim and Coptic journalists. Jawish, who would soon be released from prison, continued his attacks on Butrus Ghali, vilifying him as a traitor to the nation, while expanding his attacks on the entire Coptic Egyptian community, accusing them of collaboration with the British.[34] Some of the more radical Coptic newspapers, such as *al-Watan* (The nation) and *Misr* (Egypt), were as militant as Jawish in their attacks on Muslims and Islam, prompting scores of accusations and counteraccusations.[35] The severity of the attacks on both sides was best expressed by the contemporary Coptic Egyptian chronicler Mikha'il Sharubim.

Hatred was surfacing on many levels. . . . Many wrote hateful letters and editorials in political party newspapers, especially those belonging to the Watani Party, which attacked and insulted Coptic Christians and Christianity. The country was plagued by the likes of the *Maghribi* Sheikh [referring to Jawish's Tunisian ancestry] 'Abd al-'Aziz Jawish. Whenever the situation began to settle down and peace and unity began to take hold, he lighted the fuse of religious strife once again. . . . The situation was worsened by the retaliations of the Coptic press, which answered each of the wrongs of the Watani press with two wrongs.[36]

Sharubim also blamed the publication of Lord Cromer's book, *Modern Egypt*, which was "filled with attacks against Islam" and what he labeled as the "behind-the-curtain machinations of Sir Gorst, who would revive religious tensions whenever they died down."[37] It is doubtful, however, that Gorst intentionally inflamed religious tensions in Egypt. His correspondence with Sir Edward Grey at the Foreign Office indicates clearly that he was fearful of Coptic-Muslim religious tension and did all he could to contain it.[38]

On February 20, 1910, tension between Muslims and Copts climaxed with the assassination of the Egyptian prime minister, Butrus Ghali. Most Egyptian nationalists never forgave Ghali for his role as chief judge in the prosecutions of the Dinshaway villagers, and his appointment in November 18, 1908, as prime minister infuriated many. His popularity decreased even more because of the strong role he played in legislating the press law and his support for the proposed extension of the Suez Canal concessions.[39] Thus, when 'Ibrahim al-Wardani, the 25-year-old assassin of Butrus Ghali, was asked upon his arrest why he shot the prime minister, he unhesitatingly replied, "Because he betrayed the nation."[40]

The assassination of Ghali was politically motivated, as Eldon Gorst made sure to stress in his report to the British foreign secretary: "As I stated at the time, and now repeat, the crime itself was political and not fanatical." It was, nonetheless, still viewed by many in the Egyptian Coptic community as religiously motivated, which threatened to increase religious tension to an even higher level. Gorst was unsympathetic to the Coptic cries of persecution, judging that the "feeling of alarm and angst amongst the Copts in general" was in part a result of their minority status and their readiness to "cry out before they are hurt."[41]

However, the case can be made that the sense of alarm within the Coptic community was justified, especially considering some of Jawish's rants. This panic was exacerbated by al-Wardani's almost immediate memorialization by many nationalists as a heroic national figure. Almost immediately after his arrest, several nationalist and tabloid newspapers wrote editorials about al-Wardani's daily life behind bars. Articles discussing his sleeping, waking, reading, eating, drinking, and washing habits abounded. *Al-Liwa*, for example, stated that al-Wardani slept extremely comfortably and well. And *Misr al-Fatah* wrote that al-Wardani lunched on two cutlets of lamb and a plate of pasta. Cartoons, pictures, and drawings of al-Wardani, along with *azjal*, poetry, and ballads venerating his assassination of Ghali, filled the pages of the press. According to Sharubim:

The low and vulgar newspapers set out to immediately venerate the killer while glorifying his deed by drawing his picture on the pages of their publications along with low colloquial poetry and trivial remarks. . . . Upon hearing the newspaper sellers of these types of newspaper, the masses and the rabble descend upon them, buying and reading them. Typically the reading of such a newspaper attracts all kinds of unemployed lowlifes who laugh, giggle, and celebrate what is written with spontaneous and meaningless remarks such as "oh boy" and "oh man" [*'aywa ya 'am*] and other such nonsense. Typically this type of scene continues until the police arrives and either arrests them or separates their gathering.[42]

In July 1910, a newly available book containing thirty-nine nationalist poems and *azjal* and edited by a certain 'Ali al-Ghayati appealed to the masses and called for resistance against the Egyptian government and the British occupation.[43] Contributing to the book's legitimacy were introductions written by none other than Muhammad Farid and 'Abd al-'Aziz Jawish, accompanied by their photographs. This "volume of seditious poems," as Gorst described it to the Foreign Office, "constitutes a specimen of subversive literature of a dangerous type."[44] Several of the *azjal* and poems glorified al-Wardani as a national hero, including a poem detailing the day of al-Wardani's trial; others compared al-Wardani to the Indian Dhingra or insulted the khedive and accused him of being a collaborator. According to the Egyptian government, the book broke three penal codes by (1) acting as an apology for a crime, (2) being an affront to the office of the khedive, and (3) attempting to bring the government hatred and contempt. Al-Ghayati disappeared after a warrant was issued for his arrest and, according to Gorst, he most likely left the country.[45] Ample evidence suggests that the perception of al-Wardani as a national hero was widespread and was expressed in the streets. Law school students, who were most certainly members or sympathizers of the Watani Party, posted pamphlets on the walls of their school that declared, "al-Wardani is dead . . . Long live al-Wardani," and many others were arrested for shouting other pro-Wardani chants and slogans.[46]

PASSIVE RESISTANCE:

LAUGHING AT KITCHENER AND CROMER

Hey Lord! Go ahead and leave
and don't let the door hit you on your way out
. . .
Those who were hanged are greeting you
saying their heart will always be with you
Those who were flogged or orphaned
They declare their eternal love for you
Those who were imprisoned or had their houses demolished
hold you in great favor
Truly all of your good works speak for themselves
and all are covetous of you
But Lord! Please leave
and don't let the door hit you on your way out
                              —'Izat Saqr, *Diwan 'Amir Fann al-Zajal*

'Izat Saqr's *zajal* (the poem that opens this section) was written almost immediately after Lord Cromer resigned from his position as consul-general.[47] The satire and humor of this *zajal* is derived from the irony of contrasting Cromer's repeated claims that he was loved by the Egyptian fellah with the realities of what happened in Dinshaway. Popular jokes also expressed the collective abhorrence of Lord Cromer by the Egyptian people, especially after he published his book on modern Egypt.[48] Many of the jokes revel in the fact that, because of the Dinshaway incident, Lord Cromer could never return to Egypt in any official capacity. For instance, one of these jokes expresses the desire of Cromer to return to Egypt and conveys the impossibility of doing so: "A reliable informant has reported to us that he saw Lord Cromer sitting in an Egyptian coffee shop [*qahwa baladi*] in London with a long beard and wearing a *galabiyya* and *'abaya* [traditional Egyptian dress]." A similar joke satirizes Cromer's desperation: "Cromer is wishing to return to Egypt even if he is assigned a position as an assistant worm [*musa'id duda*]."[49]

Eldon Gorst, who replaced Cromer in 1907, was more diplomatic than his predecessor and was perceived, rightly or wrongly, by many Egyptians as being "softer" than Cromer. So when Gorst became gravely ill in the summer of 1911 and soon passed away, news that his replacement would be Lord Horatio Kitchener (1850–1916) caused a great deal of alarm in Egypt. Kitchener was a known commodity because of his previous position as sirdar of the Egyptian Army in Sudan; he had a reputation as a tough and unpleasant character. The appointment of Kitchener by the Foreign Office was in no doubt partly motivated by the desire to counter the relative disorder that was taking place.

Even before arriving in Egypt, Kitchener was viewed with suspicion and was depicted in the Egyptian press as an "exact replica of Lord Cromer."[50] In anticipation of a stricter policy than Gorst's, the satirical magazine *al-Sayf* (The sword) printed an article titled "Welcome to Harsh(er) Policies" (*Marhaban bil-Shidda*). The writer sarcastically welcomes Lord Kitchener and his reputed forceful policy by announcing that Egyptians are used to more aggressive governance by their rulers and that his appointment will only make resistance and nationalism more effective. The writer then asks, "Why were England and France liberated, and how did the American Republic rise? Was it not because of oppressive and forceful rule? Show us this forceful rule you speak of. We most certainly welcome it" (*'ayna hiyya al-shidda? Marhaban bil shidda*). In conclusion, the writer declares that "nations are often revived and resuscitated through their reaction to oppressive policy. So we welcome your repression!"[51]

The jokes of the time also reflected the consternation of the masses regarding Kitchener's appointment. For instance, one joke announces that Kitchener was asked at a parliament meeting, "Will you always be frowning like this, when you take over your position in Egypt?" A frowning Kitchener responds to the Parliament committee, "I will not crack a smile even if they start tickling me."[52] Presciently, another joke pronounces that "the reason that Lord Kitchener was late in coming to Egypt was because he was taking extensive notes and advice from Lord Cromer."[53] Indeed, Cromer was in correspondence with Kitchener and often directly advised him on policy issues relating to Egypt. One of these letters makes it clear that Cromer did perceive Kitchener as an extension of himself and his policies; it also supports the other jokes that allude to the fact that Cromer sorely missed his old position in Egypt: "It is a real consolation to me to think that under your auspices the work of my lifetime will not be thrown away; until your advent I confess that I began to fear that such would be the case."[54]

Long before newspapers and other communication technologies arrived, proverbs, jokes, and rumors were an integral part of a coping mechanism in premodern societies, helping people to deal with oppression, whether colonial or local. Indeed, as we have seen, humor and jokes, especially in an urban setting, have a tremendous impact on people's biases and thoughts and can arguably give us the most accurate glimpse of popular opinion. The printing of the most current jokes in some of the satirical periodicals was yet another example of the ongoing relationship between the oral and the textual, which undoubtedly enhanced the national circulation and popularity of these jokes.

## *TAQATIQ (TA'ATI')* AND THE CULTURE MARKET, 1907–1919

The primary motivating drive for music writing today is commercial. I am not exaggerating when I say that the record companies often ask us to write over one hundred pieces at a time . . . and they only demand the types of songs that increase their profits and attract large audiences, which undoubtedly is of the *taqtuqa* variety.
—Yunis al-Qadi, *al-Masrah*, March 15, 1926

To the chagrin of some of the conservative elite, the Egyptian culture industries, like all industries, were primarily concerned with profit, and hence they catered to the tastes of the mass consumers of culture. This meant not only that the de facto language of choice for most cultural productions was colloquial Egyptian but also that the subject matter needed to be light enough to be palatable to mass consumers. The songs and plays that were most in demand, and hence most profitable, were reproduced in greater numbers and listened to by more people. As Pierre Bourdieu has shown in his *Distinction: A Social Critique of the Judgment of Taste*, "taste classifies," and it seems that by the 1910s and 1920s a sort of mass taste, shared by most Egyptian culture consumers, was developing.[55] This emergent mass taste was in sharp contrast to the more rigid and hence far from universally accessible taste of the Egyptian cultural elite. Allowing the masses such a powerful input in what would effectively become the dominant national culture contributed to the perpetual attacks that some of the conservative elite made on most forms of mass culture.[56] This does not mean that the Egyptian elite did not listen to or watch popular colloquial Egyptian songs or plays. In reality, Egyptians of all classes—including some of the very critics who were staunchly attacking colloquial culture in the press—enjoyed the full range of colloquial Egyptian cultural production.

For the first time cultural production was driven by the desires of mass consumers, and the continual demand was for colloquial songs and plays. The record industry, in particular, was aware of the needs of the market and was always scouting for new talent. Record sales were increasing as mass-scale manufacturing of gramophones and discs made them cheaper and more accessible to a greater number of Egyptians. For example, an

American-made gramophone that sold for 3 £E (Egyptian pounds) in 1904, cost only 2 £E in 1906 and included five free discs and a five-year warranty. These prices made it possible for many urban coffee shops to buy phonographs, especially if they could not afford live entertainment. There were even "mobile phonographs" carried by their operators, who charged a small fee for playing songs on demand.[57] As Virginia Danielson has shown, even some villagers in the Egyptian countryside—in this case a young Umm Kulthum—had access to recorded music by listening at the house of the village *'umda*.[58]

With the notable exception of the records made by the Mechian Corporation, an entirely Egyptian-based operation, most of these Arabic records were recorded in Egypt and later mass-produced in Europe or the United States.[59] Although we do not have exact figures for how many records were imported into Egypt in the first quarter of the twentieth century, we can reasonably piece together a picture of an active and profitable industry. From 1900 to 1910 the Gramophone Corporation alone recorded 1,192 different records in Egypt.[60] The 1913–14 Egyptian catalogue for the Odeon Corporation listed 458 records. Unfortunately, we do not have any official figures for the Polyphon, Baidaphon, Pathé, and Mechian corporations, which were also active during this period.[61] In 1912, Germany exported 65,000 records to Egypt; these were most likely for the German Odeon label. By 1929 the estimated number of records imported by Egypt from the United States, the United Kingdom, Germany, and France was 728,000.[62]

The increasing exposure of more Egyptians to recorded music created the beginnings of a democratization and, to a certain degree, a homogenization of popular music culture. As more Egyptian men and women from all social classes were exposed to the same music, an increasingly national taste was forming. Most of the differing forms of colloquial mass culture were essentially produced by the same colloquial writers, who were valued and sought after for their mastery of colloquial Egyptian and hence their ability to convey ideas to all Egyptians, regardless of class or education. Because of these new market demands, the price of a *zajal* dramatically increased during the first quarter of the twentieth century, for not only did dozens of satirical periodicals need colloquial writers for their printed *azjal*, but also the burgeoning theater and music industries began contracting these same writers to write theatrical monologues, comedic sketches, plays, and *taqatiq*.[63] For instance, as Marilyn Booth has shown, the colloquial writer Bayram al-Tunsi "left a textual legacy that encompasses a range of genres and media: poetry, short stories, essays, verse and prose parody, serial dialogues, musical-comedy theater, film scripts, songs, and radio serials."[64] This was also true for other colloquial writers,

including 'Amin Sidqi, Badi' Khayri, and Yunis al-Qadi, who were vital
to the growth and development of these new media.[65] In this growing
market, competition was fierce between the different record companies
as demand for recorded colloquial music rapidly increased and good colloquial writers, especially composers, were in short supply.

During the first two decades of the twentieth century, record companies were competing for composers, songwriters, musicians, and singers.
Yunis al-Qadi (b. 1888), a prominent colloquial songwriter and playwright, describes how the Gramophone record company had exclusive
deals with the *zajjal* 'Ahmad 'Ashur Sulayman—who was also one of
the newspaper editors for *al-'Arnab* (The rabbit) and *al-Babaghlu* (The
parrot)—and the musician Dawud Husni to write the words and music
for their *taqatiq*.[66] Odeon, which started recording Egyptian artists as
early as 1905, soon built up its reputation by signing a contract with
the legendary Salama Hijazi and several popular female singers, including 'Asma al-Kumsariyya and Bahiyya al-Mahalawiyya.[67] According to
Pekka Gronow, in 1906 there was such an "extraordinary demand for
Arab records in Egypt" that the Odeon Corporation had contracted a
famous Egyptian singer (most likely Salama Hijazi) for the unprecedented
sum of 10,000 francs. To "recoup this investment, it was claimed that the
company would have to sell at least 100,000 records."[68]

### Munira al-Mahdiyya (1884?–1965)

By 1908, most of the well-known Egyptian performers were contractually
bound to either Gramophone or Odeon.[69] For instance, Gramophone paid
the singer 'Ibrahim al-Qabbani (1852–1927) 200 £E a year just to guarantee exclusive rights to his recordings.[70] Not to be outdone, Baidaphon,
owned by the Lebanese Bayda brothers, signed an exclusive contract
with Munira al-Mahdiyya, the most famous singer in Egypt at the time.[71]
Al-Mahdiyya's real name was Zakiyya Hassan Mansur. She was born in
the mid-1880s in the town of Zaqaziq. Her father passed away when she
was a child, and she was raised by her eldest sister. She attended a French
convent school but did not finish her primary education. Al-Mahdiyya left
home at a young age to pursue a career as a professional singer in Cairo,
where she quickly rose to stardom.[72] She later expanded her repertoire,
transforming herself into a theater actress and joining the 'Aziz 'Id troupe
and later the Salama Hijazi troupe, where "she performed the male roles
written originally for Hijazi."[73] In 1917, al-Mahdiyya started her own
theater company, where she was featured as the main singing and acting
star. According to Virginia Danielson, al-Mahdiyya "personally assumed
management responsibilities for her troupe, negotiating with the theater

owners, composers, lyricists, and singers, planning schedules and meeting payrolls, as well as performing herself."[74]

The artistic and economic power that al-Mahdiyya held within the Baidaphon company was also significant. Although the company had 'Ahmad Ghunayma as its exclusive composer, al-Mahdiyya often composed her own songs and, according to al-Qadi, made executive decisions within the Baidaphon Corporation.[75] Before al-Qadi could be hired as the primary songwriter for al-Mahdiyya, for example, Butrus Bayda, the owner of Baidaphon, had to acquire her approval.

At seven o'clock, he brought me to his office and sat me next to a lady who was wearing the traditional black Egyptian *milayya laf* [wrapping sheet] and veil. He then told her that this is the [prospective] writer of the company. I began to wonder, Who was this Egyptian woman? And why does she care who the writer of the company is? Is she one of the owners of the company? And is she merely a consultant, or does she have an executive privilege? . . . The owner declared, "This lady is Munira al-Mahdiyya," and I soon realized that she has executive-privilege and as the brightest star, is the be-all and end-all [*al-kul fil-kul*] of the company.[76]

In a tongue-and-cheek manner, yet another theater magazine describes the power Munira al-Mahdiyya held over Baidaphon: "It is said that the company [Baidaphon] has an exclusive monopoly on recording the voice of Munira al-Mahdiyya, but in reality, Lady Munira is the one with exclusive controlling rights of the company. The owners of the company do not dare sign or record any new singer without conferring with Lady Munira, the official consultant of the company."[77]

As the diva of Egyptian popular culture at the start of the twentieth century, al-Mahdiyya's earning power was significant. In addition to the money she collected from Baidaphon, she made a considerable amount from her theatrical productions, and by singing for just 40 minutes a night in the Alhambra Casino in Cairo, she earned an additional 124 £E a month.[78] Al-Mahdiyya was only one among dozens of female actresses and singers who played an important role in these thriving national productions. As mentioned in Chapter 4, *taqatiq* were an almost exclusively female art form, and record companies scoured Cairene and Alexandrian coffeehouses to find talented female singers to fill their recordings, transforming some of them into national stars (see Figure 6).[79]

Al-Mahdiyya was also not the only Egyptian female artist with music-writing experience. Na'ima al-Misriyya, who was famous in her own right, was known to write some of her own music. Sayyid Darwish, who was to revolutionize music composition in twentieth-century Egypt, used to frequent al-Misriyya's house in order to solicit her musical opinion. According to Yunis al-Qadi, Darwish believed that al-Misriyya was

FIGURE 6. *Munira al-Mahdiyya as Cleopatra. From* al-Naqid, *March 19, 1928.*

among "the best singers and song critics and knew more about music composition than most composers." Al-Qadi stressed that if al-Misriyya approvingly selected one of Darwish's songs, he was certain that it would become a hit.[80] Al-Misriyya had a similar background to al-Mahdiyya. Born in Cairo, she was raised in a lower middle-class family and took up professional singing as a way to support her family after her divorce at a young age. Like Munira al-Mahdiyya, al-Misriyya rose to the top of her profession, purchasing the famous Alhambra Casino in 1927, "which she managed herself, appearing as the star singer and planning the other entertainment."[81]

### *Sayyid Darwish (1892–1923)*

Sayyid Darwish was born in the popular quarter of Kom al-Dika in Alexandria and started his career playing and singing in coffee shops.[82] In 1914, he got his first professional break when he was hired as a composer (and singer) for the Mechian record company.[83] Darwish was the single most important figure in early twentieth-century Egyptian musical production. His revolutionary compositions were instrumental in the creation of "modern" songs that were in high demand, and record companies competed for his services. Darwish was also instrumental in transforming traditional "oriental" music, with its stuffy Ottoman classicism, into a distinctly Egyptian and "modern" compositional style that was catchy and short and perfectly suited the needs of the record companies and their overwhelming demand for new *taqatiq*.[84] Most *taqatiq* were of the light variety, with sexually suggestive and flirtatious themes, although, as we will soon examine, growing numbers of *taqatiq* had nationalist themes or addressed current social and economic concerns. One of the earliest examples of this type of *taqtuqa* was Darwish's 1914 "*'Ista'gibu ya 'Afandiyya*" (Isn't it shocking, oh gentlemen), which describes the kerosene and gasoline shortage and the subsequent rise in prices on the eve of World War I. After commiserating that 1 liter of kerosene now cost the same as a 5-liter tin (*safiha*) did,[85] the song then angrily continues, "Who would have imagined that this would happen . . . even matches are now just a memory and gas lamps are almost legendary . . . costing more than a franc and a half."[86] Another Sayyid Darwish song, ironically titled "*al-Kutra*" (Abundance), takes an even more direct approach to criticizing Egypt's deteriorating wartime economic condition. The general feeling of disenfranchisement, the unavailability of essential goods, and the increasing poverty were subtly blamed on British wartime rationing and foreign-owned capital.

> We live in the Nile valley, yet our drinking
> is rationed by water meters
> From gas, salt and sugar
> to the tramways of *khawaga* Kiryaniti
> May you never experience our desperation
> Our pockets are clean [empty] and our houses even cleaner
> Even the clothes we are wearing are already pawned
> What a ghastly life[87]

Many of these songs became instant hits and were sung and played on gramophones throughout the country. "The Fortune-Teller" ("*Bassara Barraja*"), one of Darwish's early songs, was written specifically for Munira al-Mahdiyya, and in its original version it had subtle nationalistic overtones, with the fortune-teller declaring to her client, "It is apparent you are Egyptian . . . and that you have countless enemies and almost no fortune/luck." In an obvious allusion to the British, the fortune-teller continues, "May God punish your enemies . . . for they are enslaving your people!" This reference, however, was not enough for al-Mahdiyya, who added another "improvised" line to the song in her recorded (and probably her live) version: "I am Munira al-Mahdiyya and for me the love of my nation is a passion. . . . For freedom and for my country I would sacrifice my life . . . and what does fortune have to do with that?"[88]

In what would arguably become his most popular song, Darwish composed the music for a *zajal* by Badi' Khayri that celebrated the return of the survivors of the approximately 1-million-man Egyptian labor force, recruited (often under coercion) by the British to help with the war effort. Many of these men had been sent to foreign destinations, including France, Malta, Syria, and Palestine. "*Salma ya Salama*" (Welcome back to safety), with its nationalistic theme of yearning for the homeland, struck a chord with most Egyptians; it became extremely popular and was widely sung throughout Egypt.

> Welcome back to safety
> We went and returned safely
> Blow your horn, oh, steamboat, and anchor
> Let me off in this country [Egypt]
> Who cares about America or Europe
> There is no better than this country
> The ship that is returning
> is much better than the one that is departing
> . . .
> Welcome back to safety
> We went and returned safely
> . . .
> Who cares about the British Authority, it was all for profit
> We saved as much as we could
> We saw the war and the violence
> We saw the explosions with our very eyes
> There is only one God and one life, and here we are
> We left and now we returned
> . . .
> Welcome back to safety
> We went and returned safely[89]

The speed with which this song turned into a national hit, heard and to a great extent sung by everyone, was unprecedented. Indeed, this was only the beginning of a growing and constantly changing repertoire of Egyptian songs, a national anthology of songs heard and, more important, sung by most Egyptians.[90] This certainly would not have been possible without the gramophone and the recording industry, making recording media at least as important as print media in transforming the way Egyptians perceived their identity. With the transformation of songs into a mass medium, discourse and praxis often converged, in the sense that unlike novels, newspapers, and other printed texts, listeners often participated in the experience of discourse dissemination by simply singing along. Although periodicals, especially colloquial satirical newspapers, were often read out loud in coffee shops—dramatically increasing their reach—songs were directly consumed by their listeners without intermediaries or translators. More important, because of simple melodies and lyrics, literate and illiterate alike could easily memorize and redisseminate songs, reaching a much larger audience.

Some evidence suggests that early on in the Egyptian music industry, listener and consumer participation in the process of music dissemination was encouraged. Sheet music was printed by the thousands and distributed by record and theater companies for consumption by their viewers and listeners.[91] Because of its accessibility to a much greater number of people and its ambiguous status between discourse and practice, recording media played an important complementary role to print media in the development of national identity.[92] During World War I, the importance of the music and theater industries was enhanced even further as a result of the enforcement of martial law, which vigorously imposed censorship of the press. Censorship of songs and plays was less stringent and harder to enforce, allowing a great deal of flexibility for writers who took advantage of this gap and filled the need for cultural and political expression.[93]

### LAUGHTER, HORSE MEAT, AND
### THE SOCIOECONOMIC EFFECTS OF WORLD WAR I

The process of domination generates a hegemonic public conduct and a backstage discourse consisting of what cannot be spoken in the face of power.
   —James C. Scott, *Domination and the Arts of Resistance*

The assassination of Butrus Ghali, the elevated civil strife between Muslims and Copts, and the subsequent increase in demonstrations and other acts of resistance were important factors in a zero tolerance policy directed at the Watani Party, leading to the imprisonment or exile of most of its leadership. This suppression was especially intensified with the application of martial law during World War I, and it left a temporary, though significant, leadership vacuum in the Egyptian nationalist movement. During the first couple of years of World War I, the British were worried about political instability in Egypt. The fact that at the time the Ottoman sultan was considered the caliph of all Sunni Muslims and the official sovereign of Egypt certainly contributed to this fear and forced the British administration to act swiftly to minimize any risk of rebellion.

Thus, like clockwork, on the night of October 31, 1914, several hundred "Turkish, Khedivist and nationalist agitators" were arrested; some were deported to Malta. General Maxwell, the commanding British officer, placed Egypt under martial law on November 2, and on November 5 Britain declared war on the Ottomans.[94] Britain declared its protectorate over Egypt, and Ottoman suzerainty over Egypt was officially severed on December 18. On the morning of the next day, 'Abbas Hilmi II was deposed and replaced by Sultan Husayn Kamil.[95]

The reaction of the Egyptian street was surprisingly calm, which in part at least could be explained by the harsh martial law policies, which severely punished public disorder. In examining the Foreign Office correspondence, it seems that the British were starved for intelligence reports and "expert" opinions about the attitudes and reactions of the Egyptian people with regard to the war. A curious nine-page intelligence report by the Indian Aga Khan, who vacationed frequently in Egypt, described to the British Foreign Office the situation in Egypt at the beginning of the war: "Our first impression, which still remains unchanged, was that except for the evidence of considerable military activity for the defense of the country, there was no outward sign that the Egyptians were in any way perturbed by the Great War, which had drawn into its vortex and ranged on opposite sides the British and Ottoman Empires."[96]

Public gatherings of five people or more were criminalized, and this law was regularly enforced. Special proclamations were posted regarding the "possession or introduction into Egypt of arms, explosives or seditious literature." A British-run military censorship office was established and headquartered at the Egyptian Ministry of the Interior. Newspapers and periodicals were more vigorously censored, and censorship was extended to all letters and telegrams entering or leaving Egypt.[97] This resulted in the eradication, for the time being at least, of many of Egypt's smaller periodicals (including a significant number of satirical magazines). As we examined in Chapter 4, the imposition of the press law in 1909 together with the political repressions of World War I resulted in a sharp decline in Egyptian journalistic activities throughout the 1910s. For instance, in the 1900s there were 278 new Arabic periodicals in Egypt. This number declined in the 1910s by more than 70% to only 80 new magazines and newspapers; however, this was only temporary, as an extraordinary 442 new Arabic periodicals were published in the following decade.[98]

Aside from a sudden increase in political repression, the war had a tremendous economic impact. Shortages of most essentials, from grain and meat to clothing and paper, were commonplace. Unemployment and inflation were rampant as prices soared. The economic hardships were felt across class lines, and many landowners were bankrupted, in part because the British kept cotton prices below market value to ensure a steady supply of cheap raw materials for the war effort. The countryside was devastated as farm animals and especially beasts of burden were confiscated to help supply the British armies in the region, and, as mentioned, Egyptian peasants were recruited to work in labor gangs.[99]

Despite tighter censorship enforcement, some of the surviving newspapers were able to express the frustrations felt by the Egyptian people over wartime rationing, price fixing, and inflation. This anger was best expressed by Bayram al-Tunsi, who wrote a short poem in *al-'Ahaly* newspaper describing in a play of words how the pricing (*tas'ir*) committee was in reality the hardship (*ta'sir*) committee. Al-Tunsi sarcastically continues to describe how the pricing committee has "decided the price of lunch with every individual grain of wheat, rice, and sesame costing one dirham."[100] *Al-Masamir* (The nails), subtitled "A Critical, Literary, and Humorous Nationalist Periodical" [*Jarida Wataniyya Fukahiyya 'Adabiyya 'Intiqadiyya*], was one of the few satirical newspapers that survived the censorship purges of the war. *Al-Masamir* was filled with comedic sketches and *azjal* expressing wartime frustrations.[101] For example, a *zajal* appearing in the July 21, 1918, issue implicitly attacked the British for draining the Egyptian land of crops.

> Due to neediness we find the poor
> even in the *'Id* are re-stitching their clothes
> Some patch up their shoes
> even changing the leather of their *tarbush* [fez]
> And others can't afford even this
> for they own nothing in this life . . . oh brother!
> This despair, how do we put an end to it
> and who will push it away from us?
> In our land we plant plenty of goodness
> yet evil comes in and plows it away
> The moist fertile branches are withered and dried out in their own land[102]

*Al-Masamir* was also full of colloquial dialogues similar in style to the social dialogues written by 'Abdallah Nadim a generation earlier. Written in an everyday colloquial language, the dialogues offer a glimpse of actual conversations and concerns during those trying times, and many emphasized the poverty and economic inequities facing the urban middle class. For example, the following dialogue, consisting of an everyday

conversation between Fahmi and Ramzi, reflects the hardships that the
lack of basic necessities and wartime inflation had imposed on most
Egyptians:

FAHMI: The poor, how do they survive in these harsh times, considering that
their salaries are around 150 or 200 piasters and they probably have five or
six kids? What are they supposed to do? How do they eat, drink, and cloth
themselves and their kids?

RAMZI: By God, you are right, Fahmi, since these days, their salaries barely cover
the price of bread alone! Only millionaires can afford to even see a loaf of
bread today![103]

Not surprisingly, class resentment was developing at the time, which was
reflected in plays and songs and in the press. An anti-elite *zajal* written for
the September 16, 1918, issue of *al-Masamir* powerfully reflects the poor
economic conditions suffered by the urban middle classes and the natural
resentments that the have-nots felt toward the well-to-do foreigners and
Egyptians.

You have jewelry and your pockets are full of gold
but it's not my business?
I can barely dress and I don't have a penny
but it's not your business?
You inherited property and have tons of money in the bank
but will you give me any?
I work an honest living so I can eat and don't ask you for any handouts
I don't have property or wealth, only what sustains me
but do I take anything from you?
What is annoying though, oh, Bey, Pasha or *Khawaga* is that I am a man
like you!
. . .
So at the very least you should respect me like I respect you
If you don't
then your eminence can go to hell [*mal'un abu sa'atak*][104]

As would be expected, Egyptian jokes during the war were quite reve-
latory of the economic and political troubles experienced by the masses.
More than any other mass culture source, they truly give a glimpse of the
daily realities, fears, and tribulations experienced by the urbanite middle
class. Some of these jokes specifically targeted the *dhawat*, or notables
(Egypt's traditional landed gentry), who, as mentioned, lost a great deal
of money because of below-market prices for Egyptian cotton. Because
many large landowners were experiencing economic troubles, the jokes
exaggerated their hardships—in a sort of mass gloating exercise—which
in retrospect made the urban lower and middle classes feel marginally
better about the dramatic decreases in their standard of living. For in-

stance, a popular joke at the time describes how "a group of thieves broke into the house of a notable and instead of stealing something, left some pocket money for him to spend."[105] Another joke recounts how "one of the notables wanted to teach his children mathematics, so he taught them to divide a loaf of bread into ten equal parts."[106]

Curiously, instead of just talking about the scarcity of staples, many of the jokes that emphasized scarcity were concerned with the unavailability or, rather, the unaffordability of meat. For example, during *al-'Id al-'Adha*, when Muslims are supposed to sacrifice sheep and feed the poor and butcher shop windows are typically overstocked with meat, the following joke was in circulation: "One of the notables looked at the butcher shop window during the 'Id and immediately passed out." Another meat-related joke describes how "one of the *dhawat* [landowners] bought meat for 2 dirham but he made the butcher swear not to say a word to any of his relatives" (so that he would not have to share the meat with them).[107] It is doubtful that any of the notables who lost money during the war were destitute or could not afford to buy any meat, but exaggerating the relative "hardships" that the notables were having must have helped the middle- and lower middle-class people cope with their worsening financial situation.

Continuing this obsession with meat, dozens of jokes during the war were about butchers selling horse and donkey meat.[108] As with most jokes, this reflected real events that were taking place at the time. With the price of meat skyrocketing, some butchers were caught selling horse meat, and in Alexandria a law was passed allowing horse meat to be sold.[109] Two of these jokes stand out in particular for their complicated language play. Replacing the letter *sin* with *sadd*, the word *'ahsan* (better) becomes *'ahssan* (horselike or horsier) and removing a *hamza* from the word *bi'aghla* (most expensive) transforms it into the word *baghla* (mule).

A butcher was asked: "Do you have any lamb meat?" The butcher replied: "I have meat that is horsier/better [*'ahssan/'ahsan*] than lamb."

A butcher was asked: "For how much do you sell your meat these days?" The butcher replied: "For a mule-like/high [*baghla/bi'aghla*] price!"[110]

Jokes like these reveal the daily concerns of average Egyptians during this time of scarcity. Everyday concerns overshadowed all others, and the average Egyptian was, above all, hoping for economic relief. When the war ended, there was a sense of optimism that was loaded with anticipation for economic and political improvements in everyday life. This mass anticipation was expressed in a long *zajal* printed in two parts in the December 15 and December 22 issues of *al-Masamir*. The *zajal*, which celebrates the end of the war, appropriately ends with a list of banal yet significant concerns and questions: "When will the goods we need start arriving? . . . oils, leather and boxes of pasta . . . shoes, clothes, and well-made fezzes?"[111]

## THE EVOLUTION AND CULTURAL INFLUENCE OF
## VAUDEVILLE DURING THE WAR, 1914–1918

There was the increasing vogue and availability of theaters and opera houses: an influence comparable to that of twentieth-century cinema, with everyone eager to adopt the admired accents and turns of phrase used on the stage.
—Eugen Weber, *Peasants into Frenchmen*

Because of the war, European theater companies could no longer travel to Egypt, leaving a large entertainment vacuum filled by a growing number of indigenous vaudeville theater troupes, which in the first couple of years of the war performed Franco-Arab plays.[112] In addition, despite the application of martial law and the overall repression imposed by the British during World War I, the budding Egyptian entertainment industry, and especially the comedic theater, was allowed to continue to operate with only limited censorship. 'Ibrahim Ramzi (1884–1949), who wrote some of these early vaudeville plays, described how "because the war was raging, in 1916, theatrical companies were especially performing comedic and satirical plays in order to alleviate the cloud of fear and worry that lingered in every heart and mind."[113] Indeed, it is possible that the British authorities allowed these sources of entertainment to continue as a safety valve for those who were feeling economic and political repression during the war.

According to newspaper advertisements, during the second decade of the twentieth century the price of general admission for most plays presented by the professional theater companies in Cairo and Alexandria—including the theaters of al-Rihani, al-Kassar, al-Mahdiyya, and Salama Hijazi—was 5 piasters.[114] Najib al-Rihani mentions in his diary that in his theater in late 1917, there was also a 10-piaster second-class section and a 15-piaster first-class section.[115] All these plays were open to female audiences, and many of the advertisements specifically mentioned the fact that admission was for both men and women. In addition, to maximize the number of women attending the theater, Tuesday afternoons were often designated exclusively for women and Sundays for families.[116]

'Aziz 'Id was the first theater manager to have a professional theater company entirely devoted to colloquial vaudeville comedies (see Chapter 4). The Arabic Comedy Troupe (al-Juq al-Kumidi al-'Arabi), which he established in 1907, performed a variety of plays in some of the mainstream theaters of Cairo.[117] 'Id regularly performed these plays until the end of 1909, when he virtually disappeared from the pages of the press.[118] After the start of the war, 'Id reconstituted his troupe and reappeared more permanently on the Egyptian theater scene with a number of even more controversial and groundbreaking plays, opening the way for the unprecedented success of the competing troupes of Najib al-Rihani and 'Ali al-Kassar. 'Id's play *Ya Siti ma Timshish Kida 'Iryana* (Lady, don't walk naked like this) was especially controversial, as the main star, Ruz (Rose) al-Yusuf, appeared on stage wearing just a bathing suit.[119] Al-Yusuf, who would soon become a major celebrity, was named the vaudevillian beauty (*al-fudfilia al-hasna'*) in the press, and in 1925 she was able to capitalize on her fame and transition into a successful career in journalism by starting and running *Ruz al-Yusuf*—arguably the most successful and most politically influential illustrated magazine in Egyptian history.[120]

Many of 'Id's plays were translated from French into Egyptian Arabic by 'Amin Sidqi, an up-and-coming colloquial writer who would later become the exclusive writer for 'Ali al-Kassar's comedic troupe. However, one of 'Id's most successful plays, *Dukhul al-Hamam Mish Zay Khuruguh* (Entering the public bath is easier than exiting it), was not a translated foreign adaptation.[121] Rather, this colloquial comedy, written by 'Ibrahim Ramzi, was an indigenous social critique of traditional Egyptian society, which according to its writer attempted to "reveal some of the flaws of the Shari'a courts, especially when it comes to personal status laws."[122] *Dukhul al-Hamam* was so popular that 'Id went on tour, performing the play throughout Egypt and giving some of its proceeds to the Red Cross to help with the "war's victims."[123] This was not unusual, as many singers and theatrical troupes performed songs and plays with the majority of the proceeds going to a variety of charitable causes.[124]

Many of the theatrical events during this period, in true vaudeville fashion, involved an elaborate medley of acts and performances in order to maximize their audience. An advertisement titled "This Afternoon," appearing in the February 23, 1917, issue of *al-'Afkar* newspaper, illustrates an extreme version of these carnivallike variety shows.

All of the inhabitants of the capital will race to see the show, which will be performed at the Carousel [Theater] this afternoon. In addition to the performance of European games [gymnastics], theatrical sketches, dancing, tumbling, magical acts, clowning, etc., the Munira al-Mahdiyya troupe will perform the play *'Ayyda* [Aida]. The lady [*al-sayyida*] Munira will perform the play's most important acting roles and sing all of its songs. This will be followed by the play *Khala'at al-Nisa'* [The loose behavior of women] performed by Kish Kish Bey [Najib al-Rihani], and then the play *al-'Umda al-'Abit* [The imbecile village chief] performed by Muhammad Nagi. General admission is 5 piasters.[125]

Najib al-Rihani (1891–1949) was an actor and writer in 'Id's troupe until leaving in May 1916 to perform his own comedic sketches and eventually starting his own theater company.[126]

By the end of 1917, al-Rihani expanded his one-act plays and comedic sketches to longer, more elaborate plays. His theater company would soon entirely eclipse the troupe of his former mentor and employer 'Aziz 'Id. Al-Rihani, who specialized in playing the role of Kishkish Bey, an *'umda* (village chief) from the countryside lured to the city with its many temptations, became the undisputed king of the stage by the end of the war. As discussed earlier, all the comedic plays, including al-Rihani's, relied on and included a great deal of music, mostly *taqatiq*. The popularity of these plays and songs was unprecedented, creating for the first time a national community of listeners who "collectively" heard and sang the same songs.

You see today the Egyptian masses singing in the streets the songs of Kishkish Bey and others like it from the theater. And you see girls who have memorized these songs and are singing them at home. . . . The producers of such plays (and songs) have even printed the words and music of such songs in specialized booklets. Do you know how many of these booklets were distributed just in *Dar al-Tamthil al-'Arabi?* 15,000 booklets and that's just in a short period of time."[127]

Badi' Khayri, who wrote most of al-Rihani's songs and plays, recalls in his memoirs that many of the fans of Kishkish Bey would "exit the theater memorizing his songs, and the music would spread everywhere."[128] This observation is corroborated by many contemporary newspaper accounts. The playwright Muhammad Taymur, for instance, declared in an editorial in *al-Minbar* newspaper that "al-Rihani has become the most famous actor on stage" and his "songs are sung by women in private, repeated by children in the streets and alleys, and chanted everywhere by all classes, from the highest to the lowest [*min rafi'ahum li-wadi'ahum*]."[129] In another article, a cultural critic declared in frustration that Kishkish's songs were "now the songs of the masses." These songs, the critic continued, "have penetrated every house door and knocked down the walls of every inner sanctum."[130]

Although many conservative intellectuals, especially theater and literary critics, publicly attacked most of these colloquial productions, accusing them of vulgarity, colloquial Egyptian culture was in fact consumed by all Egyptians regardless of class or education. For example, in his diary entry dated September 4, 1918, Sa'd Zaghlul Pasha describes a visit to his farm by the family of Isma'il Sidqi Pasha (minister of agriculture from 1914 to 1917 and future prime minister). During the visit, Sidqi Pasha's children performed sketches and songs from the vaudeville plays of Kishkish Bey for the adults.[131] According to al-Rihani, Zaghlul also frequented his theater.[132]

Most of the songs that were successful on stage were recorded by the record companies. Indeed, the theater and the music industry were inexorably linked. The writers, musicians, and composers who worked for the record companies were typically hired by the theater companies as well. This synergetic relationship proved equally useful for both industries, as each complemented the other and both benefited from bigger sales. Najib al-Rihani's *'Ululuh* (Tell him), for instance, produced at least nine musical hits, which were recorded almost immediately by the Mechian and Odeon record companies and were heard and sung all over Egypt.[133] Yunis al-Qadi, who wrote the words of many of Darwish's nontheatrical *taqatiq*, wrote in a 1927 article, "The best thing about these [Darwish] plays was undoubtedly the music, which was swiftly and astonishingly spreading from the mouths of the singers/musician to the mouths of the masses [*al-sha'b*] from one corner of the nation to the other, literally overnight."[134]

Naturally, Sayyid Darwish's music was in high demand by theater companies because it almost guaranteed a successful and profitable play. Darwish was first employed in the theater business by George 'Abyad, who commissioned him to write the music for the musical *Fairuz Shah* (also known as *Kanu ma Kanu*), a successful comedic historical fantasy that satirized Egyptian politics. The success of this play, according to Yunis al-Qadi, helped expose Darwish's "original never-before-heard style of music to more and more people." *Fairuz Shah* also caught the attention of Najib al-Rihani, who immediately offered Darwish a lucrative contract to compose the music for many of his plays, including *Wa-Law* (Even so), *'Ish* (Wow), *'Ululuh* (Tell him), *Rin* (Ring/buzz), and many others of the Kishkish Bey series. (For a more detailed record of all the plays and songs composed by Darwish, see Appendix B.)[135]

Because of Sayyid Darwish's unique musical talents and his near-guaranteed success with ticket and record sales, he could defy many of the professional codes of the time. Composers typically signed exclusive contracts with recording and theater companies, but Darwish became a free agent who wrote music for the highest bidder. He wrote songs, sometimes simultaneously, for the theaters of 'Ali al-Kassar, Najib al-Rihani, George 'Abyad, and Munira al-Mahdiyya.

Many of these vaudeville plays shared some of the same themes with the earlier colloquial Egyptian cultural expressions discussed in previous chapters, from street and puppet theater to the satirical press and *azjal*.[136] Perceived declines in morality because of Western influences, economic exploitation of native Egyptians by "conniving" *khawaga*s (foreigners), and calls for increasing national solidarity were themes featured in many of the plays. Continuity with the comedic methods was also evident, with much of the humor achieved through language play and the satirizing of non-Egyptian foreign accents. Intriguingly, Fusha was satirized, along with elite culture.

For example, the play *'Ish* (Wow), which debuted in January 1919, contained all of these elements.[137] The main plot of the play centers on Kishkish Bey (played by al-Rihani) losing all his money and his land after gambling with the Greek *khawaga* Kharalambo. The name Kharalambo is commonly used in Egyptian mass culture. The Greek name is used to exaggerate the sounds of the Greek language for comedic effect. Also, for added scatological humor, *khara* in colloquial Egyptian means excrement.

The play's theme song, a duet sung by al-Rihani and the up-and-coming singer Fathia 'Ahmad, begins by censuring Kishkish for his moral depravity. Kishkish responds by blaming his moral failings on the conniving *khawaga*.

> Kharalambo saw that my pocket was full
> He immediately stood still (mesmerized)
> His eyes were on my farmland
> He told me, let's play some poker
> Made me drink Johnnie Walker
> I played, got drunk and lost
> until I fell into the Abyss[138]

The song, however, ends on a hopeful and nationalistic note as Kishkish promises his audience that "tomorrow I will be respectable again / and will serve my country and nation. / To love the nation is something to be proud of / and I am repentant of my past failings."[139] This song, titled "*Abu al-Kashakish*," proved successful outside the theater as well, and, like many other theatrical *taqatiq*, was recorded many times and sold by Mechian and Pathé records.[140]

For comedic effect, Kharalambo and the other foreigners in the play speak in the typical *khawaga* accent used by all forms of Egyptian mass media. This formulaic foreign accent typically mixes verb tenses, confuses masculine with feminine nouns, and pronounces the letter *hah* (hard h) as *khah* and the letter *'ayn* as an *'alif*. This accent also serves the purpose of definitively marking some foreigners as "the other" and contrasting the *khawaga* character with the sympathetic *ibn* or *bint al-balad* (son or daughter of the country) characters, who speak flawless Egyptian Arabic. Those attempting to speak in Fusha (Classical Arabic) were viewed with similar skepticism and were also satirized as cultural outsiders.

One of the techniques used to satirize Fusha is the exaggerated use of the letter *qaf*, a prominent letter in Fusha but pronounced as a *hamza* (a glottal stop) in Egyptian Arabic. Most of these songs or sketches would inappropriately replace all *'alif*s and *hamza*s, even those letters supposed to be *hamza*s in Fusha, with the letter *qaf*. For example, in the song

"*'Iqra' ya Shaykh Qufa'a*" (Read, o sheikh Qufa'a) the words *'ustadh* (professor or mister) and *'abadan* (never), which are pronounced the same in Fusha and colloquial Arabic, are articulated instead as *qustadh* and *qabadan* by the sheikhs. The colloquial Egyptian word *'ayh* (what), which does not even exist in Fusha, is pronounced *qayh* by the sheikhs. Adding to the humor of the song, even when the sheikhs were laughing, they vocalized *haq haq* instead of *ha ha*.[141]

The disconnect between the Egyptian government, which uses written Classical Arabic in its bureaucracy, and the average Egyptian is portrayed in another sketch about an illiterate person named 'Atiyya who asks a professional writer to write a letter in Fusha to the government demanding an exemption from military service. As the professional writer reads the supposed "classical Arabic" prose, primarily composed of repeating nonsensical Fusha-sounding phrases, the chorus girls declare, "By God, what classical clarity!"[142] Thus, just like foreigners who spoke heavily accented Egyptian Arabic, those who unnecessarily made use of Fusha were viewed as elitists and incomprehensibly distant from everyday Egyptian life. According to the discourse of Egypt's new vernacular mass culture, the primary prerequisite of Egyptian identity or Egyptianness was speaking flawless Egyptian Arabic. This message of equating linguistic facility with Egyptian national authenticity permeated all forms of Egyptian cultural expression.

Aside from the subtle nationalistic language play, many of the plays contained more direct references to the importance of Egyptian nationalism. Najib al-Rihani's plays especially often ended with short nationalistic messages directed at his audience. For example, "*Lahn al-Siyas*" (The song of the stable boys) featured in the play *'Ish* speaks directly about the need for national unity: "If you really wanted to serve the advancement of Egypt, the mother of the world. . . . Don't tell me you're Christian, Muslim or Jewish, oh why don't you learn, oh, brother. . . . Those who are united through their nation . . . religion can never separate them."[143] Indeed, after the assassination of Butrus Ghali and the subsequent divisions between Muslims and Copts, Egyptian nationalists emphasized national unity. Vaudeville was at the forefront of this issue with repeated references emphasizing the primacy of Egyptian national identity over sectarian identity. Solidifying its commitment to Egyptian nationalism, *'Ish* ends with the following song:

> Oh, Egypt . . . we live and die in order to love you
> You are what is beautiful on this Earth and there is no other nation like you
> Your Nile always overflows with goodness and your sons are most generous
> Your bounty benefits your men and women . . . may you live long, oh
> Egypt![144]

Exposure to the theater and its accompanying music was not just a Cairene phenomenon. In fact, most of the professional troupes performed in Alexandria, especially during the summer, and occasionally toured the Egyptian countryside.[145] More important, however, a number of semi-professional traveling troupes crisscrossed the country, visiting Egyptian provincial towns "from Aswan to Bani Suwayf to the Delta and the coastal towns."[146] The most famous of these included the troupes of Ahmad al-Shami, 'Abd al-'Aziz al-Jahili, Mikha'il Jirjis, 'Awad Farid, Ibrahim Hijazi, and Husayn al-Kafuri.[147] In fact, early in his career al-Rihani worked as an actor in the traveling troupe of Ahmad al-Shami, and in his memoirs, he recounted the hardships of constantly traveling from the Mediterranean coast to Aswan.[148] Many of these traveling troupes copied the songs and plays that were popular in Cairo and Alexandria. Al-Rihani's character of Kishkish Bey and al-Kassar's Nubian (*Barbari*) character even had several specialized impersonators.

The *Barbari* character was impersonated by 'Ahmad al-Masiri, Zaki Sa'd, Mustafa al-Tawam, and 'Ali Lawz, among others. And the impersonators of Kishkish Bey included Muhammad Yusif, 'Ahmad Farid, Riyad al-Qusbaji, and 'Ahmad al-Bayumi, among others. They performed in parties set up by the ticket distributors in the countryside and in some of the cafés throughout Upper and Lower Egypt. They performed the plays of Najib al-Rihani, 'Ali al-Kassar, and some of the plays written by 'Amin Sidqi for the actor Muhammad Bahjat. . . . The music and dialogue of these plays were almost completely memorized by them.[149]

The increasing popularity of colloquial Egyptian plays and songs and their profusion not just in the northern urban centers but also in the national periphery helped to transform the Egyptian theater into an influential mass medium. However, precisely for these reasons, the developing media were viewed with a great deal of skepticism and perhaps fear by the Egyptian cultural and political elite.

## CULTURE WARS? THE VULGARIZATION OF VAUDEVILLE AND COLLOQUIAL SONGS

The denial of lower, coarse, vulgar, venal, servile—in a word, natural—enjoyment, which constitutes the sacred sphere of culture, implies an affirmation of the superiority of those who can be satisfied with the sublimated, refined, disinterested, gratuitous, distinguished pleasures forever closed to the profane. That is why art and cultural consumption are predisposed, consciously and deliberately or not, to fulfill a social function of legitimating social differences.

—Pierre Bourdieu, *Distinction: A Social Critique of the Judgment of Taste*

Pierre Bourdieu's study of cultural taste speaks to what was happening in Egypt during the first quarter of the twentieth century. From the begin-

ning of the development of colloquial mass media in Egypt, with the late
1870s publication of *Abu-Naddara Zarqa'*, Egyptian conservatives aggressively attacked colloquial mass discourse. Colloquial songs and colloquial theater also incurred the same sort of indignation and were deemed
vulgar and dangerous to the nation. This dichotomy between the more
official Fusha culture and the increasingly commercial colloquial Egyptian
mass culture perpetuated social distinctions between the cultural and intellectual elite and the masses. This was not merely a matter of aesthetics,
cultural taste, or reinforcement of class distinction but a reflection of the
conservative elite's fear of these new forms of media, which had an unprecedented influence on an increasing number of Egyptians and allowed
for regular political mobilization and mass politics.

Although the attacks by many of Egypt's cultural critics were multi-
faceted, the primary criticism was a disparagement of the "low" artistic
expressions of colloquial Egyptian, which, they argued, led directly to
the perceived decline of culture and morality in Egypt. With the overwhelming popularity of vaudeville, the pages of the press were filled
with such attacks. In a June 8, 1915, article titled "Arabic Acting: A
Dangerous Trend," *al-Ahram*'s theater critic explained the definitions
and parameters of the vaudeville theater and characterized most of its
plays as inappropriate for Egyptian audiences. The critic was as incensed
over the use of "corrupted colloquial" as he was about the "inappropriately vulgar" subject matter of the plays.[150] Some press condemnations
called for the government to interfere and ban all vaudeville plays. A
March 1916 article in *al-Minbar* went so far as to label vaudeville "morally dangerous" and accused it of "leading minds astray and corrupting
souls." The critic ended his article by questioning why the government
was so eager to censor for political reasons but not for moral reasons.[151]
Throughout this period, many articles with alarmist titles were printed,
including "Countering Pernicious Acting" (*Mukafahat al-Tamthil al-
Sha'in*) and "The Case [Against] Comedic Acting" (*Qadiyit al-Tamthil
al-Fukahi*).[152]

Many of these criticisms were laden with class references, describing
the "vulgarity" of the lower classes and opposing their representation on
the stage. For example, in a review of the colloquial play *'Amina Hanim*,
performed by the traveling troupe of Ahmad al-Shami, the theater critic
was disappointed that the contractor, one of the major characters in the
play, was portrayed as a "low class man who speaks with words only
spoken by those who wear blue *jalabiyyat*."[153] Another critic declared
that "these plays . . . are nothing but a collection of revolting pedestrian
scenes encountered by ordinary folks in the streets, alleys, and cafés, and
witnessed by those who frequent taverns and brothels."[154]

Unlike 'Abdallah Nadim, who retreated somewhat before the anti-colloquial attacks of the conservative elite (see Chapters 2 and 3), the colloquial writers of the emergent vaudeville and music industries had the implicit backing of tens of thousands of viewers and listeners and could afford to respond aggressively to their critics. 'Amin Sidqi, who would later write most of the plays of 'Ali al-Kassar, vigorously defended vaudeville and colloquial songs in the pages of the press. He responded to the *Ahram* rebuke of vaudeville with a forceful letter to the editor. Sidqi first accused the critic of plagiarizing his article from the Egyptian French language press, where a similar debate had taken place and where Sidqi had already responded to similar criticisms. He then explained that an essential component of all comedies is to exaggerate social behavior, especially what is thought of as immoral. This, according to Sidqi, not only creates laughter but indirectly counters the socially or morally corrupt behavior and does not condone it, as his critics claimed.

As for those who claim that this type of storytelling [i.e., vaudeville] is inappropriate for this day and age, I strongly disagree; for I am one who is never fooled by mere sloganeering. Egyptian audiences, and most especially those who attend my plays and laugh uncontrollably, are the ones who more than ever need moral education [*tarbiyya*]. . . . Acting was not specially created for the likes of the honorable critic, who can't even express his own opinion. The theater was created for the masses and the majority [of Egyptians] who are illiterate or barely literate, and for this reason I never hesitated when I was asked by the director of the theater company ['Aziz 'Id] to retranslate these plays in colloquial Egyptian. A joke is not humorous unless it is completely understood by everyone, and since the majority of people [in Egypt] are as I have described above, the Arabic language [i.e., Fusha], as it stands today, makes jokes and comedic speech impossible.[155]

Yunis al-Qadi, who wrote the lyrics for many of Sayyid Darwish's and Munira al-Mahdiyya's *taqatiq*, was regularly accused with writing "low and trivial" songs. Like Sidqi, he was not afraid to fire back at his critics.[156] Al-Qadi, however, defended modern *taqatiq* in a series of articles titled "Between the Old and the Modern" (*Bayn al-Qadim wa al-Hadith*).[157] The main thesis of these articles, which al-Qadi amply supported, was that there was no difference in content and subject matter between the "modern" *taqatiq* and the ones sung by earlier generations, making a mockery of the alarmists' claims that modern *taqatiq* were causing cultural decay. "I want to emphasize once again that those ignoramuses that are writing for *al-Ahram*, the largest daily newspaper, are falsifying history by declaring that the older traditional songs were not like the modern *taqatiq* [in their sexualized subject matter]. This is entirely false and demonstrates complete historical ignorance." To make his case, al-Qadi methodically lists sixty-three traditional colloquial songs with sexual innuendo.[158]

Sometimes colloquial songwriters and playwrights used their songs and plays to respond to and satirize culturally conservative critics. 'Ali al-Kassar's *Wi-Lissa* (More to come), which debuted in February 1919, simultaneously satirized the inaccessibility of Fusha and the attempts of the Egyptian cultural elite to "enlighten" the Egyptian masses through literal adaptation of "high culture" European plays.[159] A musical sketch titled "The Actors" sets up a dialogue between two groups of actors: comedic vaudeville actors who perform in colloquial Egyptian and drama actors who typically perform Western tragedies in Fusha. When the classically trained actors complain to the colloquial actors that vaudeville is destroying their livelihood, the vaudeville actors respond:

Why don't you come and join us
and enough of your Romeo and Juliet
Your plays are laughably out of fashion
and you will always be in poverty
"Thou shall be obeyed o your highness"
and such incomprehensible jibber-jabber
Your words are harsh on the ears
and displease young and old
. . .
If you want to succeed
in your branch of drama and excel
perform plays like us with Egyptian themes and then you will succeed
What do people care about John and Raul or a play set in Liverpool?
People want to see relevant events and people that look and dress like
    them.[160]

As this comedic dialogue indicates, when it came to mass entertainment at least, the Egyptian people of all classes and persuasions played the decisive role in this debate by voting with their wallets. In just seven years, 'Ali al-Kassar's theater earned an estimated 47,000 £E, and remarkably, during the 1918 season alone Najib al-Rihani's theater earned an unprecedented 28,500 £E.[161] Colloquial music records and vaudeville tickets were selling in high numbers, whereas no one seemed to be attending the "culturally superior" Fusha plays.[162] A theater critic writing for *al-Minbar* newspaper in the fall of 1918 corroborates this by blaming "Egyptian audiences for not appreciating the genius of a great actor like [George] Abyad and turning away from his theater and toward the (irritating) comedic theater." The critic disappointingly describes how the "theaters that are playing vaudeville and the like are overstuffed with men and women, who are exposed to [lessons in] lewdness and public indecency. In the meanwhile, a small theater like Abyad's is often barren with few spectators."[163]

CONCLUSION

The key driving force in the emerging Egyptian media capitalist system was monetary gain. The motivation for bigger sales increasingly called for the use of colloquial Egyptian as opposed to Fusha, and with it, an overall catering to the cultural tastes of the urban masses. In turn, the mass culture industries simultaneously shaped mass taste through their unprecedented standardization of cultural production. The result was a virtual dialogue between the consumers and producers of mass culture, strengthening the "authenticity" and ensuring the popularity of these new productions.[164] Achieving success as a colloquial writer was predicated on having just such a dialogue with everyday Egyptians in the everyday language. Indeed, many colloquial Egyptian writers preferred to write in coffee shops—which were typically open to the street—where they were exposed daily to the latest news and jokes and where their command of Egyptian street language and the accents and mannerisms of Egypt's diverse foreign communities was honed and perfected.[165]

The cafés on Imad al-Din Street, where most of the vaudeville theaters were housed, played an important role in the rise of the vaudeville theater industry. At least three major cafés on Imad al-Din Street were frequented by actors, singers, writers, and musicians: Qahwat al-Fann (The Arts Café), Qahwat Barun (The Baron Café), and Qahwat Misr (The Egypt Café). For instance, 'Ibrahim Ramzi, who wrote for 'Aziz 'Id, described how he wrote many of his plays in Qahwat al-Fann. Ramzi also acknowledged that Yunis al-Qadi "prefers to write only in coffee shops."[166] Badi' Khayri also acknowledged the importance of Cairo's coffee shops, helping him more fully "experience people and the colors of everyday life." He relates that "these cafés were the most important school for inspiring my theatrical writing. I learned the Egyptian dialects and the differing Arab dialects from sitting in these cafés." Even Najib al-Rihani confesses in his autobiography that early in his career, he was practically living in Qahwat al-Fann.[167]

By integrating and using the languages and discourses of the street and of everyday life, the writers of these new media tapped into a growing demand for comprehensible, realistic characters, songs, and stories. This emergent media capitalist system—combining print, sound, and performance media—allowed for an increasing number of Egyptians to more fully participate in a variety of expanding public spheres. The market-driven forces fueling the commercial production of theatrical and recording hits had revolutionary social implications, not only because they increased the level of homogeneity of national taste but also because they trumped the exclusivist Fusha cultural models pushed by the cul-

tural elite and the Egyptian state. Thus in the first quarter of the twentieth century, mass cultural production, which followed the dictates of the
developing culture market, was counterhegemonic primarily because it
was independent of the Egyptian state and competed with, and in many
ways mocked, the classicist traditions of the cultural conservatives.

## CHAPTER SIX

# The Egyptian Street

## *Carnival, Popular Culture, and the 1919 Revolution*

Pardon us, Wingate! But our country has had enough!
You took our camels, donkeys, barley, and wheat aplenty.
Now leave us alone!
. . .
Laborers and soldiers were forced to travel, leaving their land.
They headed to Mount Lebanon and to the battlefields and the trenches!
And now they blame us?
Behold all the calamities you caused! Had it not been for our laborers, you
(and your rifles) would have been helpless in the desert sand!
You who are in authority! Why didn't you go all alone to the Dardanelles?
Maxwell! Now you feel some hardships.
so why don't you drink it up!
The Egyptian is resilient; and now he is willing and able and can do anything.
His achievements are worthy of praise and he will do his all to gain a
     constitution.
We are the sons of the Pharaohs, which no one can dispute.
When necessary we can fight with clubs, sticks, and even head butts.
Long live Egypt! Long live Egypt! Best of all nations; mother of the brave;
and this has been for all times.
A new life! O glorious Egypt! We have gained our eternal purpose.
There is no disputing that
so leave us alone!
. . .
O Wilson, we have gathered together but to whom shall we address ourselves?
    For we have no real newspapers—only those lunatics in the *Muqatam.*
. . .
We want it to be known—total independence is our goal!
If only "they" leave our nation! We would surpass Japan in civilization.
Return to your country! Pick up your belongings! What audacity and rudeness.
You are a true calamity! Do you have to stick to us like glue?

—Popular song, 1919

These lyrics from a popular colloquial Egyptian song called "Pardon us, Wingate"—which was widely sung in the streets during the 1919 Egyptian revolution—accurately portray many of the deep-rooted causes of the revolt and explain, in part, the unprecedented and unforeseen mass mobilization of the Egyptian people.[1] As discussed in Chapter 5, World War I imposed new economic burdens that affected most social classes in Egypt, from the peasants and urban masses to the landed elite. The peasants were hit hard by the requisitioning of their "camels, donkeys, barley, and wheat" and by being recruited by the British authorities to serve as their wartime labor corps. To cheaply supply its factories, the British kept raw Egyptian cotton prices artificially low, allowing them to reach only 56% of the world market price. This greatly angered the Egyptian landed gentry and was certainly one of the motivating factors in the overwhelming support the elite gave, early on at least, to the independence movement.[2] The middle classes were increasingly resentful because of the ever-expanding number of British bureaucrats employed in large numbers during the war. Most of the urban population was angered over inflation, high prices, and the unavailability of basic goods. In addition, repressive British policies during World War I, which included tight censorship of all newspapers and the wide application of martial law, heightened everyone's resentment and contributed to a growing sense of injustice and oppression. This cumulative mass anger needed only a spark to trigger a nationwide revolt. Conveniently enough, this spark was provided by the March 8, 1919, arrest and exile of Sa'd Zaghlul and three members of what would become the Wafd (delegation) Party.[3]

In this chapter I focus on the street politics of the revolution and, as much as possible, cover the lives of ordinary Egyptians who acted en masse in the public sphere during the spring of 1919. Accordingly, Egypt's streets, and by extension its many *midan*s (public squares), cafés, bars, theaters, mosques, and churches, served as focal points of most of the events covered in this chapter. The role of illicit publications and circulars on the Egyptian streets, especially in light of the tight censorship imposed on the officially recognized press, is closely examined. Finally, I scrutinize the almost instantaneous celebrations and depictions of the events of the revolution in theater and in song and the role that these mass media played in the actual revolution and, perhaps more important, in shaping its memory in the Egyptian national imagination. However, before examining the street politics of the revolt, it is necessary to frame these actions within their historical context through a brief examination of the events leading up to the revolution.

### THE WAFD PARTY AND ZAGHLUL:
### FROM ELITISTS TO POPULISTS?

The 1910 assassination of Butrus Ghali not only elevated civil strife between Muslims and Copts to new heights (see Chapter 5) but also was an important factor in a repressive policy directed at the Watani Party, leading to the imprisonment or exile of most of its leadership. This suppression was especially intensified with the application of martial law during World War I and left a significant leadership vacuum in what was an increasingly populist movement. Ironically, the mantle of nationalist leadership was inherited by the nonpopulist Sa'd Zaghlul Pasha and other members of the 'Umma Party, which predominantly consisted of the Egyptian landed gentry.[4]

Zaghlul, who had previously been the Egyptian education and justice minister and had been pushed out of governing circles by 'Abbas Hilmi II and Lord Kitchener, found temporary solace and a renewed sense of national prestige by being elected in 1913 to the Legislative Assembly (al-Jam'iyya al-Tashri'iyya). With the advent of World War I and the establishment of the British protectorate, however, the Legislative Assembly was suspended; Zaghlul spent most of the duration of the war in a self-imposed exile at his Egyptian countryside estate.[5] Even though the Assembly was suspended during World War I, sixty-six of its ninety-one elected members retained some legitimacy as representatives of the people.[6] Zaghlul, for example, always emphasized his 1913 election by the Egyptian people. Well into the 1920s he consciously sought to enhance his legitimacy and political clout by signing his official letters with the title "The Elected Representative to the Legislative Council."[7] After World War I ended, Zaghlul and a number of his colleagues from the Assembly, including 'Abd al-'Aziz Fahmi Pasha and 'Ali Sha'rawi Pasha, began petitioning the British to send a delegation (*wafd*) of their choosing to represent Egypt at the Paris Peace Conference, with the aim of securing Egypt's "independence." How much independence Zaghlul and these well-seasoned politicians expected from the British at this stage is unclear, although it was generally believed in Egypt that because of Egyptian economic and political sacrifices during the war, the British owed Egypt at least nominal independence.[8]

On November 13, 1918, Zaghlul, Fahmi, and Sha'rawi officially inaugurated the Wafd Party on the national stage by demanding Egyptian independence at a publicly orchestrated meeting with the British high commissioner, Sir Reginald Wingate.[9] According to 'Abd al-Rahman

Fahmi, the general secretary of the Wafd Central Committee in Cairo, news of that meeting spread quickly throughout the city and then to other large urban centers, and "soon most of the country was conversing about these events." Sha'rawi's declaration to Wingate that "we (Egyptians) want our friendship with the British to be that of freemen and not of slaves to their owner" was repeated throughout Egypt.[10]

After the November 13 meeting, the Wafd Party took immediate steps to enhance its legitimacy and consolidate its core membership. The original members of the party were Sa'd Zaghlul, 'Abd al-'Aziz Fahmi, 'Ali Sha'rawi, Muhammad Mahmud, 'Ahmad Lutfi al-Sayyid, 'Abd al-Latif al-Mikabati, and Muhammad 'Ali 'Aluba. From the very beginnings of the Wafd as a movement, there was a concerted and fairly successful effort to create national unity between Copts and Muslims. The first Coptic Christians to join the Wafd leadership were George Khayyat and Sinut Hanna, who, like the other Wafd leaders, were from wealthy landowning families.[11]

In the early days of the movement, the Wafd Party was fully cognizant of the need to appeal to the masses and actively relied on the publication of petitions and pamphlets to both legitimize and advertise its nationalist goals. Several public petitions made their way through the Egyptian provinces and collected tens of thousands of signatures.[12] Public meetings were also organized at mosques, churches, clubs, and coffee shops; many of the speeches given at these meetings were collected and published. For instance, a January 13, 1919, speech given by Zaghlul in which he demanded an immediate British withdrawal from Egypt was immediately published and distributed throughout the country.[13]

The Paris Peace Conference and President Woodrow Wilson's Fourteen Points raised the average Egyptian's expectations for acquiring major concessions from the British, if not complete independence. As the song lyrics at the beginning of this chapter demonstrate, in the first four months of 1919, the Egyptian streets were filled with hopeful expectations: Woodrow Wilson and the Americans were viewed as literal saviors who would unilaterally grant Egypt its independence. The Wafd Party, initially at least, also took Wilson's Fourteen Points at face value and had high hopes for the Americans.[14] On February 16, 1919, Zaghlul sent a telegram to Woodrow Wilson pleading with him for a hearing at the peace table in Paris. How could the "[peace] conference officially hear the Syrian delegation which was until recently a part of the Turkish Empire," Zaghlul asks, and "refuse to listen to the voice of all Egyptians?" He then reproached Wilson by asking, "Is it reasonable to you that those who were fighting against the Allies have the right to voice their demands and

Egypt, which participated in the war on the side of the Allies, is denied this right?" The telegram however, was intercepted by British censors.[15]

EXILE AND "REVOLUTION"

The Wafd Party continued to be a thorn in the side of the British authority. By early March, British officials were discussing how to deal with the "Wafd problem" and by March 6, 1919, they began formulating a decision to exile Zaghlul.[16] On March 8, 1919, Zaghlul, Isma'il Sidqi Pasha, Muhammad Mahmud Pasha, and Hamd al-Basil Pasha were arrested and exiled to Malta.[17] The decision to exile Zaghlul and "some of his associates" was predicted to produce a calming effect and "a temporary reaction" in favor of the British. Reginald Wingate went so far as to confidently declare to the Foreign Office that the exile of Zaghlul "should discourage and discredit the extremists."[18]

It did not take long to disprove Wingate's theory, as news quickly spread about the exile of Zaghlul and the others. The next morning the streets of Cairo witnessed a large and "noisy demonstration" composed mainly of students—310 arrests were made.[19] On March 10, unrest cropped up in Alexandria, and the demonstrations expanded in intensity as students were "joined by riff-raff of the town" and rioting took place.[20] By March 11, unrest spread from Cairo and Alexandria to the countryside and to the peripheral towns and cities in the Delta, such as Tanta and Damanhur.[21] According to British reports, by mid-March the situation in the Delta was deteriorating fast: "Reports from the provinces show trouble at Damietta and demonstrations at Mansura and attempts are being made to interrupt communications. Telegraph lines have been cut in several places, apparently with the view to isolating Cairo and railway lines from Tanta to Menouf."[22] Unrest also spread into Upper Egypt with large demonstrations and the cutting of railroad tracks and telegraph wires.[23] The British authority's desperation can be gleaned from the following excerpt from a March 18, 1919, report to the Foreign Office: "Telegraph wires and poles being destroyed in all directions. There is no communication other than by wireless telegraph and aeroplane between Cairo and the provinces."[24]

Airplanes, however, were not just used for communication; the British attempted to stop the destruction of the railways using air power.

During last two days aeroplanes have machine gunned with excellent effect crowds engaged in damaging railways and are now ordered to use bombs when targets offer. Have formed five squadrons from training squadrons and over 100 machines are now occupied. General situation is such as to necessitate considerable military measures being taken, and the acting Commander-in-Chief has come to Egypt to direct operations."[25]

Collective punishment was also used; it became standard policy to burn the village closest to the damaged railway tracks. In a note to the Foreign Office, Sir Ronald Graham stressed the importance of censoring any news of the above policy from Parliament: "I would advise that any communiqués from Egypt dealing with the burning of villages etc., should be carefully censored before publication, otherwise questions in Parliament are almost certain to arise."[26]

Despite these purges, almost daily demonstrations and unrest continued throughout Egypt for the remainder of March. To the surprise of the British authorities, elite Egyptian women also demonstrated in March, led by Huda Sha'rawi (1879–1947), who would become the leading feminist voice in Egypt in the first half of the twentieth century. The first women's demonstration was held on Sunday, March 16, 1919, and was followed by yet another one on Thursday, March 20, 1919. Elite women would continue to play an important and increasingly public nationalist role throughout the spring and summer of 1919 and beyond.[27]

When the hard-line approach appeared not to be working, the British completely reversed course, and on April 7, 1919, they freed Zaghlul and his colleagues, triggering "spontaneous outbursts" of celebration throughout Egypt.[28] However, the release of Zaghlul and the other exiles, as well as the granting of permission for the Wafd leaders to travel to Paris to argue the Egyptian case for independence, proved futile for the nationalists. The British were successful in diplomatically isolating the Egyptian delegation; the Wafd leaders were snubbed by the French and the Americans, who officially accepted the continuation of the British protectorate over Egypt.[29] Strikes, sporadic demonstrations, and general disorder continued for months as the British began to negotiate with an increasingly fragmented Wafd leadership. As these negotiations foundered, in February 1922 Great Britain unilaterally renounced its protectorate and Egypt gained nominal independence.[30]

Although the stated goal of "complete" independence was not achieved, the 1919 Revolution was a resounding success in another way: For the first time in Egyptian history, a mass movement encompassing most of the Egyptian population was able to gain perceptible concessions from the ruling authority. In the remainder of this chapter I focus on the street politics of the revolution. The collective voice of the Egyptian masses, as embodied in the forms of conversations, rumors, speeches, demonstrations, and publicly performed dances, chants, and songs, is the lens through which we will examine the turbulent events of the spring and summer of 1919.

### DANCING IN THE STREETS:
### A CELEBRATORY CARNIVAL?

I saw America's . . . armistice celebrations in Philadelphia and Boston. . . . America's peace carnivals, however, were as Sunday school exercises when compared with the mad delirium of patriotic fervor that swept Cairo into the streets for two days of oration on the proclamation of Gen. Allenby freeing the nationalist leaders exiled in Malta. . . . Occasionally the one chorus was varied by cheers for America and for Mr. Wilson and for France and for Saad Zaghlul and for the peace conference. Mostly, though, it was tirelessly, "Yahia el Watan! Yahia el Watan!" [Long live the nation]. The frenzy grew with the crowds. . . . Anybody could see that this was a festival of joy, with animosity to nobody. There were no parties or classes in this freedom carnival. Egypt was indulging in a joyous and innocent orgy of national consciousness. The slums sent their worst and the palaces sent their best to mingle in a common and tumultuous street filling procession of patriotism, which kept up an overpowering and unbelievable din.

—William T. Ellis, *Washington Post*, June 21, 1919

As William T. Ellis—a correspondent to the *Washington Post* and the *New York Herald*—describes on April 7, 1919, when news leaked out that Zaghlul and the rest of the Wafd delegation were released from Malta, Cairo exploded in celebratory demonstrations.[31] In his memoirs, 'Abd al-Rahman Fahmi recalled these celebrations and especially took notice of the role played by the female urban masses. After recounting how in celebrating the release of Zaghlul, the elite women "paraded in their cars, waving flags and throwing flowers," Fahmi described how the "lower class women [*'ammat al-nisa'*] were not to be outdone as they rode on the back of trucks [and donkey-drawn carriages] and proceeded to dance and chant to the rhythm of drums and trumpets."[32] In his editorial Ellis went to great lengths to describe the public dancing taking place in the streets while assuring his prudish readers of the "non-vulgar" propriety of these expressions: "With no thought of vulgarity, but only as an instinctive, spontaneous expression of enthusiasm . . . scores of women mounted carts, and with castanets on their fingers, did the muscle dances which are tabooed by the police of American cities" (see Figure 7). Describing the temporary carnivallike egalitarian qualities of the assembly, Ellis related: "The social standing of these women is represented by a minus sign rather than a zero: yet they rode unrebuked side by side with the elegant automobiles of the veiled daughters and wives from the harems of the princes and pashas and beys. Egypt was never before as democratic as on this day of days: the fiesta was a cross section of the nation's life. From royalty to fellaheen and Bedouin, all clamorous with 'Yahia el Watan' [Long live the nation]."[33] Egyptian men also danced

FIGURE 7. *Egyptian women celebrating release of Saʿd Zaghlul.*
*From* L'Illustration *(Paris), May 3, 1919. Picture taken on April 8, 1919.*

that day, as Ellis observed them on multiple occasions in front of the Shepheard Hotel.[34]

The next morning (April 8, 1919), Cairo's streets witnessed a more organized demonstration, replete with musicians playing nationalist songs and bearers carrying Egyptian flags. At the forefront of the entire procession, a student carried what became the recurring symbol of national unity: a large flag with the cross and the crescent depicted on it. According to an eyewitness, an "'Azhari Sheikh was seen carrying a picture of the Coptic Christian patriarch along with a flag depicting the cross and the crescent, while chanting: 'Long live our holy union' and the gathering crowd enthusiastically repeated his chant."[35] Also, British reports confirmed that Jewish Egyptians participated in the nationalist celebrations: "A noticeable feature of this afternoon's procession which I myself saw was two carriages full of Jews, amongst whom, was one of the chief Rabbis. . . . They were carrying the Jewish Flag [i.e., a flag with the Star of David] attached to the Egyptian Flag and the Rabbi made several speeches which were loudly cheered."[36] As we shall discuss in more detail later in this chapter, these carnivalesque displays—in which many social, religious, and gendered distinctions were momentarily suspended—were frequently on display in the streets of Cairo during the spring of 1919.[37]

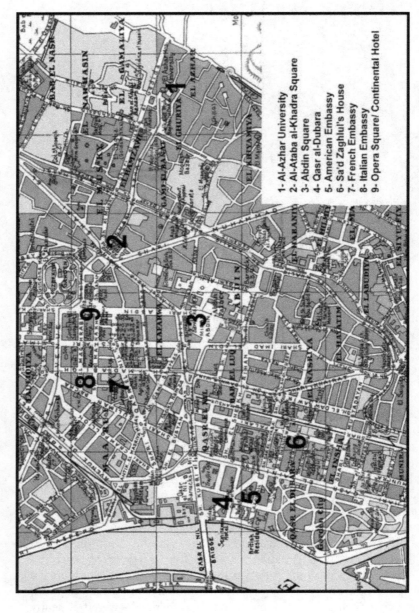

1- Al-Azhar University
2- Al-Ataba al-Khadra Square
3- Abdin Square
4- Qasr al-Dubara
5- American Embassy
6- Sa'd Zaghlul's House
7- French Embassy
8- Italian Embassy
9- Opera Square/ Continental Hotel

FIGURE 8. *Map of April 8, 1919, demonstration route. Adapted from Alexander Nicobossoff's Map of Cairo (Alexandria, Egypt: Etablissement des Arts Graphiques, c. 1930).*

## CITY SQUARES AND THE URBAN STREETS

The April 8 demonstrators marched through the streets of Cairo and, as had become customary, assembled outside Zaghlul's home to listen to nationalist speeches. Safiyya Zaghlul, the wife of the exiled leader, frequently met with the "delegations of men and women flocking to the house to pledge their support" and "address[ed] the crowds that used the house as a rallying point."[38] The Zaghlul house, which by now was called *Bayt al-'Umma* (house of the nation), played an important role as the focal point of nationalist and Wafdist politics. Locating *Bayt al-'Umma* as the nerve center of the revolution and the Wafd Party was guaranteed by Safiyya Zaghlul, who insisted, despite her husband's exile, to continue holding Wafdist meetings in her house.[39] This calculated move not only ensured her husband's position as the leader of the Wafd Party but also "gave Safiyya an opportunity to play a pivotal role in the movement."[40] As Beth Baron has shown, Safiyya Zaghlul, who would soon become known as the Mother of Egyptians (*'Umm al-Misriyyin*), actively "manipulated maternal symbolism to carve out a political role for herself."[41]

One of the speakers assembled in front of *Bayt al-'Umma* during the April 8 demonstrations declared to the crowd, "No one must cease from demonstrating, no one must go back to their work, no one must rest, until Egypt has her independence." Alluding to this demonstration, he said that "in any case it is sweet to die if one is dying for one's country."[42] Speech after speech fed off the exuberance of the crowds, reinforcing the feeling that their collective actions and voices had a direct impact on the release of Zaghlul and encouraging all Egyptians to continue to resist and to "strike while the iron is hot."[43] The protestors then slowly proceeded to 'Abdin Square, Opera Square (facing the Continental Hotel), and the main square near the train station. At each of these locales, they stopped and listened to speeches and declarations concerning the revolution.[44]

The significance and size of the public space outside the Continental Hotel was an important reason for its transformation into one of the key protest sites during the revolution. It not only overlooked the open spaces of the 'Azbakiyya Park to the east but also the large Opera Square (sometimes called *midan al-tiyatru*, or theater square) to the southeast. In addition, the presence of large numbers of foreigners in the hotel served to propagandize and advertise the revolution to the outside world. It is precisely for this reason that many of the planned demonstrations stopped momentarily in front of important foreign embassies. For instance, a pamphlet distributed on April 7, 1919, the day that Sa'd Zaghlul was released from Malta, announced the exact route of the celebratory demonstration planned for the next morning[45] (see Figure 8). The route of the demonstration—which according to the pamphlet was planned by students of al-'Azhar University—began at al-'Azhar and was intended to stop along key assembly points, including the Italian, French, American, and Spanish embassies, Sa'd Zaghlul's house, the main square at Cairo's train station, 'Abdin (palace) Square, and several of Cairo's other large squares.

As is evident from examining the map in Figure 8, the demonstrations that took place during the 1919 Revolution greatly benefited from Cairo's newer and more expansive public spaces. The demonstrators were able to march and assemble in large numbers in the wide streets, boulevards, and squares of the city, facilitating mass action and "physical" lateral comradeship on an unprecedented scale. The layout of the streets and public squares also facilitated mass public viewing of the revolutionary events as they materialized (see Figure 9). Those who were not physically involved in the revolts or demonstrations could still participate: by listening to the sounds of the songs and chants, perhaps by singing along, or by merely observing the street theater unfolding before their eyes. In these crowded carnivalesque environments, hearing, seeing, and speaking were further embodied by physical contact, as demonstrators, viewers, and listeners literally touched shoulders. The reverberations of sound from the chants,

FIGURE 9. *Egyptian crowds with Italian flag. From* L'Illustration *(Paris),*
*May 3, 1919.*

clapping, music, and other noise were also physically felt by all who were present. Undoubtedly, this was also an olfactory experience for everyone involved, perhaps subconsciously highlighting the embodied physical presence of these events by adding yet another sensory dimension.

## COFFEE SHOPS AS REVOLUTIONARY HUBS

No city has a more active café life than Cairo. Even in the morning the little iron tables on the pavement are thronged. Whenever you pass a café there are numbers of tarbushes to be seen both outside and inside. A few people may be playing dice or Dominoes. But the mass are reading newspapers and talking politics.

—H. Hamilton Fyfe, *The New Spirit in Egypt*

Fyfe's observation, made in 1911 when he traveled to Egypt from America, illustrates the importance of cafés and café culture in the Egyptian public sphere. To put the importance and prevalence of coffee shops in perspective, 'Ali Pasha Mubarak's 1887 survey of Cairo counted 1,067 coffee shops compared to only 264 mosques.[46] In Egypt's urban centers, coffee shops were (and continue to be) an extension of the street, in that their spatial boundaries usually expanded beyond their officially "enclosed" space. Weather permitting, most Egyptian cafés sat more people outside on the sidewalks and on the pavement than inside. This meant that passersby, be they paperboys, street vendors, entertainers, or simply pedestrians, could observe and listen to, if not participate in, the coffee shop experience.

In the Egyptian urban sphere, politics and coffee shops were synonymous, especially after newspapers and newspaper culture became prevalent in the 1870s. As discussed in earlier chapters, listening to recorded and performed music and sharing newspapers and reading them aloud often took place in Egyptian coffee shops. The 1919 Revolution, in particular, demonstrated the importance of cafés as meeting places and as essential communication hubs where the male urban masses received and interpreted the latest news and information. Coffee shops served as revolutionary centers where impromptu speeches were delivered, nationalistic songs were performed, counterhegemonic ideas were debated, and illicit newspapers and circulars were distributed, posted, and read.[47] The British spy network, well aware of these activities, struggled to keep up with the plethora of "seditious" acts taking place in the cafés. For instance, an April 8, 1919, intelligence report declared, "All the talk in the Cafés is hatred for the British and the desire to finally rid the country of them, and there is no doubt that feeling is running very high."[48] Another intelligence report emphasized how all Cairene cafés and bars were crowded with patrons busy discussing how to resist the British. The report called attention to the fact that there were many "conversations emphasizing the fact that the Egyptian Nation must be prepared to lose thousands of men before their ideals are realized."[49]

Aside from providing the backdrop for conversations, coffee shops also served as a public forum for revolutionary speeches, as another British report related: "Groppi's, last night in particular, has never been so crowded and it was almost impossible to get a seat." This excitement spilled over into the streets "as small groups were walking about arm in arm shouting 'Long live independence.'"[50] For most of the spring of 1919, it was common for people to make impromptu speeches in the streets, often near a landmark, a *midan*, or anywhere with large gatherings of people. The crowds listened and observed, and, later on no doubt, they conversed about these revolutionary discourses, spreading them even further afield.

Acts of communal coercion and collective shaming were quite common on the streets as well. Throughout the spring of 1919, public voices that called for moderation were quickly attacked and marginalized. When a school principal who was sitting at a coffee shop declared that students should end their "strike" and return to school, he was "spat on and called a 'traitor in the pay of the British.'"[51] After a coordinated strike by government employees in April, much of the public discourse on the streets and in the cafés reproached and intimidated workers who returned to work.[52] For instance, on the night of April 23, a man named 'Abd al-Karim Fahmi stood up in a popular café and delivered a long diatribe attacking the employees who had gone back to work, calling them traitors to the nation.[53] In an April 26 editorial, *al-Akhbar* newspaper reported that "lower-class women, street sweepers, and other riffraff" shamed and discouraged government employees from returning to their jobs.[54] British reports also took note of the street intimidations: "Government employees are very annoyed and in some cases frightened of the intimidation meted out to them when going to their offices, and expect a stop to be put to it. Apparently both the rabble and also the native women are specially hired for the purpose of accosting and insulting employees."[55] The role of lower-class urban women during the 1919 Revolution was significant, although it was not as highlighted as the role of the elite women's demonstrations in the contemporary press and even in the current historiography.

The British frequently raided coffee shops, confiscating illicit circulars and arresting those who were deemed troublemakers. These raids only momentarily subdued revolutionary discussions and debates: "The raids on the cafés make a certain amount of impressions even if only of a temporary nature. Each time raids are made there is a very subdued tone amongst the frequenters of the cafés and bars for several days following."[56] Cafés, however, were not the only public places where revolutionary activities took place. From the beginning of the March revolt, mosques and churches played a similar role as congregational centers for revolutionary activities.

### SECULARIZING AND GENDERING THE SACRED:
### MOSQUES AND CHURCHES AS REVOLUTIONARY SPACES

So, day after day, morning, noon and night, the strikers and the nationalists assembled by the thousands in El Azhar to discuss their grievances and demands, as well as methods of procedure. It is a grand and glorious carnival of speechmaking. Moslem ulemas and sheikhs, Coptic and Armenian priests and bishops, lawyers, doctors, professors, students, merchants and whoever has something to say, gets up to address the crowd. When the audience does not like a man or have had enough of him they say so. Up to date the most popular speaker is a Christian priest, a Copt, named Sergius. The only woman ever to speak at Azhar was a Jewess, a nationalist.
—William T. Ellis, *Washington Post*, June 25, 1919

Like the coffee shops, mosques and Coptic churches provided critical meeting places for subversive activities throughout the 1919 Revolution. Although coffee shops were regularly raided by the British and the Egyptian police, mosques and churches proved to be a safer forum for regularly scheduled public discussions and meetings. Egyptians of all religious, ethnic, and socioeconomic backgrounds participated together in these meetings. As we will examine, al-'Azhar University became the nerve center of the revolution. The university, with its large enclosed spaces, functioned as a protective "public" sphere where everyone could participate in secular revolutionary activities.

In part, to counter any anticipated British accusations that the 1919 revolt was sectarian and to demonstrate national unity, Coptic Christians and Muslims regularly attended and participated in meetings held at each other's houses of worship. In addition, unlike coffee shops, which were at this time a predominantly male public space, Egyptian women attended and actively participated in many of the mosque and church meetings.[57] For instance, many upper-class Muslim and Christian women were present during a large nationalist meeting held for the occasion of the Sham al-Nasim holiday at a Cairene Coptic church.[58] The meeting was attended by many important 'Azhari sheikhs and Coptic priests. According to British intelligence reports, during the meeting the Coptic patriarch made an anti-British speech, in which he declared that "Copts were now united with Muslims."[59]

Egyptian women also actively participated in and delivered important speeches at many of these mosque and church meetings. Muslims and

Copts of both sexes held a meeting on the afternoon of May 3, 1919, in a Coptic church located on Clot Bey Street, where a Muslim woman stood up and "preached for a general strike."[60] The next morning several Egyptian ladies walked into the Sayyida Zaynab Mosque in Cairo and made speeches about the Egyptian revolution. Because of the coordination and frequency of such activities, British authorities suspected that these "Egyptian ladies" were being "induced to go to the mosques and make seditious speeches."[61]

As mentioned, al-'Azhar University provided a safe house for revolutionary activities, putting nationalists to a certain extent outside the reach of the British authorities. Although the British authorities made sure not to forcibly enter al-'Azhar University and other mosques, which would certainly have caused an escalation in violence, they nonetheless had regular spies who attended many of the meetings and wrote lengthy reports detailing subversive activities.

A reliable agent, well acquainted with the affairs of Al Azhar and having intimate relations with persons of consequence there, gives the following report: "The meetings have become so degraded and common that a respectable person would be really ashamed to attend them. The university has actually become a sort of public café where people of the most common type go loiter around and spend their spare hours. Newsboys go in freely and sell seditious and other newspapers. The walls and pillars of Al Azhar are simply covered with seditious circulars, notices, etc., some of which are of a most vulgar nature."[62]

Despite British surveillance, the daily mass meetings held at al-'Azhar University provided a political forum for discussion at which ordinary people of both sexes and all religious backgrounds expressed their opinions about the revolution and current events. Coptic priests, women, young students, railroad workers, and even shoemakers delivered speeches, leading some nationalist leaflets to label the daily 'Azhar meetings as the "Egyptian Congress."[63]

According to British intelligence reports, at many of the 'Azhari meetings Copts gave more violent speeches than Muslims.[64] As alluded to in the report quoted, one of the leading and most subversive speakers at al-'Azhar University was a Coptic priest named Murqus Sergius, who quickly developed a national reputation for his vehement patriotic speeches. His reputation was further enhanced as his eloquent sayings spread in Cairene circles. In one such line he declared, "As a servant of God my duty is to celebrate marriage and funeral rites, and I long to bury the authority of England and to marry Egypt to liberty and independence."[65] Sergius's activities extended to other mosques as well; he gave another "violent speech" on Friday, April 4, 1919, at the Ibn Tulun Mosque, urging all Egyptians to "unite and rise against the English."

To prevent British forces from surrounding the Ibn Tulun Mosque to keep people from entering, the nationalists used large stones to block the road connecting the al-Sayyida Zaynab district to the mosque.[66] Sergius would soon be incarcerated, further enhancing his status as a staunch nationalist.[67]

The Egyptian press reflected and actively encouraged the ongoing religious fraternization between Copts and Muslims. During Easter, for example, the pages of the press were filled with Easter greetings from Muslims.[68] During Ramadan, on May 30, 1919, a large deputation of Coptic notables and leaders visited al-'Azhar University and "conveyed the good wishes of the Coptic community." In a host of "congratulatory and patriotic speeches" it was decided to continue to strive toward unity and "the attainment of independence." During the meeting, some Copts even pledged to fast for ten days during the month of Ramadan to demonstrate their solidarity with their countrymen and, according to British reports, to demonstrate the "inability of English intrigues to separate them."[69]

The stark contrast between Muslim-Coptic relations in 1919 and those earlier in the decade (see Chapter 5) raises the question of the degree to which this rapprochement was genuine and how much of it was a marriage of convenience. Although this distinction is nearly impossible to determine, what is certain is that the nationalist leadership and the higher-ranking clergies of both religions used every tool at their disposal to preempt any possible sectarian fissures. The ongoing exchange of clergy, with priests speaking in mosques and sheikhs speaking in churches, coupled with a multimedia blitz emphasizing the unity of the revolution, achieved overwhelming success in this regard.[70]

This visible rapprochement and unity between Muslims and Copts also extended to the provinces. In the town of Damanhur in Buhayra (in the Egyptian Delta), a large meeting of Muslims and Copts was held on Sunday, April 13, 1919, at a Coptic church. According to British informants, there were "cheers for 'unity' and 'independence.'" However, the report also qualifies, to a certain extent, this atmosphere of brotherhood and goodwill, stating that "this week-end, the Copts seem to be showing a genuine distress at the idea that perhaps Moslems should attend the Easter services."[71]

### CENSORSHIP AND THE OFFICIAL EGYPTIAN PRESS

Because of the rigorous censorship laws in place, most Egyptian newspapers provided limited coverage of the ongoing uprising, and early on at least, the press was generally restrained in its enthusiasm for the revolution. Any material deemed objectionable to the censors was immediately removed; many newspapers were sold with some columns almost entirely blanked out. Of the officially recognized Arabic newspapers, only *al-Muqattam* and *al-Watan* were categorically against the demonstrations and called for an immediate return to "public order."[72] Initially, *al-Ahram, Misr, Wadi al-Nil* (The Nile Valley), *al-Mahrusa* (Cairo), and *al-Masamir* (The nails) were hesitantly supportive of the student demonstrations and blamed any excessive violence or looting on urban riffraff (*al-ri'a'*).[73]

The Wafd leaders soon began courting some of the more sympathetic periodicals, urging them to openly support the revolution; by May 1919, newspapers such as *Misr, Wadi al-Nil, al-Nizam* (Order), and eventually *al-Ahram* were pro-Wafd and explicitly supported the nationalist movement. It is also probable that some Egyptian periodicals switched more openly to the nationalist camp for business rather than patriotic reasons, as pro-nationalist periodicals were simply selling more newspapers. By April, *al-Ahram* devoted most of its second page to covering nationalist issues in a new section titled "*Al-Ahram* Is an Egyptian Paper for Egyptians." This section, however, was heavily censored, and the newspaper was often printed with numerous empty segments on its second page. *Misr, al-Mahrusa,* and *al-'Afkar* (Thoughts/ideas) were not only frequently censored but also temporarily suspended and charged for "inciting violence."[74]

Because of these ongoing press purges, many newspapers walked a fine line between restraint and insinuation. Throughout this period the censors allowed some general expressions of patriotism (e.g., references about loving the nation), yet descriptions of current revolutionary activities or references to key nationalist figures were strictly forbidden. In the March 30, 1919, issue of *al-Masamir*, the lead editorial, titled "The Days," discussed the uncertainties of the current political situation in Egypt without referring to any specifics. The writer also shrewdly used the masculine form of the word *happiness* (*sa'd*) instead of the more common feminine version (*sa'ada*): "Ah! These days! No misery and no happiness [*sa'd*], no playfulness and no solemnity, no scarcity and no abundance, no strength and no weakness, no life and no death."[75] Referring to Sa'd Zaghlul in this manner was common, and, aside from newspapers, many songs, poems, and theatrical sketches used similar wordplay. In a *zajal* in the May 18, 1919, issue of *al-Masamir*, the colloquial poet celebrated the revolution and national unity and declared his yearning for the beloved (i.e., Sa'd Zaghlul). As expected, Zaghlul was never mentioned by name; instead all references to him were implied.[76]

The British also tried to use some Arabic-language newspapers to support their agenda. Aside from *al-Muqattam*, which was always over-whelmingly pro-British, British sympathizers made regular overtures to other newspapers and regularly posted articles supporting their cause. Increasingly, however, the political climate made it almost impossible for the British to find Arabic newspapers willing to publish their "propaganda." The following report to the British Foreign Office demonstrates British frustrations over the "switching over" of many newspapers to the nationalist side:

Al Lataif [*al-Lata'if al-Musawwara*] has lately gone over to the nationalist side, and I have ceased to use it for propaganda. It is not licensed as a political organ. Nevertheless, the editor, Selim Makarius, a Syrian related to the Nimr group, is doing his best to keep alive the interest in Saad Zaghlul and his doings. In this week's issue he proposed to publish photographs of Saad at different ages with a short biography and a panegyric, hoping that God will give him strength to obtain all of Egypt's demands.[77]

Although the censors suppressed this photographic display, they did allow a significant nationalistic spread on the front cover of the April 7, 1919, issue of *al-Lata'if al-Musawwara* (Illustrated pleasantries). It featured a large Egyptian flag flapping in the wind and the following phrases in large bold print: "Long live the nation . . . Long live Egypt . . . Long live the munificent Egyptian homeland . . . Long live the Egyptian Youth . . . Long live the Egyptian ladies." The same day that this magazine issue was printed, news of the release of Zaghlul and the other exiles from Malta spread quickly, and most of the other newspapers printed patriotic paeans celebrating the event.[78] A British press report described the state of the "native press" at the end of April as full of "abstract articles on patriotism, liberty, charity and . . . reference to the position of women, poetry on female patriotism etc., abounds."[79] These articles had to be "abstract" and general enough to be printed, although by collectively celebrating Egyptian identity, they served the nationalist movement and the ongoing revolution.[80]

## PAMPHLETS, PAMPHLETEERING, AND THE "ILLICIT" PRESS

Although most of the officially recognized newspapers supported the revolution, the censorship laws in place made them impractical for directly serving the nationalists. The demand for current information and, to some extent, disinformation helped launch several illicit periodicals and hundreds of revolutionary circulars. Pamphlets were produced by several autonomous groups and contained a variety of information, serving different short-term and long-term nationalist goals. The Wafd Party and al-'Azhar University were the leading publishers of these revolutionary pamphlets, in addition to a significant number of independent parties, organizations, and even individuals.[81] Some of the material produced by the Wafd Party was clearly marked as such and contained official information about it as a political organization. In early May, for example, the Wafd published an elaborate booklet titled *The White Book*, which contained a "collection of the telegrams, letters, notes, speeches, etc. made by Sa'd Pasha Zaghlul in connection with the Independence Movement." According to British reports, the booklet was clandestinely sold in the streets for 5 piasters.[82]

Private presses and sometimes established newspapers' presses were secretly used to publish these materials. For instance, during the spring and summer of 1919, Badi' Khayri was a member of a "secret society dedicated to printing revolutionary circulars." Khayri said in his memoirs that these circulars were clandestinely printed on "the farm of Prince Isma'il Dawud in the village of Mahalit Ruh, near al-Mahala al-Kubra and covertly distributed in Cairo."[83] On a larger scale, Mahmud 'Abd al-Fattah, the editor of the Alexandria-based *Wadi al-Nil* newspaper, admitted in a 1921 book that he discreetly used his press to publish revolutionary circulars. He also specifically confessed to secretly publishing Wafdist papers, including the "speeches and journals of Sa'd Zaghlul and Husayn Rushdi." According to Abd al-Fattah, these circulars were immediately "distributed in the cafés and clubs" of Cairo and Alexandria.[84] Aside from official Wafdist publications, the Wafd Party also produced a variety of more "illicit" unsigned pamphlets managed by the Wafd secretary, 'Abd al-Rahman Fahmi. 'Ahmad 'Amin, a prominent Egyptian writer, worked closely with Fahmi in several Wafdist propagandist efforts and described some of these activities in his memoirs.

When the fires of the revolution were blazing, I was among those who contacted 'Abd al-Rahman Bey Fahmi, the secretary of the Wafd who had many young men volunteering to help with the effort. He chose me to supervise two tasks: the first was to administer the making of political speeches in mosques after Friday prayers . . . so I regularly met with colleagues and organized with them the topics to be discussed and assigned each of them to give the speech in a different mosque. The second task I was given was to write circulars, detailing the latest and most important events of the day. The most important of these circulars was the one I wrote about the effects of the March 16, 1919, ladies demonstration . . . which was promptly printed and distributed.[85]

The Wafd Party also produced *al-Wafd al-Misri* (The Egyptian delegation), a weekly periodical that expressed the party's official policy with regard to the revolution and the independence movement. The newspaper had at least two mottoes: "The nation's progress is through its liberal press" and the more confrontational "Fight till you drive them out." Many of *al-Wafd al-Misri*'s articles were consistent with the second motto; for instance, in the May 12, 1919, issue they printed several articles describing England as the typhoid of Europe.[86]

### Illicit Periodicals

A short walk in the Native quarter would convince anyone that a spirit of revolt was around. It is particularly noticeable in the streets round about Al Azhar and the mosque of Sayed El Hussein. One can see every evening students of every denomination who gather round them groups of ignorant and illiterate natives and read them extracts from the native press.

—"Intelligence Report on the Egyptian Situation," June 28, 1919

As discussed in earlier chapters, the reading aloud of newspapers and other printed materials was a common occurrence in Egypt's streets and urban coffeehouses. This was especially true during the 1919 Revolution, when the demand for information far exceeded the limited supply of news that was allowed through by the censors. To help fill this information vacuum, many "illegal" newspapers appeared along with *al-Wafd al-Misri*. Most of these periodicals consisted of a large single sheet of paper, and they were all rabidly anti-British. *'Abu al-Hul* (The sphinx), *al-Ra'd al-Misri* (The Egyptian thunder), *al-Balabil* (The nightingales), *al-Misri al-Hurr* (The free Egyptian), and *al-'Istiqlal al-Tam* (Complete independence) were just some of the newspapers that attempted to fill the information void caused by the stringent censorship of the officially recognized press.[87] *Al-'Istiqlal al-Tam* typified this type of periodical. The main editorial in the fourth issue of this single-sheet newspaper was a "violent article attacking General Allenby" and his aggressive repression of the uprising. The rest of the issue was given over to a call for government employees to continue with a general strike.[88]

Bayram al-Tunsi's *al-Masala* (The obelisk) was arguably the most famous of these periodicals, with dozens of *azjal* violently criticizing the British and anyone who seemed to sympathize with them. A brief British intelligence report incredulously described how *al-Masala* was "attacking everybody, even H. H. the Sultan in the most insulting terms."[89] Al-Tunsi wrote a series of scorching *azjal* attacking Sultan Fu'ad and the Egyptian royal family. The *azjal* questioned the timing of the marriage of the sultan and alluded to the popular perception that it was performed to cover up the premarital pregnancy of his bride.[90] Because of al-Tunsi's Tunisian family origin, he was technically under the protection of the French

Consulate and thus, for the time being at least, out of direct reach of the Egyptian and British authorities, allowing him to publish his periodical for a total of thirteen weeks.[91] The British eventually pressured the French to shut down the periodical. Undeterred, al-Tunsi started another periodical, *al-Khazuq* (The impalement stake), which featured yet another *zajal* attacking the Egyptian royal family.[92] The magazine was promptly closed down after its first issue. The last straw for al-Tunsi was a popular *zajal* he wrote that continued on the same theme and again openly questioned the legitimacy of the newborn Prince Faruq. This prompted a direct appeal by Sultan Fu'ad to the British, who convinced the French to order al-Tunsi's exile from Egypt on October 21, 1919.[93]

### Revolutionary Pamphlets

In addition to the weekly unlicensed periodicals appearing at this time, hundreds, perhaps thousands, of pamphlets circulated in the Egyptian streets. These revolutionary pamphlets, which were produced during the spring and summer of 1919, can generally be grouped into four broad but often overlapping categories. The first type of circular functioned as a revolutionary call to action. Some of these were nonspecific and were intended to motivate Egyptians broadly to fight for independence. Others were more targeted and demanded the enforcement of strikes and the boycotting of British goods or simply announced the locations and times of public meetings and demonstrations. For example, in early to mid-May 1919, an anonymous pamphlet titled "A Patriotic Appeal to Boycott English Commerce" was circulating. The pamphlet declared that "no Egyptian must deal with any English firm or promote English commercial interests."[94] News pamphlets, the second category of revolutionary pamphlets, were also common, especially because the censorship laws severely limited the amount and type of news that could be published. Often, events that happened in the morning were printed up and distributed by the evening. However, these pamphlets were hardly accurate and contained a great many inaccuracies and rumors. The third category of circulars consisted of libelous attacks on the British and Egyptian "collaborators." These abuses were sometimes general, although more often they specifically targeted individuals. Last, many of the circulars contained *azjal* and songs meant to be read aloud or sung, which effectively propagated the revolutionary message to a much wider audience.

The British struggled to keep track of the many circulars appearing every day. On April 30, 1919, the British intelligence report detailed a list of six newly published "seditious circulars." Three of these circulars addressed government employees and warned them against going back to work. Another warned all Egyptians not to believe the "rumors that the Powers have agreed to maintain the British Protectorate in Egypt." And another pamphlet exclusively targeted students, labeling them the "men of the future," and incited them to continue their strikes for the sake of their country.[95] On May 2, 1919, British intelligence reported seven new pamphlets circulating in Cairo and many of the surrounding areas. These included "a circular entitled 'The First Sacrifice Among the Egyptian Ladies.'" It described the death of an Egyptian woman named Shafiqa during one of the demonstrations and called her "the Egyptian Miss Cavell."[96] Aside from celebrating heroes, some of the circulars condemned those who were deemed traitors or collaborators. A circular distributed in Fayyum and Cairo in early May blamed the *mudir* (mayor or district administrator) of the district of Fayyum for allowing the British to open fire on demonstrators on March 18, 1919. The circular, titled "The Mudir of Fayum Is a Traitorous Spy," ended with the following words: "What are men, who act like this traitorous Mudir, aiming at? Do they want the *Times* to eulogize them? Do they expect to visit England and receive an ovation? Do they expect King George to condescend and relinquish to them Malta, or some other island, for them to sell or mortgage and live on the proceeds?"[97]

The practical importance of these pamphlets, and the speed with which they dealt with the realities on the streets, is best seen with circulars, which appeared immediately after Woodrow Wilson and the American delegation at the Paris Peace Conference officially recognized the British protectorate over Egypt. On the morning of April 22, 1919, the Egyptian papers printed the communiqué containing President Wilson's acceptance of the protectorate, giving the Egyptian nationalists "a very unpleasant and unexpected shock." For a while at least, it took the wind from the sails of the nationalist movement.[98] To counter some of the effects of the declaration, within just a few hours, dozens of nationalists "came down to all the bars and cafés armed with pamphlets, and urged all to take no notice of the proclamation."[99]

Coffeehouses and bars were crucial distribution and dissemination points for most of these pamphlets. The colloquial Egyptian code word for these circulars was *al-busta* (the mail) and the person delivering them was labeled *al-bustagi* (the mailman).[100] The "mail" was regularly and almost ritualistically distributed every evening in Egypt's urban coffeehouses.

The extremists are still making their presence very much felt, especially in public meeting places. In every bar are gathered groups of these young Effendis discussing, making speeches, and distributing pamphlets. . . . Propaganda is being openly distributed now in Bars and Cafés, and the arrival of the "mail" is usually about half past six, when the crowd is at its greatest.[101]

A later Foreign Office report elaborated: "The arrival of the 'mail' always causes intense excitement: students and others even get up on chairs and make speeches, and usually the popular song of the moment is sung."[102] However, these circulars were not always distributed so openly. In a game of cat and mouse, for a few days after the British closed down printing presses and raided coffee shops looking for circulars, the "mail" was still secretly distributed: "The 'postman' delivers his pamphlets rolled up like a spill, and hands them surreptitiously only to those whom he knows."[103] Also, as another British intelligence report indicates, paperboys were regularly employed to covertly distribute pamphlets, which they inserted in the newspapers they were selling: "It came to my notice yesterday that a vendor of the 'Ahram' refused to supply an interpreter from this office with a copy of the paper because he was in uniform. This suggests that the real reason was that there was an illicit paper wrapped up with the 'Ahram.'"[104]

As these events highlight, the interaction between print and oral/aural communication was especially strong during moments of national crisis, when "reading" was more often than not an almost embodied communal event—loud, messy, and unashamedly alive. For the observers and participants in these active communal readings, there was participatory listening, chanting, celebrating, and mourning of important events, news, and even gossip. There was no need to "imagine" a national community privately in the "lair of the skull," as framed by Benedict Anderson.[105] For the time being at least, this emergent nationalism was brightly and loudly experienced through the sights, sounds, smells, and textures of the cafés and the urban streets.

### SINGING IN THE STREETS

The song quoted at the beginning of this chapter was only one among many colloquial Egyptian songs and *azjal* that were printed, mass-distributed, and collectively sung in the streets. These types of leaflets were arguably the most effective of the revolutionary circulars, because the words they contained were meant to be read aloud or performed. The British reports were full of references describing how "copies of revolutionary and very anti-British poems are being freely circulated."[106] Many of these *zajal*/song pamphlets attempted to motivate mass action through appeals to the listeners' and readers' patriotic sentiments.

> Egypt, exert some effort
> for we're a race of freemen
> Patriots and sons of freedom

heirs of our brave forefathers
Soon will 'Abbas come hither
on arms and shoulders carried
We'll all be joyful and merry
and live in joy and glory.[107]

In part, because of his forced abdication in 1914 (see Chapter 5),
'Abbas Hilmi II retained a great deal of popularity in Egypt throughout
World War I and during the revolution. A few of the popular songs and
street chants circulating at the time mentioned him as a heroic, almost
messianic figure who would return from exile and rescue Egypt from
the British. Another British intelligence report noted that in the popular areas of Cairo, "street-boys, lower-class natives, seed vendors, etc.,
have been publicly singing a new song in the vernacular in which open
insinuations are made regarding the arrival in Egypt of the ex-Khedive
['Abbas II] and Enver Pasha." This song, the report continued, also contained "uncomplimentary remarks about the G.O.C. [General Officer
Commanding]."[108]

Revolutionary circulars were successfully distributed beyond Cairo
and Alexandria, to the towns and the villages of Upper Egypt and the
Delta. Students returning to visit their villages and hometowns were
the primary carriers of these leaflets; they would often conceal them in
their personal possessions or even in the clothes they wore.[109] A report
filed in July 1919, for instance, remarked how a "'National Hymn' was
found at Port Said," intended to be "taught to women and children and
sung at national festivals." The hymn was "mostly exhorting the sloth-
ful Egyptians to wake up and be patriotic."[110] Although the report did
not include a text of the hymn, it was likely that the song in question
was the Sayyid Darwish theatrical ditty "*'Um ya Masri*" (Stand [wake]
up, o Egyptians), which was released just two months before the report
was filed.[111]

Some printed songs were performed in the streets directly by *zajjalun*
(sing. *zajjal*) and singers. Outside the Continental Hotel in Cairo was
one of the prime locations for such performances, as observed by a British intelligence officer: "Many popular poems are being circulated and
sung. I heard one of them myself in front of the Continental Hotel this
afternoon, which was sung by a priest from El Azhar. It was greeted with
cheers and laughter."[112] The Continental Hotel was also the favorite performance location for the *zajal* writer 'Isa Sabri (b. 1883), who was an
accomplished *zajjal*, artist, and calligrapher. Sabri wrote countless *azjal*
for *Humarit Munyati*, *al-'Arnab*, and *al-Babaghlu al-Misri*. He eventually
started his own satirical newspaper, *al-Rasaam* (The painter/sketch artist),
which was filled with his satirical cartoons and *azjal*.[113] Sabri was also

known for his nationalistic songwriting and singing. According to some of his contemporaries, "his voice was beautiful and strong," and he often used it to arouse the masses in the streets. During the 1919 Revolution, Sabri, surrounded by a large crowd, "stood on the bed of a pickup truck parked in front of the Continental Hotel, beat on his drum [*tabla*], and sang patriotic songs to fellow demonstrators."[114] The following excerpt is from one of the songs that Sabri performed that day:

> Ye who seek independence
> long live our nation, o, Egyptians
> We are on strike from all work
> and we locked the doors of all institutions
> O prime minister—he's held hostage [Zaghlul]
> you know his rights, of this I am certain
> We as freemen demand a constitution
> and will resist the schemes of the occupiers[115]

All through the spring of 1919, revolutionary pamphlets flooded the Egyptian streets. The prevalence of these underground leaflets and the near instantaneous speed and flexibility with which they disseminated information to the masses were remarkable and extremely effective in mobilizing dissent. These leaflets played an essential role in fueling, motivating, and sustaining many of the revolutionary activities, which took place in the urban streets. Because the songs were intended to be sung aloud, the pamphlets had an especially powerful impact on the illiterate and semiliterate masses. The collective singing of such songs in public reinforced a sense of nationalism and national unity and served the goals of the revolution. This street-based revolutionary song culture was stimulated by and in turn influenced the growing mass media music industry.[116]

## "PERFORMING" THE REVOLUTION
### IN THE STREETS AND ON STAGE

The play ['*Ululuh*] was to be performed in the wake of all the demonstrations—in which the entire nation in all its classes participated. So we made sure to place at the heart of the play nationalist songs representing the manner and language of all the varied socioeconomic groups that demonstrated in the streets.

—Najib al-Rihani, *Mudhakkirat Najib al-Rihani*

On the eve of the 1919 Revolution, a theater critic complained about the vulgarity of Najib al-Rihani's vaudeville plays. Al-Rihani, who by this time had become a national star specializing in the comedic role of

Kishkish Bey, was so successful that he earned an estimated 28,000 £E (Egyptian pounds) a year.[117] The writer declared that Kishkish's songs were "now the songs of the masses." These songs, the critic continued, "have penetrated every house door and knocked down the walls of every inner sanctum."[118] As we have examined in the last two chapters, the record companies took full advantage of the popularity of these compositions, recording and selling thousands of discs. Most of the successful songs in al-Rihani's theater were composed by Sayyid Darwish and were written by Badi' Khayri, whose simple compositions and realistic, everyday colloquial Egyptian lyrics were instrumental in transforming the songs into nationally recognized hits.[119] This is how a contemporary of Khayri accounts for the popularity of his writings and song lyrics:

Badi' Khayri chose a different path than others in choosing the topics and style with which to address the masses. He chose a [linguistic] style with which he can simultaneously communicate with the noneducated Egyptian fellah, with the students in primary schools, and with the big-headed intellectuals. He spoke to all in a language that speaks to everyone. He spoke to everybody in one common language that benefited each and every one. Other nations speak to their masses, so why don't we do the same without all of these difficulties and pretenses?[120]

Khayri's colloquial lyrics were complemented by Darwish's music, which reflected and in a sense mimicked the sounds of the Egyptian streets. For example, before he could compose the music for a song about urban water sellers, Darwish sat for hours in a coffee shop near Harit al-Sa'ayyin (the water sellers' quarter in Cairo), listening to the tone and pitch of the water sellers' calls.[121] According to his colleague Yunis al-Qadi, when Darwish was writing "*Dingi Dingi*," a song about the Sudanese in Egypt, he frequented a traditional Cairene bar (*buza*) called Buzat al-'Ilwa[122] in the district of Bab al-Khalq patronized by the Sudanese population. By singing along with the Sudanese patrons of the bar, Darwish culled some of the rhythms of Nubian and Sudanese music and replicated them—albeit stereotypically—on stage.[123] This dynamic dialogue between the streets and musical and theatrical productions was the primary reason for the popularity of vaudeville and the music industry; it helps to explain their power and influence on the Egyptian urban masses.

As discussed in Chapter 5, for several years before the 1919 Revolution, the Egyptian recording industry and the vaudeville music theater openly supported the Egyptian nationalist agenda. This trend dramatically accelerated during and after the revolution. An ongoing dialogue existed between the masses, who demonstrated in the streets, and the cultural productions emanating from Egypt's mass media. Not only were some of the songs sung in the streets during the 1919 revolt taken directly from the records and plays of Egypt's vaudevillian mass culture, but also, perhaps more important, the writers and musicians were mining the streets for nationally authentic material, and many of the songs and plays openly or clandestinely discussed the events of the revolution.[124] These audiovisual reenactments and celebrations of the revolutionary events in particular and of Egyptian nationalism in general strengthened and reflected a growing sense of national identity.

Because of the revolution, the British temporarily suspended all theatrical activities for about one month, starting on March 10, 1919.[125] When the theaters were closed down, many of the actors, actresses, and musicians took to the streets, sang nationalist songs, and actively participated in the revolt. Mustafa 'Amin, Safiyya Zaghlul's nephew, who lived as a child in Zaghlul's house during the revolution, had a chance to see many of the demonstrations firsthand because they typically assembled outside what became known as *Bayt al-'Umma*. 'Amin specifically remembered that Najib al-Rihani and his entire troupe were particularly active in many of these demonstrations. He also singled out the actress Zaynab Sidqi as a vigorous demonstrator who was at the head of the "actors and actresses group demonstration."[126] In his memoirs, Badi' Khayri recalled singing in the streets *"Lahn al-Siyas"* (The song of the stable boys), with its theme of national unity (see Chapter 5).

The song spread from the theater to the street. All of us went out into the streets—the entire troupe, along with Sayyid Darwish, Najib al-Rihani, and I— and we rode on horse-drawn carriages with flags in hand. Some flags had crosses on them, the others crescents, and some with crosses in the middle of crescents. We continued on in this large nationalist demonstration, singing this song, until we arrived at the Ibn Tulun Mosque.[127]

By the first week of April, the theaters were reopened and vaudevillian troupes once again performed to packed audiences. 'Ali al-Kassar, the main competitor of al-Rihani, was one of the first to reopen his theater on April 6, 1919, and continued performing his play *'U'bal 'Andukum* (May you have the same).[128] Al-Kassar specialized in making blackface comedies; he played the recurring role of 'Uthman 'Abd al-Basit, a heavily stereotyped Sudanese/Nubian man who, like Kishkish Bey, had instructive comedic misadventures. Al-Kassar's plays and music were also openly nationalistic, and the record companies produced many of his theatrical songs.[129]

Al-Rihani reopened his theater in early May and continued to be the number one draw on stage, with tremendous popularity and packed theaters.[130] The popularity of Kishkish's theater was clearly expressed in some of the newspaper reports at the time; as a journalist who wrote for *al-'Ikspress* newspaper related, "We attempted to go to al-Rihani's theater, but unfortunately we were not able to penetrate the tremendous crowd which was assembled in front of the theater door and extended to seemingly forever. We were told that entering tonight would be impossible and that we would have to come another day and attempt to beat the crowds."[131]

Out of all the vaudeville plays that dealt with the events of the revolution, Najib al-Rihani's *'Ululuh* (Tell him) was by far the most significant, producing the most memorable of Sayyid Darwish's hits, many of which are well known even today.[132] After the British banned the play in March 1919, an updated version of it began playing in early May. Al-Rihani described how he and the writers explicitly "made sure to place at the heart of the play nationalistic songs representing the manner and language of all the varied socioeconomic groups that demonstrated in the streets."[133] *'Ululuh* continued to play to packed audiences well into June.[134] The most overtly nationalistic of the play's songs was "*'Um Ya Masri*" (Rise up, o Egyptian), which had a rhythmic martial music beat, purposely designed to motivate the masses to action. The song addressed many of the events taking place in the streets and actively motivated Egyptians to continue to resist.

Rise up o Egyptian
Egypt always calls for you
Lead me [Egypt] to victory
My triumph is a debt you must repay
The day that my happiness
was needlessly taken away right before your eyes
Restore my glory
the glory which [in the past] you wasted away
. . .
Did you see
o Egyptians a country with such beauty
that compares
with your country with its rich soil
Her Nile brings forth
happiness in abundance
. . .
Love your neighbor
more than you love your own existence
What's the difference—Christian
Muslim or Jew[135]
The real essence
is that we're all descendants of the same ancestors

According to al-Rihani, this was the song most frequently performed by his theater troupe in the Egyptian streets during the 1919 demonstrations. Indeed, as we have seen, throughout the spring of 1919 the "boundaries" between the "street" and the "theater" were especially fluid. The streets, the balconies, and the backs of trucks and donkey carts literally functioned as stages where the Egyptian urban masses actively participated (see Figure 9). This "embodied" dialogical conversation physically enacted in the public sphere as a carnivalesque mass ritual had a tremendous impact on its participants, listeners, and observers.

## Happiness, Pigeons, and Sweet Dates

Every subordinate group creates, out of its ordeal, a "hidden transcript" that represents a critique of power spoken behind the back of the dominant.
—James C. Scott, *Domination and the Arts of Resistance*

Although the song "*'Um Ya Masri*" strongly advocated national unity among the different religious communities in Egypt and openly called for Egyptians to rise up, some of its lines contained hidden meanings. For instance, the line "The day that my happiness . . . was needlessly taken away right before your eyes" (*Yum ma Sa'di . . . Rah hadar 'udam 'inayk*) indirectly referred to the forced exile of Sa'd Zaghlul. The phrase "my happiness [*Sa'di*]" also meant within the context of the song "my Sa'd," that is, my Sa'd Zaghlul.

Referring indirectly to Sa'd Zaghlul was common at the time and was done, in part, to avoid censorship, because the British were particularly keen on limiting Zaghlul's growing popularity among the Egyptian masses. From March 1919 until the mid-1920s several songs expressed the deliciousness of zaghlul dates (*balah zaghlul*).[136] The most famous of these songs was by Na'ima al-Misriyya and was recorded many times.

> O zaghlul dates, how pretty they are
> O those dates, those zaghlul dates
> God bless, how sugary and sweet
> Lord almighty—zaghlul dates!
> I call out to you in all the valleys
> I yearn for and need—zaghlul dates!
> You're my country's produce
> I envy my own happiness [Sa'di]—zaghlul dates!
> O soul of your country, why the long separation
> Return and take care of your children—zaghlul dates![137]

Not to be outdone, Munira al-Mahdiyya soon recorded a song about zaghlul pigeons, a small breed of Egyptian pigeons. In a similar fashion, al-Mahdiyya declared her yearning for zaghlul pigeons.

> The pigeons were lifted and placed down again
> from Egypt to the Sudan
> It's a *zaghlul* [pigeon] and my heart aches for it
> I call on it when I need it
> You can understand its language if you attend to it
> It says *hamayham ya hamam*
> My passion for those *zaghalil* is an obsession
> and loving them is my destiny[138]

Although many songs contained couched references, most were so obvious that they were hardly hidden. Why then did so many artists continue with this charade? I suggest that using these techniques dramatically increased the emotional power of the song (or theatrical dialogue) by drawing in the participation of the audience. By giving the impression that only the performers and the intended audience possessed the tools necessary to decipher the nationalistic message and by "allowing" the listeners to participate—and in some sense become complicit—in this "illicit" decoding, the effectiveness of these cultural expressions dramatically increased.

### RELIVING THE REVOLUTION ON THE STAGE
### AND IN SONGS

As examined in this and the preceding chapter, Munira al-Mahdiyya's contribution to nationalistic mass media productions was significant. She hired Sayyid Darwish to compose the music for the play *Kullaha Yumayn* (In just a couple of days), an allegory of the events in Egypt from the start of disturbances in March until the debut of the play in December 1919. Even the title of the play, "In a Couple of Days," refers to the belief that the entire "independence crisis" would soon be favorably resolved.[139] The play's two main antagonists are Munira (played by Munira al-Mahdiyya), who represents Egypt, and the villain Marco, who represents the British and other moneyed foreign interests. The first crisis in the play begins with Marco lighting Munira's house on fire, which sets up a song titled "The Firemen" ("*Rigal al-Matafi*").

> Attack the fire, be strong hearted
> Don't let the hose [*al-Khartum*] slip from your hands[140]
> Sacrifice your life for your brothers' sake

Fire! Fire! But it's better than dishonor
Rise, Egyptians, and lend a hand
Every supporting hand helps
Sacrifice your life for your brethren
You and your brothers can save your nation
Sacrifice your life for your brothers' sake
Fire! Fire! But it's better than dishonor
Here are the true Egyptian men
Those who protect our lives
They saved us from the oppressors
They risked their lives for our sake
Fire never harms those who are true
Egypt's hellfire is paradise[141]

Here the "fire" clearly represents the 1919 uprising; the song unabashedly relives the events of the revolution and celebrates them onstage. The song also calls for more national sacrifices, if necessary, to save Egypt from the "oppressors." The appeals to the masculinity and honor of Egyptian males are also clearly on display in this particular song, especially because Egypt is represented as a female (Munira al-Mahdiyya) and the male firemen are urged to die while fighting the fire rather than face dishonor.[142]

In the end, the fire destroys Munira's house as well as the deeds to her property, allowing Marco to take possession of her land through "legal" trickery. Impoverished and homeless, Munira gets by in the countryside selling "country" butter.[143] As the local prosecutor (representing Sa'd Zaghlul) begins investigating Marco, hope is restored. In the shadow of the great pyramid and in homage to its builder, the fourth dynasty pharaoh Khufu (Cheops), Munira makes a pact of unity with others who were exploited by Marco.

Sleep o Khufu, and rest in safety
We confronted [the enemy] and we saw suffering and pain though no more
Who can ever forget this experience?
O glorious one, builder of the pyramid
Christians and Muslims, all volunteer to be in your service
Their unity is an enduring one, and tomorrow we will be the most civilized
    nation[144]

The play ends happily: Marco is evicted and imprisoned, and all of the stolen land is returned to its owners.[145] Reenacting the revolution in song and onstage just months after the violent events of March and April, even while sporadic street violence was still occurring, not only further legitimized these acts but also gave citizens a way to actively participate in and relive these events.

CONCLUSION:

THE 1919 REVOLUTION AS A CARNIVAL?

In a carnival everyone is an active participant, everyone communes in the carnival act. Carnival is not contemplated and, strictly speaking, not even performed; its participants *live* in it, they live by its laws as long as those laws are in effect; that is, they live in a *carnivalistic life*. Because carnivalistic life is drawn out of its usual rut, it is to some extent "life turned inside out," "the reverse side of the world" ("monde à l'envers"). The laws, prohibitions and restrictions that determine the structure and order of ordinary, that is noncarnival life, are suspended during carnival: what is suspended first of all is hierarchal structure and all forms of terror, reverence, piety, and etiquette connected with it—that is, everything resulting from socio-hierarchal inequity or any other form of inequity among people (including age). All *distance* between people is suspended, and a special carnival category goes into effect: *free and familiar contact among people*. . . . People who in life are separated by impenetrable hierarchical barriers enter into free familiar contact on the carnival square. The category of familiar contact is also responsible for the special way mass actions are organized, and for free carnival gesticulations, and for outspoken carnivalistic word.

—Mikhail Bakhtin, *Problems of Dostoevsky's Poetics*

Mikhail Bakhtin's conception of the carnival and carnivalistic life, which he partly defines as a "temporary suspension of all hierarchic distinctions and barriers," supplies a useful tool with which to examine the events of the 1919 Revolution.[146] For Egypt's urban lower classes, women, and religious minorities, the almost spontaneous development of carnivalesque and hence nonhierarchical political expressions provided an important avenue of dissent. Marginalized voices were loudly heard through collective and direct action in the streets and other "carnival squares," where revolutionary discourse continued for a while longer. Bakhtin defines the "carnival square" as a space where "carnival acts" occur. He later elaborates that any "places of action" that provide "meeting- and contact-points for heterogeneous people—streets, taverns, roads, bathhouses, decks of ships, and so on—take on this additional carnival-square significance."[147]

Thus for a few weeks in the spring of 1919, through the use of songs, chants, circulars, speeches, and violence, a counterdiscourse and, for a brief time, alternative centers of power were created. The streets, and by extension the public squares, cafés, bars, mosques, and churches, became the necessary carnivalesque spaces outside the reach of the centralized authorities where illicit counterhegemonic opinions were debated and exchanged. Even al-'Azhar University transformed temporarily into a secular, gender-neutral, socially egalitarian space of open counterhegemonic subversion. Muslims, Christians, and Jews; men and women; rich and poor; young and old participated fully in open acts of resistance within the carnival square of al-'Azhar University.

In time, on the surface at least, physical order eventually prevailed in the streets, and traditional authority regained relative control of most public spaces. Yet, after the carnival, things were never quite the same, as the reestablished order was somewhat different. The veil was cast aside, albeit briefly, and genuine dialogue among normally suppressed voices revealed a common humanity underneath the socioeconomic and political inequities of the established order. At the same time, vaudeville theater, colloquial Egyptian music, *azjal*, and satirical periodicals continued to provide a "virtual" carnival square where hierarchal distinctions were suspended and resistance still actively took place.

# Conclusion

The purpose of this book was twofold. First, I wanted to document the impact of modern colloquial Egyptian mass culture, from its beginnings with privately owned newspapers in the 1870s to vaudeville and the recording industry, which became powerful cultural vehicles in the first two decades of the twentieth century. More important, through the lens of these new media, I undertook a more comprehensive examination of the rapid changes in Egyptian collective identities from the last third of the nineteenth century to the 1919 Revolution. During this relatively short time span, more and more inhabitants of the Nile Valley, from Aswan to Alexandria, began to identify strongly with being Egyptian. Although studies on Egyptian nationalism have examined this change, they have overlooked colloquial Egyptian sources and consequently have conceptualized the growth of Egyptian nationalism as a top-down enterprise. The reality, however, was quite different: Most Egyptians did not read, nor were they exposed to the intellectual writings of Taha Husayn, Lutfi al-Sayyid, or Salama Musa or even the nationalistic novels of Muhammad Husayn Haykal, Najib Mahfuz, and Tawfiq al-Hakim. This does not mean that the masses disregarded or disrespected the iconic writings of these intellectuals. Simply put, the vast majority of Egyptians were illiterate, and for those who could read, most of these works were not in a "language" or format that resonated with them. Instead, it was newspapers (especially the satirical press), recorded and performed colloquial Egyptian songs, and the vernacular theater that were the principal and most effective mediators and broadcasters of cultural ideologies, including the idea of a collective Egyptian identity.[1]

Modern Egyptian mass culture—especially vaudeville and the music industry—transcended the bounds of literacy and gave room for (Cairene) colloquial Egyptian culture to develop a common, increasingly national forum for comprehensible, universally accessible, and socially relevant public discussions about political community, the state, and British imperialism. It is the totality of these media, working together as a media system, that entertained, informed, and, in the process, provided new shared discourses about nationhood and identity.[2]

These newly formed mass media were especially effective at mediating between the written Fusha discourses of the "bourgeois nationalists" and the colloquial expressions of the Egyptian urban masses, creating virtual Egyptian communities that were written, acted out, and sung on pages, stages, and phonograph records.[3] As I have shown, this was by no means a top-down enterprise, because the consumers and producers of these cultural forms had an ongoing dialogue. Most of the men and women who were involved in the newspaper and entertainment industries were part of a growing Egyptian urban middle class, and this membership greatly enhanced their mediating and authenticating engagements with the Egyptian street. Indeed, the form, content, and colloquial languages of these vernacular media were stimulated by and principally echoed the interests and the social multiplicities of everyday Egyptian life. The demand from below was for entertaining, culturally relevant, and linguistically comprehensible media. In other words, the primary role of the music and theater industries was to entertain, attract a large audience, and make a profit. These media were not designed to intellectualize the finer points of Egyptian national identity. Unlike dense Fusha editorials or books, threeminute songs or jingles—despite their seemingly shallow and simplistic nationalist themes—did not require their listeners to be literate and could be easily memorized and sung in the streets, aiding the mass diffusion of nationalist ideas.

The laws of the market shaped the content and form of these new cultural products. As demonstrated in this book, the Egyptian public's appetite for plays and songs performed in Fusha was virtually nonexistent. On the other hand, colloquial vaudeville plays and music sold exponentially more tickets and records, fueling the growth of popular entertainment as a big business. Also, the popular press (especially satirical periodicals), with its cartoons, light vernacular *azjal*, and colloquial dialogues, was more popular and influential than the dense intellectual treatises of the Egyptian intellectuals. Thus it was not just print capitalism, as claimed by Benedict Anderson, but media capitalism and the resulting professionalization and commercialization of Egyptian popular entertainment with Cairo as its hub that increasingly exposed more and more Egyptians to the same urban mass culture, creating in the process a nationally influential mass media. It was these predominantly colloquial media, from

the satirical press to recorded music, that were instrumental in popularizing the collective identification of Egypt as an "imagined political community" with "deep, horizontal comradeship."[4] Because the concept of
media capitalism is not visual-centric and is less focussed on texts, it is
more corporally engaged with the wider range of sensory culture, allowing for the oral and aural along with the visual and the written. Turn-
of-the-twentieth-century cultural consumers did not just "silently" read;
they also listened, watched, debated, and discussed.

## AUTHENTICATING MODERN MEDIA

An important reason for the success of these new media, aside from their
use of a universally understood colloquial Egyptian language, was that
they were "authentically" grounded in older forms of cultural expression. Egyptian vaudeville, recorded *taqatiq*, and the colloquial cartoons
and dialogues of the satirical press drew liberally from traditional music,
*azjal*, and street theater. To be sure, these older forms were completely
transformed, "modernized," and reshaped to suit the new media; however, they retained enough of the culturally authentic and locally relevant
elements to allow them to speak to most Egyptians effortlessly and famil-
iarly. New media were introduced at such a rapid pace that many of the
performers reinvented their careers many times to adapt to these changes.
'Ali al-Kassar and Najib al-Rihani, for instance, began their careers as
traditional comedic sketch artists, successfully transitioned into vaudeville actors in the 1920s, and morphed again into successful film actors by
the end of the 1930s. Indeed most writers, singers, and actors migrated,
along with their scripts, jokes, songs, and even vaudeville stage personas,
to phonograph recordings, radio, and eventually film. As Asa Briggs and
Peter Burke have shown in a recent study, media should be understood as
a system with a dynamic and ongoing division of labor "between the different means of communication available in a given place and at a given
time without forgetting that old and new media can and do coexist and
that different media may compete with or echo one another as well as
complement one another."[5] For instance, as we observed, songs that were
performed in vaudeville plays were often recorded and sold by record
companies. Both the plays and the songs were reviewed and advertised in
the burgeoning national press. The arrival of "new media," such as radio
and the movie industry, onto the scene in the 1920s and 1930s did not
spell the end of newspapers or recording, as both media simply adapted
to the new environment.

MUNDANE NATIONALISM

Egypt's new mass media reflected on relevant everyday political, economic, and cultural concerns and amplified them on the national stage in
a comprehensible, locally pertinent, and entertaining form. The repeated
themes of many of these media included bemoaning the lack of economic
opportunities for native Egyptians, portraying the economic exploitation of Egyptians by foreigners, warning of perceived declines in national
"morality," satirizing and at times insulting British and native officials,
and rousing patriotism and a sense of collective national solidarity.

However, the most effective way that national identity and a sense
of nationhood were absorbed was not only through these overstated
themes and methods but also through the *mundane* media portrayals
and representations of everyday "national" life and the internalization
of these modes in actual practice. As Michael Billig describes in *Banal
Nationalism*, nationalist ideology "might appear banal, routine, almost
invisible," but these "subconscious" matter-of-fact representations create
a commonsense "naturalness of belonging to a nation."[6] Billig explains
that often there is "continual 'flagging,' or reminding, of nationhood,"
because on a daily basis, citizens are reminded of their national identity.
This reminding, however, is "so familiar, so continual, that it is not consciously registered as reminding."[7] Mundane and unstated representations of Egyptianness abounded in most forms of mass culture, where
"Egyptians" distinctively spoke and acted and were clearly, though tacitly, differentiated from non-Egyptians. Most of the media examined in
this book implicitly addressed their listeners, viewers, and readers as
members of an Egyptian "nation." To be sure, the most influential aspect
of vaudeville and the satirical press was not necessarily the outwardly
nationalistic messages of many of their articles, cartoons, and dialogues
but the recurring and *mundane* representations of colloquial Cairene
as the de facto dialect of all Egyptians and the implicit understanding
that flawlessly speaking and understanding it was the basic marker of a
"modern" Egyptian national identity. Only an "authentic" *ibn* or *bint
al-balad* (son or daughter of the country) would use Egyptian Arabic and
grasp its multiple meanings and nuances and hence participate in this
new mass-produced colloquial culture. In fact, many of the comedic dialogues depicted in political cartoons and vaudeville repeatedly contrasted
the mispronunciations of foreigners—who often played unsympathetic
or villainous roles—with the "correct" pronunciation of affable Egyptian
characters. This repeated portrayal of Cairene as the only "authentic"
Egyptian accent reified it as an unofficial dialect of all Egyptians, even if
back in the villages and towns of the Sa'id more localized modes of ex-

pression were used. By way of media capitalism, Cairo's dialect and culture were overwhelming—colonizing, if you will—the multitude of other localized dialects and cultures in Egypt. Thus, paradoxically, Cairene Arabic was the primary tool for nationalist, anti-imperialist discourse, and simultaneously, through internal colonialism, it imposed its own culture on the "nation."[8]

## THE SENSORIUM AND THE PUBLIC SPHERE

The efficacy of the new mass media and their potential for mass mobilization were best demonstrated during times of national crisis. The 1906 Dinshaway incident and the 1919 Revolution in particular reveal how all forms of mass media functioned together to effectively document, memorialize, celebrate, and mobilize on a national scale. The growth of popular Egyptian mass culture was the pivotal factor in the popularization and dissemination of an Egyptian national identity. The evolution and universalization of a colloquial Egyptian middle culture, made possible especially through the utilization of sound and audiovisual media, allowed for a shared and "uniquely" Egyptian cultural landscape. It is primarily within this nonofficial web of vernacular mass culture, driven in large part by media capitalism, that Egyptian national identity was widely disseminated and popularized.

One crucial aspect of this study was the critical role that coffee shops played as cultural hubs. Differing mass media, from newspapers to recorded music, publicly merged and were negotiated and digested in the coffeehouses. Many of the songs initially written for musical and comedic plays were recorded and played or performed by street musicians at coffee shops and even in the streets and on the sidewalks. The role of the thousands of urban cafés and other public meeting places in the broadcasting and reception of these new cultural productions is central to understanding the potency and effectiveness of this developing nationwide culture. Indeed, coffeehouses, as Briggs and Burke remarked, "inspired the creation of imagined communities of oral communication."[9]

However, as discussed in this book, these conversations were never one-sided, because writers of these vernacular media were plugged into the streets and public squares through these very same cafés. As we have observed throughout this study, the entire vaudeville theater industry arose out of the cafés on 'Imad al-Din Street, where most of the vaudeville theaters were housed.[10] It was through these dialogical "physical" interactions with the people in the streets, marketplaces, and cafés that the writers, musicians, and performers of these media (re)calibrated the subtleties, textures, and flavors of everyday Egyptian life. As Bakhtin cautions, we must not ignore the "social life of discourse outside the artist's study, discourse in the open spaces of public squares, streets, cities and villages"; it is in these public spheres that Egyptian mass culture is embodied into everyday life, acquiring its socioeconomic, political relevance and, more important perhaps, its perceived authenticity and contemporaneity.[11] Indeed, access to any form of knowledge—be it visual, aural, tactile, gustatory, or olfactory—is corporally mediated and acquired through a living dialogical engagement. Or as Bakhtin elaborates, "The single adequate form to verbally expressing authentic human life is the open ended dialogue. . . . In this dialogue a person participates wholly and throughout his whole life, with his eyes, lips, hands, soul, spirit, within his whole body and deeds."[12] In other words, texts alone are meaningless when viewed in isolation from the socially embodied realities of their production and, more important perhaps, their reception on the street. It is in their interrelationship with social life that texts become meaningfully activated and authenticated as genuinely reflecting popular concerns and realities. As we have seen throughout this book, colloquial Egyptian culture is better equipped to engage in this dialogue with the everyday and hence to guarantee its circulation and popularity.

### THE 'AMMIYYA PARADOX

The colloquial is one of the diseases from which the people are suffering, and of which they are bound to rid themselves as they progress. I consider colloquial one of the failings of our society, exactly like ignorance, poverty, and disease.        —Najib Mahfuz

In Egypt and the rest of the Arab world, people speak a language they do not read or write and are "required" to read and write in a language they do not speak. The use of colloquial Egyptian in printed texts peaked in the 1920s and, other than in political cartoons, almost entirely disappeared from print by the 1950s (see Chapter 4). Perhaps the reason for the virtual disappearance of colloquial Egyptian from print by the early 1950s was the increase in religious and cultural conservatism in the 1930s, which viewed written colloquial Egyptian as a direct assault on Arab and Islamic traditions.[13] Radio and the movie industry, which became important entertainment media in the 1930s and mostly broadcast colloquial Egyptian content, played a role as well, through fulfilling the demand for colloquial cultural expressions in a more accessible and less controversial format. By the 1950s, Fusha had become the predominant language of print media, and it remains so today.[14] Colloquial Egyptian, on the other hand, remains the primary language of most audiovisual media. In

Egypt today, texts from school textbooks to novels and newspapers are in Fusha, whereas movies, songs, and television programming are mostly in the everyday spoken vernacular; however, with the advent of a largely unregulated Internet and the popularity of cell phone text messaging, writing in colloquial Egyptian is on the rise.[15]

Despite the fact that colloquial Egyptian has found an important niche as the language of nonprint mass media, it is still largely vulgarized, belittled, and marginalized by the intellectual elite. As the linguist Niloofar Haeri aptly points out, "Egypt's constitution makes no mention of the existence of Egyptian Arabic, educational institutions do not teach it, in textbooks no historical characters seem to have spoken in this language, and in cultural productions involving print, it is shunned."[16] This ongoing relational tension between these linguistic poles representing different cultural traditions, one transnational and rooted in classicism and the other popular and clearly national, is crucial to understanding the perpetual evolution of Egyptian mass identities. The territorially ambiguous transnationalism of Fusha as the modern heir to the language of the Qur'an and the common official language of all Arab nations is more compatible with the conservatism of religious traditionalism and the aspirations of Pan-Arabism. Colloquial Egyptian, on the other hand, is territorially bounded and hence more nationally exclusive.[17] As Joel Beinin notes, the mere "decision to write in colloquial Egyptian Arabic, even if not so intended, has often been perceived as a political act associated with a nationalist program of populism, anticlericalism (though not irreligion), and local Egyptian patriotism (*wataniyya*), as opposed to Pan-Arabism (*qawmiyya*)."[18] For this reason, I suggest that the nexus of colloquial culture, the new mass media, and mass politics, which were vital in shaping modern Egyptian identities, can also shed light on similar processes taking place elsewhere in the Arab world. Indeed, examining the importance of colloquial Arabic culture—which is regionally and nationally unique—and the ongoing duality and confrontation it has with official Fusha culture, is essential to understanding the complexity and dynamism of differing mass identities in Arab countries today. Future studies examining the history and politics of the Arab world must take this ongoing linguistic and cultural duality into account.

## LOOKING AHEAD

The effects of media capitalism on Egyptian society throughout the rest of the twentieth century were significant, although certainly uneven. Because the Egyptian government nationalized or gained effective control of most forms of mass media in the 1950s and 1960s, the dynamics of mass culture dramatically shifted. During this media etatism phase, Egyptian mass media ceased to be openly counterhegemonic, and resistance and unregulated cultural expressions were subdued. However, the advent of cheap cassette tape technology (and to a lesser extent video recording technology) in the 1970s dramatically shifted the mediascape yet again, away from government control and into the hands of small, independent entrepreneurs who sold millions of unregulated and uncensored tapes to a growing black market. Audiocassette tapes with contents ranging from lively and at times politically cutting *sha'bi* music to recorded Friday sermons circulated in the streets, allowing for a more open expression of unregulated discourse outside the controls of the state.[19] Like the *taqatiq* explosion of the first three decades of the twentieth century, which would not have been possible without phonograph recording technology, cassette tape recordings were instrumental to the creation of the *sha'bi* music phenomenon, which took Egypt by storm in the last three decades of the twentieth century.

In the last two decades, other advancements in communication technologies have allowed for almost instantaneous transnational consumption of mass media. Because of the proliferation of satellite television, colloquial Egyptian movies, songs, music videos, and television miniseries are widely consumed and understood throughout the Arab world. At the same time, twenty-four-hour news channels such as al-Jazeera and al-'Arabiyya are broadcasting news to the entire Arab world in Fusha. On the other hand, the advent of personal computers, digital audio and video recorders, the Internet, and media-enabled cell phones complicates this picture even further by giving ordinary Egyptians the ability to receive, create, and, more important, cheaply transmit texts, sounds, music, pictures, and movies. Understandably, the vast majority of the form and content of these new personal-media productions are in colloquial Egyptian. Still, it is too soon to measure the long-term implications of such media on either the issue of identity or the ongoing tension between Fusha and *'ammiyya*. This transnational identity crisis, I submit, will resolve itself only if this cultural and linguistic duality ends, with either the absorption or the eventual dominance of one form of the language over the other.

*Reference Matter*

# Appendix A

## Urbanization and Infrastructure

TABLE A.1. *Egyptian railroad statistics for 1877–1920*

| Year | Number of passengers | Transported goods (tons)[1] | Year | Number of passengers | Transported goods (tons) |
|------|------|------|------|------|------|
| 1877 | 2,265,377 | — | 1899 | 11,284,284 | 3,055,897 |
| 1878 | 1,952,426 | — | 1900 | 12,453,777 | 2,950,022 |
| 1879 | 2,172,868 | — | 1901 | 13,404,681 | 3,022,800 |
| 1880 | 3,086,478 | 1,145,000 | 1902 | 12,928,544 | 2,974,170 |
| 1881 | 3,599,281 | — | 1903 | 14,951,776 | 3,059,861 |
| 1882 | 3,331,180 | — | 1904 | 17,724,922 | 3,529,559 |
| 1883 | 2,761,126 | — | 1905 | 20,036,424 | 3,645,768 |
| 1884 | 2,883,819 | — | 1906 | 22,584,675 | 3,981,652 |
| 1885 | 3,421,610 | — | 1907 | 26,082,627 | 4,175,851 |
| 1886 | 3,223,154 | — | 1908 | 25,851,661 | 3,927,644 |
| 1887 | 3,407,070 | — | 1909 | 25,306,178 | 3,657,227 |
| 1888 | 4,004,882 | — | 1910 | 25,727,045 | 3,856,493 |
| 1889 | 4,378,453 | — | 1911 | 27,941,187 | 4,313,501 |
| 1890 | 4,696,287 | 1,724,000 | 1912 | 28,782,736 | 4,759,213 |
| 1891 | 5,612,562 | — | 1913 | 28,573,705 | 4,492,434 |
| 1892 | 7,047,295 | 2,256,556 | 1914 | 23,424,159 | 3,591,098 |
| 1893 | 9,301,081 | 2,113,002 | 1915 | 25,907,831 | 4,144,020 |
| 1894 | 9,827,813 | 2,389,682 | 1916 | 30,867,749 | 4,958,344 |
| 1895 | 9,517,892 | 2,389,233 | 1917 | 26,918,964 | 4,545,709 |
| 1896 | 9,854,365 | 2,551,827 | 1918 | 26,931,754 | 4,653,649 |
| 1897 | 10,742,546 | 2,796,096 | 1919 | 26,212,988 | 4,091,589 |
| 1898 | 11,312,399 | 2,786,779 | 1920 | 30,548,469 | 3,768,921 |

SOURCE: Sami Pasha, *Taqwim al-Nil*, v. 3, 1518–25; *Annuaire statistique de l'Egypte*, 1909, 132.

1. Cotton, cotton seed, cereals, and coal amounted to roughly 50% of all transported goods.

TABLE A.2. *Periodicals delivered by the Egyptian Post Office*

| Year(s) | Total mail (national) | Mailed periodicals (national) | Percentage of mailed periodicals |
|---|---|---|---|
| 1895–1899 (yearly average) | 17,946,000 | 6,260,000 | 34 |
| 1900–1904 (yearly average) | 25,237,000 | 9,400,000 | 37 |
| 1905 | 33,250,000 | 12,100,000 | 36 |
| 1906 | 36,970,000 | 12,940,000 | 35 |
| 1907 | 40,580,000 | 13,514,000 | 33 |
| 1908 | 41,983,000 | 13,870,000 | 33 |
| 1909 | 43,086,000 | 14,720,000 | 34 |
| 1910 | 44,523,000 | 15,251,000 | 34 |
| 1911 | 47,230,000 | 16,340,000 | 35 |
| 1912 | 48,174,000 | 15,909,000 | 33 |
| 1913 | 51,263,000 | 17,487,000 | 34 |
| 1914 | 48,849,000[1] | 16,760,000 | 34 |
| 1915 | 48,437,000 | 14,414,000 | 30 |
| 1916 | 48,830,000 | 15,206,000 | 31 |
| 1917 | 46,927,000 | 14,111,000 | 30 |

SOURCE: *Annuaire statistique de l'Egypte*, 1914, 238–44; *Annuaire Statistique de l'Egypte*, 1918, 139.

1. A general decline in postal deliveries from 1914 to 1918 was mainly due to the outbreak of World War I.

TABLE A.3. *Urbanization statistics for Cairo and Alexandria*

| Place of birth | 1907 Cairo | 1907 Alexandria | 1927 Cairo | 1927 Alexandria |
|---|---|---|---|---|
| Port Said and Ismailia[1] | 778 | 531 | 3,373 | 1,932 |
| Suez | 651 | 390 | 1,036 | 761 |
| Behera | 3,981 | 13,890 | 8,082 | 16,701 |
| Charkiyya | 9,234 | 1,401 | 21,166 | 3,269 |
| Dakhliyya | 7,829 | 3,333 | 15,854 | 5,666 |
| Gharbiyya | 10,641 | 6,393 | 27,977 | 13,925 |
| Qaliubiyya | 17,654 | 964 | 31,767 | 1,557 |
| Minufiyya | 14,107 | 3,080 | 45,759 | 9,281 |
| Dammitte | — | — | 3,501 | 1,590 |
| Beni Souef | 7,110 | 947 | 10,212 | 1,421 |
| Fayoum | 4,140 | 970 | 6,799 | 1,043 |
| Giza | 20,375 | 871 | 46,400 | 1,463 |
| Minyah | 9,197 | 1,362 | 12,764 | 1,678 |
| Girga | 12,166 | 6,668 | 28,162 | 20,932 |
| Qenah | 3,783 | 2,506 | 12,520 | 6,893 |
| Assiut | 30,083 | 8,214 | 42,288 | 16,337 |
| Aswan | 6,640 | 4,425 | 18,085 | 13,364 |
| Foreign-born | 75,221 | 65,279 | 81,835[2] | 77,105[3] |
| Unknown | 71 | 62 | 6,139 | 5,610 |
| Cairo | 410,833 | 7,064 | 614,041 | 13,276 |
| Alexandria | 9,982 | 241,659 | 16,317 | 358,614 |
| Total born outside city | 243,643 | 128,350 | 450,526 | 214,449 |
| Total population | 654,476 | 370,009 | 1,064,567 | 573,063 |
| Percentage of migrants | 37.2 | 34.7 | 42.3 | 37 |

SOURCE: *Annuaire statistique de l'Egypte*, 1914, 42; *Annuaire statistique de l'Egypte*, 1928–1929, 36–43.

1. Port Said and Suez are listed together as Canal Zone.

2. Of the 81,835 foreign-born Cairo residents, 39,490 were Egyptian citizens.

3. Of the 54,580 foreign-born Alexandria residents, 22,525 were Egyptian citizens.

# Appendix B

### *Plays and Songs Composed by Sayyid Darwish from 1918 to 1919*

| Date | Play | Troupe | Recorded songs |
|------|------|--------|----------------|
| July 21, 1918 | *Fairuz Shah* | George 'Abyad | *Ra'ayt Ruhi fi Bustan* (Baidaphon 65-66/823) |
| July 28, 1918 | *Kuluh Min Dah* (More of the same) | al-Rihani | *al-Muwazafin/Hiz al-Hilal* (Odeon 47658)<br>*Ya Abu 'Abdu 'Ul li Abu Himda* (Odeon) |
| July 31, 1918 | *al-Hawari* (Beautiful maidens) | George 'Abyad | |
| October 5, 1918 | *Wa Law* (Even if) | al-Rihani | *'al Niswan ya Salam Salim* (Odeon 4771)<br>*al-Hilwa di 'Amit Ti'gin* (Mechian)<br>*al-Sa'ayyin* (Odeon 47645) |
| January 13, 1919 | *'Ish* (Wow) | al-Rihani | *Baya'it al-Ward*<br>*Shaykh Qufa'a* (Odeon 172 and Odeon 47714)<br>*al-Nashalin/al-Suyyas* (Odeon 47713)<br>*Tugar al-'Agam* (Odeon)<br>*Abu al-Kashakish* (Mechian 651) (Pathé Records 35004/18007)<br>*Da ba'f min 'Ili Yi'alis* (Odeon 47711) |
| February 22, 1919 | *Wi Lissa* (More to come) | al-Kassar | *al-Garsunat* (Baidaphon)<br>*al-Buhyagiyya* (Baidaphon) |
| March 4, 1919 | *'U'bal 'Anduku* (*May you be so lucky*) | al-Kassar | (Could not find recorded songs from this play) |

| Date | Play | Troupe | Recorded songs |
|------|------|--------|----------------|
| May 16, 1919 | *'Ululuh* (Tell him) | al-Rihani | *Shid al-Hizam* (Odeon 171)<br>*Salma Ya Salama* (Odeon 178)<br>*al-Bahr Biyidhak* (Odeon 178)<br>*Da ba'f min ili Yi'alis* (Odeon 47711)<br>*Ya Wild 'Ami* (Mechian 827)<br>*Til'it ya Mahla Nurha* (Mechian 652)<br>*'Um ya Misri* (Odeon 170)<br>*Khafif al-Ruh* (Mechian 589)<br>*al-Qilal al-Qinawi* (Mechian 797 and 665)<br>*'Uw'aki Tisada'i* (Odeon)<br>*Ya Kiki Kiku* (Mechian) |
| July 22, 1919 | *'Ahlahum* (The best) | al-Kassar | *Ya Tufah* (Mechian 798) |
| October 17, 1919 | *'Ulnaluh* (We told him) | al-Kassar | (Could not find recorded songs from this play) |
| November 19, 1919 | *Marhab* (Hello) | al-Kassar | (Could not find recorded songs from this play) |
| December 7, 1919 | *Rinn* (Buzz/Ring) | al-Rihani | *'Ayn al-Hasud Fiha 'Ud* (Odeon 47607)<br>*Ya Halawit 'Um Isma'il* (Odeon 47607)<br>*al-Kukayin Kukh* (Baidaphon 82562) |
| December 30, 1919 | *Kulaha Yumayn* (In a couple of days) | Munira al-Mahdiyya | *al-Zibda* (Baidaphon 64-63/823)<br>*Nam ya Khufu* (Baidaphon B82492)<br>*Yahiyya al-'Adl* (Baidaphon 93-94/824)<br>*Gana al-Farah* (Baidaphon 93-94/824)<br>*'Intisarik ya Munira* (Baidaphon 61-62/823)<br>*al-Sibirtu* (Baidaphon 43-44/824) |

SOURCES: *Al-Ahram*, July 21, 1918; June 21, 1919; October 10, 1919; May 16, 1919; October 18, 1919; July 22, 1919; November 19, 1919; and December 7, 1919. *Al-Muqatam*, July 28 and 31, 1918; August 8, 1918; October 5 and 16, 1918; January 15, 1919; and March 4, 1919. *Al-Minbar*, December 30, 1919. *Misr*, February 22, 1919. Dar al-Kutub wa al-Watha'iq al-Qawmiyya, *Fihris al-Musiqa*.

# Notes

## PREFACE

1. "Intelligence Report on the Egyptian Situation," July 31, 1919, Great Britain, Public Records Office, FO 141/781/8915.

2. *Azjal* (colloquial poetry; sing. *zajal*) and songs were orally broadcast in the same manner as jokes or popular Egyptian proverbs, which often spread like wildfire with the aid of urban communal meeting places, such as popular coffeehouses.

## CHAPTER ONE

1. Scott, *Domination*, xii–xiii.

2. See Wendell, *Evolution of the Egyptian National Image*; Safran, *Egypt in Search of Political Community*; Ghali, *L'Egypte nationaliste*; C. D. Smith, *Islam*; Ramadan, *Tatawwur al-Haraka*; and Reid, *Cairo University*.

3. In the last few years many excellent monographs have been published on the role of intellectuals in Egyptian society. On Egyptian historians and historiography, see Di-Capua, *Gatekeepers*; and Gorman, *Historians*. For the role of science as a discourse, see Shakry, *Great Social Laboratory*.

4. Beinin and Lockman, *Workers on the Nile*; Cole, *Colonialism*; Chalcraft, *Striking Cabbies*.

5. Powell, *Different Shade of Colonialism*; Baron, *Egypt as a Woman*; Selim, *The Novel*; and Gasper, *Power of Representation*. Recently, a variety of innovative studies have covered varying aspects of Egyptian culture and society during the first half of the twentieth century. On masculinity and identity, see Jacob, "Working Out Egypt." On Egyptology and Egyptian modernity, see Reid, *Whose Pharaohs*; and Colla, *Conflicted Antiquities*. On marriage, modernity, and national identity, see Kholoussy, *For Better, For Worse*.

6. Ahmed, *Intellectual Origins*, 34, 113.

7. Gershoni and Jankowski, *Egypt, Islam, and the Arabs*, xii.

8. In the last decade several important studies have been published on the influence of gender on the formation of a modern Egyptian national identity, although most of them focus on the role of elite women. See Badran, *Feminists, Islam, and*

*Nation*; Booth, *May Her Likes Be Multiplied*; Pollard, *Nurturing the Nation*; Baron, *Women's Awakening*; Baron, *Egypt as a Woman*; and Russell, *Creating the New Egyptian Woman*.

9. Abu-Lughod, "Writing Against Culture," 143–47, 154. See also Geertz, *Interpretation of Cultures*.

10. See Clifford, *Predicament of Culture*.

11. Burke, *Popular Culture*, ix.

12. See Cachia, *Popular Narrative Ballads*, 16.

13. Hinds, "Popularity," 363.

14. Fine, "Popular . . . Culture," 382.

15. For a reexamination of some of the most important debates about popular culture, especially in the age of the mass media, see Mukerji and Schudson, *Rethinking Popular Culture*, 1–61. See also Storey, *Inventing Popular Culture*.

16. Abdel-Malek, *Vernacular Poetry*; and Booth, *Bayram al-Tunsi's Egypt*. See also Booth, "Colloquial Arabic Poetry"; Armbrust, "Formation of National Culture"; Armbrust, *Mass Culture*; Haeri, *Sacred Language*; Powell, *Different Shade of Colonialism*; Baron, *Egypt as a Woman*; Pollard, *Nurturing the Nation*; and Gasper, *Power of Representation*; see also Beinin, "Writing Class."

17. Holes, *Modern Arabic*, 5. Despite his estimate of the mid-nineteenth century as the "beginnings" of MSA, Holes cautions that "in practice, however, there is no chronological point at which CLA [Classical Arabic] turned into MSA, still less any agreed set of linguistic criteria that could differentiate the two."

18. Holes, *Modern Arabic*, 5.

19. For an examination of the role of Arabic in national identity, see Suleiman, *Arabic Language*.

20. On the other hand, today, with the advent of the Internet and mobile phone texting, which are largely unregulated, more Egyptians are writing in colloquial Egyptian.

21. The term *diglossia* was defined by Charles Ferguson as "a relatively stable language situation in which, in addition to the primary dialects of the language (which may include a standard or regional standard), there is a very divergent, highly codified (often grammatically more complex) superposed variety, the vehicle of a large and respected body of written literature, either of an earlier period or in another speech community, which is learned largely by formal education and is used for most written and formal spoken purposes but is not used by any sector of the community for ordinary conversation." See Ferguson, "Diglossia," 336. The coining of the term is credited to William Marçais. See Marçais, "La diglossie arab."

22. For examples, see Armbrust, *Mass Culture*, 48–55; and Haeri, *Sacred Language*, 35–51.

23. Holes, *Modern Arabic*, 342.

24. Holes, *Modern Arabic*, 342–43. Nonetheless, a thorough and practical knowledge of Fusha by the Egyptian masses is still far from universal.

25. *Annuaire statistique de l'Egypte*, 1918, 15. According to the 2005 *CIA World Factbook*, Egyptian literacy is still only 57.7%.

26. Mitchell, "Some Preliminary Observations," 70.

27. See Armbrust, *Mass Culture*, 37–62. Armbrust devotes an entire chapter

("The Split Vernacular") to the tensions between classical Arabic and colloquial Egyptian. Also see Booth, "Colloquial Arabic Poetry."

28. Bakhtin, *Rabelais*, 466.

29. Bakhtin, *Rabelais*, 88.

30. See Bakhtin, *Dostoevsky's Poetics*; and Bakhtin, *Rabelais*.

31. For instance, although far from a classic traditionalist, Muhammad 'Abduh (later to become the mufti of Egypt) made a scathing critique of Ya'qub Sannu''s colloquial newspaper *Abu-Naddara Zarqa'* in *al-Tijara*, June 3, 1879. See also Cachia, "Use of Colloquial," 20.

32. See Armbrust, *Mass Culture*, 37–62. Also see Haeri, *Sacred Language*, 1–24.

33. Miller, "Between Myth and Reality," 28–30; and Woidich, "Egyptian Arabic," 185–90. In addition, the Southern Egyptian dialect splits into the Middle Egyptian (from Giza to Assiut) and Upper Egyptian (from Assiut to Aswan) dialect groups.

34. For a definition of *ibn al-balad*, see El-Messiri, *Ibn al-Balad*, 1–8.

35. Miller "Between Myth and Reality," 35–36.

36. The magazine specialized in large, colorful political cartoons and sociopolitical satire and relied heavily on lengthy colloquial Egyptian comedic sketches.

37. Rashid Rida (1865–1935), the editor of *al-Manar* newspaper, was a religious reformer and a student of Muhammad 'Abduh. See Hourani, *Arabic Thought*, 222–44.

38. *Al-Kashkul al-Mussawwar*, January 2, 1925. For more on Egyptian perceptions of race and Nubians, see Powell, *Different Shade of Colonialism*.

39. *Wa hayat waldak* literally means "by your father's life."

40. *Al-Kashkul al-Mussawwar*, January 23, 1925.

41. As in Egypt, the pronunciations of southerners in the United States and Italy are often contrasted disapprovingly with the more "proper" accents of the north.

42. See Gramsci, *Southern Question*; and Dickie, *Darkest Italy*, 6. For an excellent discussion of the possibility of a Gramscian Southern Question in Egypt, see Gran, "Upper Egypt."

43. Attempts to standardize Fusha (Modern Standard Arabic) have been ongoing since the late nineteenth century, with the establishment of several Arabic academies. These academies were primarily set up to prevent the "encroachment" of *'ammiyya* and foreign words on Fusha. For an examination of the history of these Arab academies, see Holes, *Modern Arabic*, 44–50.

44. For the primordialist model, see Armstrong, *Nations Before Nationalism*; Connor, "A Nation Is a Nation"; Van den Berghe, "Race and Ethnicity"; and Geertz, *Old Societies*, 105–57.

45. The perennialist approach to nationalism, and the concept of *ethnie*, or prenational ethnic community, is best articulated in Anthony D. Smith's earlier works. For example, see A. D. Smith, *Ethnic Origins*; and A. D. Smith, "Gastronomy or Geology." See also A. D. Smith, *National Identity*, 19–42.

46. Breuilly, *Nationalism*; Brass, *Ethnicity*; Hechter, *Internal Colonialism*; Nairn, *Break-Up of Britain*; Anderson, *Imagined Communities*; and Gellner, *Nations and Nationalism*.

47. Chatterjee, *Nation and Its Fragments*, 5.

48. Anderson, *Imagined Communities*, 19, 36–46.

49. For a heated scholarly exchange on the applicability of Anderson's theory on Egyptian nationalism, the role of print culture, and the importance of the secularization of the liturgical language, see C. D. Smith, "Imagined Identities"; Gershoni and Jankowski, "Print Culture"; and C. D. Smith, "Cultural Constructs."

50. Haeri, *Sacred Language*, 1.

51. Gellner, *Nations and Nationalism*, 37. The overwhelming majority of Egyptian songs, movies, theatrical plays, television programming, and so on is in colloquial Egyptian, and most newspapers and books are in Fusha. Although Fusha is the official language of Egypt, colloquial Egyptian is more culturally relevant to everyday life, in the sense that it is the spoken language of all Egyptians and hence effectively the mother tongue of the nation.

52. Gellner, *Nations and Nationalism*, 38.

53. Gellner, *Nations and Nationalism*, 37–38.

54. Anderson, *Imagined Communities*, 37–46.

55. In *Imagined Communities*, Anderson mentions orality and audiovisual technology only in passing and always as secondary to print. See Anderson, *Imagined Communities*, 135–36.

56. Edensor, *National Identity*, 7–8.

57. In *Understanding Media*, for example, McLuhan describes "the inability of oral and intuitive oriental culture to meet with the rational, visual European patterns of experience" (5). In McLuhan's *Gutenberg Galaxy* this line of thinking takes on an even more extreme binary: "There can be no greater contradiction or clash in human cultures than that between those representing the eye and the ear" (68). For an excellent critique and analysis of Ong and McLuhan's theories, see L. E. Schmidt, *Hearing Things*, 1–22.

58. Corbin, *Village Bells*; Corbin, *Time, Desire, and Horror*; L. E. Schmidt, *Hearing Things*; M. M. Smith, *Sensing the Past*; and Hirschkind, *Ethical Soundscape*.

59. M. M. Smith, *Sensing the Past*, 48.

60. Anderson, *Imagined Communities*, 35.

61. Wogan, "Imagined Communities Reconsidered," 409.

62. Ayalon, *The Press*, 154–59.

63. On the embodiment of everyday life and national identity, see Billig, *Banal Nationalism*; and Edensor, *National Identity*.

64. Anderson, *Imagined Communities*, 25.

65. Briggs and Burke, *Social History of the Media*, 5, 22–23. See also Armbrust, "Formation of National Culture," 161.

66. *Annuaire statistique de l'Egypte*, 1918, 15.

CHAPTER TWO

1. For an overview on the effects of print capitalism and new communication and transportation technologies on Islamic movements in the eastern Mediterranean, see Cole, "Printing and Urban Islam."

2. For an excellent discussion on the cultural differences of Upper Egypt, see Hopkins and Saad, *Upper Egypt.*

3. Hunter, *Egypt Under the Khedives*, 9–15.

4. Gran, *Islamic Roots of Capitalism*, 12–13; Gran, "Upper Egypt," 83–84.

5. Gran, *Islamic Roots of Capitalism*, 12–14, 114–17; Cuno, *Pasha's Peasants*, 103–20.

6. Cuno, *Pasha's Peasants*, 125–29; al-Rafi'i, *'Asr Muhammad 'Ali*, 487–500.

7. K. Fahmy, *All the Pasha's Men*, 12–21.

8. Hunter, *Egypt Under the Khedives*, 36–37.

9. Marsot, *Reign of Muhammad Ali*, 232–54.

10. For a complete list of 'Ali's government departments and councils, see Deny, *Sommaire des archives turques du Caire*, 95.

11. Isma'il also built 112 new irrigation canals and increased Egypt's railroad network tenfold, reaching 2,100 kilometers by the end of his reign. See Mubarak, *al-Khitat al-Tawfiqiyya*, v. 7, 243–51.

12. The ceremony for the opening of the Suez Canal alone cost 1.4 million Egyptian pounds, an exorbitant amount at the time. See al-Rafi'i, *'Asr Isma'il*, 99.

13. Cole, *Colonialism*, 92–93; Hunter, *Egypt Under the Khedives*, 36–37, 225–26.

14. Heyworth-Dunne, *Education in Modern Egypt*, 330–41.

15. Heyworth-Dunne, *Education in Modern Egypt*, 346–66, 382–92.

16. For more on the *'afandiyya*, see Ryzova, *L'effendiyya*; Ryzova, "Egyptianizing Modernity"; Beinin and Lockman, *Workers on the Nile*, 10; and Chalcraft, *Striking Cabbies*, 11, 161.

17. Tignor, *Modernization*, 322–30.

18. Boktor, *School and Society*, 115–18; *Annuaire statistique de l'Egypte*, 1928–1929, 132–34; Sami Pasha, *al-Ta'lim fi Misr fi Sanat*, 113; al-Sahm, *al-Ta'lim*, 78–91.

19. Tignor, *Modernization*, 283–84; see also pp. 180–213.

20. For more information on the level of control established by the centralized government on the Egyptian countryside, see Mitchell, *Colonizing Egypt.*

21. Mubarak, *al-Khitat al-Tawfiqiyya*, v. 7, 243–46, 251. See also Owen, *Middle East*, 123, 128–29.

22. Al-Shirbini, *Tarikh al-Tijara al-Misriyya*, 192–96; Hunter, *Egypt Under the Khedives*, 93; Tignor, *Modernization*, 380–82.

23. Sami Pasha, *Taqwim al-Nil*, 1518–25; *Annuaire statistique de l'Egypte*, 1909, 132.

24. See al-Rafi'i, *'Asr Isma'il*, 99; and Cole, *Colonialism*, 92–93. For a look at a similar process taking place in nineteenth-century France, see Weber, *Peasants into Frenchmen*, 212–18.

25. Sami Pasha, *Taqwim al-Nil*, 1518–25.

26. Ramzi, *Masrahuna 'Ayyam Zaman*, 10–11.

27. *Annuaire statistique de l'Egypte*, 1914, 238–44.

28. *Annuaire statistique de l'Egypte*, 1914, 238–40.

29. *Annuaire statistique de l'Egypte*, 1914, 238–44; *Annuaire statistique de*

*l'Egypte*, 1918, 139. In addition to the internal mail, more than 35 million pieces of international mail were delivered by the Egyptian postal system in 1913.

30. *Misr* in Arabic also means a large city or metropolis.

31. Beinin and Lockman, *Workers on the Nile*, 12, 26; Mitchell, *Rules of Experts*, 60–62.

32. Migration to both Cairo and Alexandria continued to grow, and by 1927 more than 450,000 (42%) of the inhabitants of Cairo and 214,000 (37%) of Alexandria's residents were born outside the two cities. See *Annuaire statistique de l'Egypte*, 1914, 42; and *Annuaire statistique de l'Egypte*, 1928–1929, 36–43.

33. United Kingdom, Parliamentary Papers, *Reports*, 1908, 8.

34. According to the 1917 census, from 1907 to 1917 Alexandria's population expanded by 89,223, or 25.1%, and Cairo increased its population by 112,506, which was a 16.6% increase. The percentage growth rate of both Cairo and Alexandria expanded even more from 1917 to 1927, reaching about 30% for both cities. See *Annuaire statistique de l'Egypte*, 1918, 9–15; and *Annuaire statistique de l'Egypte*, 1928–1929, 21.

35. *Annuaire statistique de l'Egypte*, 1914, 42.

36. For more on *ibn al-balad*, see El-Messiri, *Ibn al-Balad*.

37. The term *mutamassirun* is defined by Beinin and Lockman as "people of foreign origin who had become permanent residents and had been 'Egyptianized.'" Beinin and Lockman, *Workers on the Nile*, 9. For an examination of the difficulties that many *mutamassirun* endured during the Nasser regime, see Beinin, *Dispersion of Egyptian Jewry*, 37–38. For a brief history of the foreign community in Egypt and issues of national identity, see Starr, *Remembering Cosmopolitan Egypt*, 18–23.

38. Sami Pasha, *Taqwim al-Nil*, 1571.

39. This percentage is based on Egyptian newspapers and periodicals available and listed at the Dar al-Kutub al-Misriyya (Egyptian National Library). Actual figures are probably considerably higher, because Dar al-Kutub's collection is not complete. For instance, most illegal (not government-registered) periodicals are not included in their collection.

40. For an excellent look at printing and the press in Egypt, see Ayalon, *The Press*. For an examination of books and book culture in eighteenth-century Egyptian society, see Hanna, *In Praise of Books*.

41. Nussayr, *Harakat Nashr al-Kutub*, 501.

42. *Annuaire statistique de l'Egypte*, 1914, 24; *Annuaire statistique de l'Egypte*, 1918, 15; *Annuaire statistique de l'Egypte*, 1928–1929, 30.

43. Ayalon, *The Press*, 56, 156.

44. Ayalon, *The Press*, 128.

45. For a more detailed discussion of the prevalence of reading newspapers aloud in Egypt and the availability of newspapers in cafés, see Ayalon, *The Press*, 154–59; see also Baron, *Women's Awakening*, 92.

46. Ayalon, *The Press*, 156.

47. Ayalon, *The Press*, 154.

48. See Ong, "Oral Residue."

49. Habermas, *Structural Transformation*, 42.

50. Ninet, "Origins of the National Party," 128. Ninet frequently visited Egypt in the last quarter of the nineteenth century. He wrote several books and essays supporting Egyptian nationalism. A few years later the London *Times* correspondent also documented this reading aloud phenomenon; see *The Times* (London), March 3, 1885; speaking about Ya'qub Sannu's journal *Abu-Naddara Zarqa'*, the *Times* correspondent announced that "its contents are eagerly read aloud in many a village in Egypt."

51. Sharubim, *al-Kafi fi Tarikh Misr*, v. 5, bk. 1, pt. 2, 660. Mikha'il Sharubim was an important, although rarely used, late nineteenth- to early twentieth-century Egyptian chronicler and historian who documented many of the important events of his day. The last section of the fourth volume and the entire fifth volume (three books) of *al-Kafi fi Tarikh Misr al-Qadim wa al-Hadith* [The sufficient history of Egypt from ancient times to the present] document events taking place in his lifetime. The three-part fifth volume of *al-Kafi*, which covers political events from 1892 until 1910, was not published until 1998, more than 80 years after it was written. Until now historians have used only Sharubim's first four volumes, which were first published in 1898 by the Bulaq Press in Cairo.

52. Sharubim, *al-Kafi fi Tarikh Misr*, v. 5, bk. 1, pt. 2, 660.

53. Habermas, *Structural Transformation*, 37.

54. For an examination of Cairo's soundscape at the turn of the twenty-first century, see Hirschkind, *Ethical Soundscape*.

55. See Khurshid, *al-Judhur al-Sha'biyya*, 99–104; al-Ra'i, *Funun al-Kumidiyya*, 50–68.

56. Briggs and Burke, *Social History of the Media*, 5.

57. Briggs and Burke, *Social History of the Media*, 5.


CHAPTER THREE

1. In 1869 Jalal edited along with Ibrahim al-Muwalihi a short-lived newspaper called *Nuzhat al-'Afkar* (Promenading thoughts). The newspaper was quickly shut down, however, for criticizing Khedive Isma'il. See 'Abduh, *A'lam al-Sahafah fi Misr*, 103–4.

2. The *rababa* is a traditional stringed instrument. It was the instrument of choice for the traveling performers who specialized in recounting traditional tales (in colloquial Egyptian) about historical and mythological characters, such as al-Zahir Baybars, Abu Zayd al-Hilali, and Antar 'ibn Shadad.

3. This popularity can especially be compared to the failed attempts by the cultural elite to introduce plays in Classical Arabic or European classical music. Khurshid, *al-Judhur al-Sha'biyya*, 102–10; see also al-Ra'i, *Funun al-Kumidiyya*, 50–68.

4. "Hello, *kurdash*" is a greeting typically used by Turkish soldiers.

5. Here the term *Magharba* refers specifically to North African mercenaries hired by the Mamluks in Egypt.

6. Burckhardt, *Arabic Proverbs*, 183. Here, the accent of the "Moroccans" is rendered in the first half of the proverb.

7. Burckhardt, *Arabic Proverbs*, 56, 122.

8. Burckhardt, *Arabic Proverbs*, 28–29, 83, 279. According to Burckhardt, many of these proverbs were specifically used to refer to Muhammad 'Ali.

9. Salih, *al-'Adab al-Sha'bi*, 103–13; Taymur, *al-Amthal al-Sha'biyya*, 1, 174, 221.

10. Burckhardt, *Arabic Proverbs*, 37, 82, 280.

11. Khurshid, *al-Judhur al-Sha'biyya*, 102–10.

12. Lane, *Manners and Customs*, 308.

13. Lane, *Manners and Customs*, 384–85.

14. See al-'Allati, *Kitab Tarwih al-Nufus wa Mudhik al-'Ubus*, v. 1, 3. See also al-Ra'i, *Funun al-Kumidiyya*, 84–86.

15. See Riyad and al-Sabah, *Tarikh 'Adab al-Sha'b*, 123–36, 149–53, 177–88, 231–37. For instance, Muhammad al-Najar (or al-Shaykh al-Najar) edited *al-'Arghul* (The flute) from 1894 to 1900; Muhammad Tawfiq edited *Humarat Munyati* (The idiocy of my desires) from 1899 to 1908; Ahmad 'Ashur Sulayman (al-Shaykh 'Ashur) was one of the editors for *al-'Arnab* (The rabbit) and *al-Babaghlu* (The parrot); Muhammad Fahmi Yusuf edited *al-Baghbaghan* (The parrot); Husayn Shafiq al-Misri edited *al-Sayf* (The sword) and several other periodicals; and 'Isa Sabri edited *al-Rasaam* (The painter).

16. Abu Buthayna, *al-Zajal wa al-Zajalun*, 27–30.

17. Abu Buthayna, *al-Zajal wa al-Zajalun*, 43–44; Riyad and al-Sabah, *Tarikh 'Adab al-Sha'b*, 62–63.

18. See Khurshid, *al-Judhur al-Sha'biyya*, 102–10.

19. See Gendzier, *Practical Visions*, 46–50; Sadgrove, *Egyptian Theater*, 89–124; Moosa, "Ya'qub Sanu'"; and Landau, "Abu Naddara."

20. See *al-'Adab wa al-Tamthil*, April 1916; Riyad and al-Sabah, *Tarikh 'Adab al-Sha'b*, 98–100; al-Khozai, *Early Arabic Drama*, 169–71; and al-Ra'i, *Funun al-Kumidiyya*, 119–20.

21. *'Aysh wassal wahid zayyak yidrabni, ya kalb, ya ghagar, ya sakkari, ya hashash, ya 'ars, ya harami.* See *Rawdat al-Madaris al-Misriyya*, no. 5, June 4, 1871.

22. *Rawdat al-Madaris al-Misriyya*, May 5, 1871, to July 4, 1871. The play was printed from the third issue of the second year (15 Safar 1288 H [May 6, 1871]) to the seventh issue of the second year (15 Rabi' 1288 H [July 4, 1871]).

23. Badawi, *Early Arabic Drama*, 68–71.

24. Jalal published three of Racine's plays in 1892. See 'Uthman Jalal, *al-Riwayat al-Mufida fi 'Ilm al-Trajida*.

25. See *al-'Adab wa al-Tamthil*, April 1916; Riyad and al-Sabah, *Tarikh 'Adab al-Sha'b*, 98–100; al-Khozai, *Early Arabic Drama*, 169–71; al-Ra'i, *Funun al-Kumidiyya*, 119–20; and Najm, *al-Masrah al-'Arabi*, v. 4.

26. In his *Studies in the Arab Theater and Cinema*, Jacob Landau mistakenly states that Jalal "translated the tragedies . . . into modern literary Arabic." Landau, *Arab Theater*, 109.

27. George Abyad's troupe regularly acted Jalal's comedic plays. See al-Ra'i, *Funun al-Kumidiyya*, 135–37.

28. Gendzier, *Practical Visions*, 9–12; Landau, "Abu Naddara," 31–32. Sannu''s

father, Rafael Sannu', was from Leghorn, Italy, and was among the thousands of European workers arriving in Egypt early in the nineteenth century. He was employed as an adviser to Prince Ahmad Pasha Yeken, the grandson of Muhammad 'Ali.

29. Gendzier, *Practical Visions*, 16–18; Moosa, "Ya'qub Sanu'," 402.

30. The subsidizing of Sannu''s theater by the Egyptian government was not unusual. Early in his reign, Isma'il set out to modernize Egypt's infrastructure with countless public works projects. Isma'il built schools and encouraged the arts, which included the funding of theatrical troupes. See al-Rafi'i, *'Asr Isma'il*, v. 1, 201–37; v. 2, 9–32; and Vatikiotis, *Modern Egypt*, 74–75.

31. The scripts of all seven of Sannu''s surviving Arabic plays and one short theatrical sketch were published in Najm, *al-Masrah al-'Arabi*, v. 3. The seven plays enclosed in Najm's book are *Bursat Misr* (The Egyptian stock market), *al-'Alil* (The sick man), *Abu Ridah al-Barbari wa Ka'b al-Khayr* (Abu Rida the Nubian and Ka'b al-Khayr), *al-Saddaqa* (Friendship/faithfulness), *al-Amira al-'Iskandaraniyya* (The Alexandrian princess), *al-Durratayn* (The co-wives), and *Molière Misr wa ma Yuqasihi* (The Egyptian Molière and what he endures).

32. During the first half of the twentieth century, this theme became common in Egyptian literature. It is, for example, one of the major subplots in Muhammad Husayn Haykal's *Zaynab* and Tawfiq al-Hakim's *al-'Ard*. Yahya Haqqi's *Qindil 'Umm Hashim* is one of the few novels written during this period that complicates this modernist narrative through its ambivalence toward the superiority of modern medicine over traditional medicine.

33. These comedic characters were transferred to the early Egyptian cinema and are still alive in today's movies and television serials.

34. See Powell, *Different Shade of Colonialism*, 185–95.

35. See Najm, *al-Masrah al-'Arabi*, v. 3. Here are some examples of the non-Egyptian characters in Sannu''s plays:

Nubian characters: Farag in *al-Bursa*, 'Abu Rida in *'Abu Rida al-Barbari wa Ka'b al-khayr*

Greek characters: Theresa in *al-Bursa*, Carolina and Kharalambo in *al-'Amira al-'Iskandaraniyya*

Syrian characters: Ni'mat Allah in *al-Saddaqa*

Other foreigners and tourists: Dr. Kabrit Bey in *al-'Alil*, Na'um in *al-Saddaqa*, Victor in *al-'Amira al-'Iskandaraniyya*, the English tourist in *al-Sawah wa al-Hammar* (a one-act farce)

36. Jacque Chelley, "Le Molière Egyptien," *Abu-'Naddara*, August 1, 1906; Abul Naga, *Les sources françaises*, 76; 'Anus, *Masrah Ya'qub Sannu'*, 31–33; Moosa, "Ya'qub Sanu'," 404–5; Landau, *Arab Theater*, 65–67; Gendzier, *Practical Visions*, 34–38.

37. See Landau, "Abu Naddara," 34; Gendzier, *Practical Visions*, 46–50; Cole, *Colonialism*, 137; Landau, "Prolegomena," 138–43; and Sadgrove, *Egyptian Theater*, 89–124.

38. See al-Ra'i, *Funun al-Kumidiyya*, 135–37. For an early attack on Sannu''s use of "low and vulgar language" by Muhammad 'Abduh, see *al-Tijara*, June 3, 1879. For other examples, see Chapter 4.

39. *Al-Tankit wa al-Tabkit* (Humor and criticism) was published from June 6, 1881, to September 9, 1881.

40. See Landau, "Abu Naddara," 34; Gendzier, *Practical Visions*, 44–48; Cole, *Colonialism*, 137–38; Landau, "Prolegomena," 138–43; and Keddie, *Sayyid Jamal ad-Din al-Afghani*, 92–93. See also Sadgrove, *Egyptian Theater*, 89–124.

41. Landau, "Abu Naddara," 33.

42. Gendzier, *Practical Visions*, 65.

43. *The Times* (London), March 12, 1885. Sannu' frequently changed the name of his paper to evade the censors. Other names for the paper include *Abu-Naddara*, *Abu Suffara* (The man with a whistle), *Abu Zummara* (The man with a trumpet), and *al-Hawi* (The magician).

44. Ninet, "Origins of the National Party," 128.

45. Annually (sometimes biannually), Sannu' bound together in one volume his entire journal issues for that year for resale.

46. *The Times* (London), March 12, 1885. If just one-third of those estimated 7,000 issues reached their destination, then *Abu-Naddara* would claim a circulation of approximately 2,300 copies, sizable for the time.

47. Gendzier, *Practical Visions*, 70; Ninet, *Arabi Pacha*, 226.

48. *Abu-Naddara* (Paris), November 15, 1907. Muhammad Sabri is sometimes called al-Sorboni (from the Sorbonne). He earned his bachelor's degree (1919) and his doctorate (1924) from the Sorbonne. For a brief biographical description, see Goldschmidt, *Biographical Dictionary*, 172–73.

49. For a closer look at Sannu''s European public opinion campaign and his French discourse, see Z. Fahmy, "Francophone Egyptian Nationalists."

50. The year of Nadim's birth is in dispute. Gilbert Delanoue and 'Ali al-Hadidi maintain that he was born in 1845, Hourani selects 1844, and 'Abd al-Min'im al-Jumay'i claims that 1843 is the correct year.

51. It was during this period that Nadim was first exposed to the ideology of Jamal al-Din al-Afghani.

52. The *'umda* (village chief) of Bidawy village was al-Shaykh Ahmed Abu-Sa'da, who owned 1,000 acres in al-Daqahliyya. This period was important in Nadim's life, because he became personally aware of the problems facing the Egyptian fellah. For more on Nadim and Sannu' and especially their representation of the Egyptian peasant, see Gasper, *Power of Representation*.

53. Delanoue, "'Abd Allah Nadim," 75–79; al-Hadidi, *'Abdallah al-Nadim*, 14–64; al-Jumay'i, *'Abdallah al-Nadim*, 33–43.

54. *The Times* (London), August 30 and September 8, 1879; Delanoue, "'Abd Allah Nadim," 80–83; al-Hadidi, *'Abdallah al-Nadim*, 64–84; al-Jumay'i, *'Abdallah al-Nadim*, 44–50; Keddie, *Sayyid Jamal ad-Din al-Afghani*, 116–23; Cole, *Colonialism*, 98–109, 153–54; Schölch, *Egypt for the Egyptians*, 108–12.

55. *Al-Tankit wa al-Tabkit*, June 19, 1881.

56. See Cole, *Colonialism*, 110–32.

57. *The Times* (London), March 3, 1885.

58. *The Times* (London), March 3, 1885.

59. Ninet, "Origins of the National Party," 128. Ninet actively supported the 'Urabi revolt and wrote several books and essays supporting Egyptian nationalism. For example, see Ninet, *Arabi Pacha*.

60. Sharubim, *al-Kafi fi Tarikh Misr*, v. 4, 324–25. See also, Cole, *Colonialism*, 124–25.

61. In his June 1879 article, the Cairo correspondent of *L'Europe diplomatique* wrote: "Le mois passé . . . j'ai pu aller entendre Ahmad Salem [Ahmad Salim], le grand chanteur arabe du Caire. . . . Mais ce soir-la, il arriva qu'un vendeur clandestine de l'Abou Naddara put se glisser, je ne sais comment, au travers de l'assemblée. En moins de rein c'étais fait, loin des yeux de la police il avait vendu près de trois cents exemplaires. . . . Chacun de tourner le dos au chanteur et de se mettre, entouré d'un petit groupe, à lire le journal prohibé. . . . Et les invités ne consentirent à rester qu'à la condition qu'Ahmed Salem leur chanterait la chanson du proscrit Abou Naddara!" (Last month I was able to go and listen to the famous Cairene Arabic singer Ahmad Salim. But during this night, somehow, a clandestine newspaper seller of *Abu Naddara* was able to stealthily hide among the assembled crowd. In no time at all, far from the eyes of the police, he was able to sell close to 300 copies of the journal. In their turn, most of the spectators turned their backs to the singer and assembled in small groups while reading the prohibited journal. The audience then insisted, on threat of leaving [the concert], that Ahmed Salim sing for them a song written by Abu Naddara [Sannu'].) Quoted in Sabry, *La genèse*, 127–28.

62. Sharubim, *al-Kafi fi Tarikh Misr*, v. 4, 261–62.

63. Quoted in Cole, *Colonialism*, 208–9. A *mulid* is a carnivalesque religious festival celebrating the birth of a celebrated religious figure.

64. According to Alexander Schölch, the petitioners consisted of merchants, religious scholars, members of the Egyptian Chamber of Deputies, senior military officers, and high government officials and nobles. See Schölch, *Egypt for the Egyptians*, 87–93.

65. Schölch, *Egypt for the Egyptians*, 89–99; *The Times* (London), August 30 and September 8, 1879; Delanoue, "'Abd Allah Nadim," 80–83; al-Hadidi, *'Abdallah al-Nadim*, 64–84; al-Jumay'i, *'Abdallah al-Nadim*, 44–50; Keddie, *Sayyid Jamal ad-Din al-Afghani*, 116–23; Cole, *Colonialism*, 98–109, 153–54; Sharubim, *al-Kafi fi Tarikh Misr*, v. 4, 264–67.

66. Al-Hadidi, *'Abdallah al-Nadim*, 64–84; al-Jumay'i, *'Abdallah al-Nadim*, 44–50; Keddie, *Sayyid Jamal ad-Din al-Afghani*, 116–23.

67. *Abu-Naddara*, March 6, 1880. In an attempt to evade the censors, Sannu' changed the title of this issue of *Abu-Naddara* to *al-Naddarat al-Misriyya* (The Egyptian spectacles).

68. *Abu-Naddara*, March 6, 1880.

69. Sharubim, *al-Kafi fi Tarikh Misr*, v. 4, 289–90; al-Naqash, *Misr li al-Misriyyin*, v. 4, 84–87. Rifqi was replaced by Mahmud Sami al-Barudi, who although from Circassian stock, was an 'Urabi sympathizer.

70. Sharubim, *al-Kafi fi Tarikh Misr*, v. 4, 300.

71. *Al-Tankit wa al-Tabkit*, August 7, 1881, and September 11, 1881.

72. Al-Naqash, *Misr li al-Misriyyin*, v. 4, 94–99. See also Riyad and al-Sabah, *Tarikh 'Adab al-Sha'b*, 62–63.

73. Sharubim, *al-Kafi fi Tarikh Misr*, v. 4, 296–98; al-Naqash, *Misr li al-Misriyyin*, v. 4, 101.

74. Sharubim, *al-Kafi fi Tarikh Misr*, v. 4, 300, 305–10; al-Naqash, *Misr li al-Misriyyin*, v. 4, 90–96; Cole, *Colonialism*, 235–37.

75. See *Abu-Naddara Zarqa'*, February 1882.
76. Al-Naqash, *Misr li al-Misriyyin*, v. 4, 194–97.
77. *The Times* (London), March 3, 1885.
78. *The Times* (London), September 5, 1882.
79. Sharubim, *al-Kafi fi Tarikh Misr*, v. 4, 360–72; al-Naqash, *Misr li al-Misriyyin*, v. 4, 271–77; Cole, *Colonialism*, 238–41; Hunter, *Egypt Under the Khedives*, 36–37, 225–26.
80. Based on the 1897 census, the literacy rate in Egypt was 5.8%.


### CHAPTER FOUR

1. For the cultural importance of recording technology and its effects on identity, see J. Smith, *Vocal Tracks*, 1–15.
2. This expression can still be heard in Egypt today to describe a sense of shock or disbelief. It is similar in meaning to the English expression "I'll be damned!"
3. Delanoue, "'Abd Allah Nadim," 83–95; al-Hadidi, *'Abdallah al-Nadim*, 80–108; al-Jumay'i, *'Abdallah al-Nadim*, 51–55, 125–60, 336–48; Cole, *Colonialism*, 123–24, 244–48.
4. Tignor, *Modernization*, 48–50, 66–69.
5. See *Abu-Naddara*, 1882, no. 3.
6. *Abu-Naddara*, December 1902.
7. *Abu-Naddara*, April 18, 1885.
8. *Abu-Naddara*, August 30, 1889, and May 28, 1891.
9. Sannu''s cartoon character of *al-'aguz al-shamta'* (the mindless old lady) was modeled after "la vieux Albion," featured in Anglophobic nineteenth-century French cartoons. See H. D. Schmidt, "Idea and Slogan."
10. This is a reference to "John Bull," or Great Britain. *Bul* in Arabic also means urine. *Abu-Naddara*, June 9, 1893; May 1, 1893; October 18, 1893; and September 25, 1895.
11. *Abu-Naddara*, May 16, 1885; June 15, 1893; and February 20, 1898.
12. *Rawdat al-Madaris al-Misriyya*, November 17, 1876; *al-Ahram*, December 1, 1876; October 10, 1877; and January 14, 1885.
13. *Al-Ahram*, March 17, 1885.
14. See *al-Ahram*, March 17, 1885; January 9, 1886; and January 15, 1886.
15. See *al-Ahram*, January 3, 1887, and February 11, 1887; and *al-Qahira*, April 25, 1887.
16. *Al-Qahira*, November 19, 1888.
17. *Abu-Naddara*, May 1, 1893.
18. For more on Wilfred Blunt, see Berdine, *Accidental Tourist*.
19. Shafiq Pasha, *Mudhakkirati fi Nisf Qarn*, v. 2, 35–36. Nadim was pardoned on February 3, 1892, and returned to Egypt on May 9, 1892. Marsot, *Egypt and Cromer*, 156–57; al-Jumay'i, *'Abdallah al-Nadim*, 179.
20. *The Times* (London), March 31, 1893; March 20, 1893; April 1, 1893; and May 29, 1893. The *Muqattam*, a pro-British Arabic daily, also published several anti-Nadim articles. See *al-Muqattam*, May 20–24, 1893.

21. From 1878 until 1910, Sannu' published all his papers from Paris.

22. See *al-'Ustadh*, August 24, 1892.

23. For example, see *al-'Ustadh*, September 6, 1892, and September 20, 1892.

24. *Al-'Ustadh*, January 3, 1893. Nadim breaks down the distribution of his 2,288 issues into 1,506 issues distributed by mail, 492 issues distributed to subscribers in Cairo, 190 issues sold through newsstands in Cairo, and 100 sold through newsstands in Alexandria.

25. Delanoue, "'Abd Allah Nadim," 95. The December 1910 issue of *Abu-Naddara* was the last issue of Sannu''s journal and was entirely dedicated to making his final farewell to his readers. However, Gendzier mistakenly claims that Sannu' retired in 1907: "Without formally taking leave of his readers, the *Abu-Naddara* and *L'univer Musulman* abruptly ended in November 1907." See Gendzier, *Practical Visions*, 138. Scholars relying on Gendzier for Sannu''s biographical information are continuing to date 1907 as the year of Sannu''s retirement from journalism. For example, see Beinin, "Writing Class," 194; and Gasper, *Power of Representation*, 68.

26. *Dar al-Kutub al-Misriyya*.

27. For an example, see the memoirs of Muhammad Lutfi Jum'a, *Shahid 'Ala al-'Asr*, 58.

28. Al-Rafi'i, *Mustafa Kamil*, 24–29, 31–49; *al-'Ustadh*, February 28, 1893.

29. Letter dated July 12, 1891, written by Kamil to his brother, 'Ali Fahmy Kamil. See Kamil, *'Awraq Mustafa Kamil: al-Murasalat*, 136. Also see al-Rafi'i, *Mustafa Kamil*, 24–29, 31–48.

30. See Zaydan, *Tarajim Masha'ir al-Sharq*, v. 1, 295; al-Jumay'i, *'Abdallah al-Nadim*, 199–225; al-Rafi'i, *Mustafa Kamil*, 24–29, 31–49; and *al-'Ustadh*, February 28, 1893.

31. Marsot, *Egypt and Cromer*, 156–57; Cromer, *Abbas II*, 1–10; Berque, *Egypt*, 163–69.

32. Shafiq Pasha, *Mudhakkirati fi Nisf Qarn*, v. 2, 50. In his article "The Egyptian Nationalist Party," Goldschmidt misquotes Shafiq's memoirs and dates Kamil's meeting with 'Abbas to February 1892 instead of November 28, 1892. See Goldschmidt, "Egyptian Nationalist Party," 312.

33. Hilmi, *Khedive of Egypt*, 136.

34. Adam, *L'Angleterre*, 144–45; al-Rafi'i, *Mustafa Kamil*, 51–54; Marsot, *Egypt and Cromer*, 156–57.

35. See *al-Ahram*, December 28, 1894; January 4, 1895; January 28, 1895; February 4, 1895; February 23, 1895; and March 4, 1895. Kamil began writing nationalist articles in the local press in early 1893. See *al-Ahram*, February 11, 1893; February 16, 1893; February 24, 1893; March 8, 1893; April 20, 1893; July 20, 1894; July 31, 1894; August 3, 1894; September 1, 1894; and September 8, 1894.

36. *Al-Surur*, February 28, 1895; *al-Hilal*, February 1, 1895. See also Badawi, *Early Arabic Drama*, 70.

37. Ramzi, *Masrahuna 'Ayyam Zaman*, 10–11, 15, 43.

38. For a brief biography of Mikha'il Jirjis, see *Ruz al-Yusuf*, March 10, 1926; and Isma'il, *Tarikh al-Masrah*, 171–78.

39. Ramzi, *Masrahuna 'Ayyam Zaman*, 10–11.

40. *Jaridat Misr*, October 6, 1899; *al-Muqattam*, July 24, 1891; October 20, 1893; December 11, 1894; and February 10, 1898; *al-Mu'ayid*, July 9, 1891; *al-Ahram*, March 10, 1894, and March 29, 1894.

41. Al-Ra'i, *al-Kumidiyya al-Murtajila*, 35–36.

42. Al-Ra'i, *al-Kumidiyya al-Murtajila*, 30–33.

43. Al-Ra'i, *al-Kumidiyya al-Murtajila*, 38–39. Al-Far's full name is Ahmad ('Afandi) Fahim al-Far. According to al-Ra'i, the title of 'Afandi was given to him to differentiate him from another comedic sketch artist named Ahmad al-Far, who wore a turban instead of a fez. Al-Far recorded his animal sound sketches with Gramophone. See Gramophone 7874 and 11098.

44. Landau, *Arab Theater*, 4. For more on al-Far, see Landau, "Popular Arabic Plays."

45. *Al-Muqattam*, August 13, 1907; *Misr*, May 9, 1906, and July 28, 1907.

46. See al-Ra'i, *al-Kumidiyya al-Murtajila*, 33–38, 66–67; and Khurshid, *al-Judhur al-Sha'biyya*, 102–10, 114–16.

47. For example, see *al-Mu'ayid*, April 11, 1907; *Misr*, April 6, 1906; and *al-Ahram*, July 19, 1906.

48. *Al-Ahram*, July 19, 1907. See also *al-Muqattam*, July 16, 1907.

49. Al-Fil, *Ru'yat wa Bayan Halat al-Masrah al-'Arabi*, 410.

50. *Al-Mu'ayid*, September 4, 1907; *al-Ahram*, September 7, 1907; September 14, 1907; and September 21, 1907; *al-Watan*, October 4, 1907.

51. See *al-Tamthil*, April 1916; and al-Fil, *Ru'yat wa Bayan Halat al-Masrah al-'Arabi*, 401–3, 410–11.

52. Many comedic artists, actors, and even singers simulated these linguistic duels in their theatrical acts.

53. Smith, *Vocal Tracks*, 15.

54. Dar al-Kutub wa al-Watha'iq al-Qawmiyya, *Fihris al-Musiqa*, 168–72. The actual number of records made by Sayyid Qishta is likely more than forty-three. This figure is based on the number of his records available at Dar al-Kutub.

55. See Lagrange, "Musiciens," 130.

56. Dar al-Kutub wa al-Watha'iq al-Qawmiyya, *Fihris al-Musiqa*, 168–72.

57. Dar al-Kutub wa al-Watha'iq al-Qawmiyya, *Fihris al-Musiqa*, 27–29. For example, al-Far performed "*Ghina' al-Barbari*" (The singing of the Nubian), "*'Afiyat al-Barabra*" (The Nubians' verbal duel), and "*Tarkib al-Tilifun 'And al-'Abd*" (Telephone installation at the African slaves' house) (all were recorded by Gramophone). For an analysis of Nubian and Sudanese racial sketches, see Powell, "Burnt-Cork Nationalism."

58. See Sayyid Qishta, *Qafiyat al-Turk* (The Turk's verbal duel), Columbia Records 3339, n.d. This record was also released as Odeon 47881. See also Dar al-Kutub wa al-Watha'iq al-Qawmiyya, *Fihris al-Musiqa*, 171.

59. Dar al-Kutub wa al-Watha'iq al-Qawmiyya, *Fihris al-Musiqa*, 171–72. "*'Afiyat al-Fiqi*" was released by Zonophone (see Zonophone 102706) and "*'Afiyat al-Nahu*" was released by Baidaphon (Baidaphon 12675-2).

60. Smith, *Vocal Tracks*, 3.

61. By 1905, for example, it cost 2 Egyptian pounds for a phonograph and five free discs. See *Misr*, October 3, 1905, quoted in Racy, "Musical Change," 79–80, 82.

62. Lagrange, "Musiciens," 113–14.

63. Baidaphon, which was started by the Lebanese-Egyptian brothers Butrus and Jibran Bayda, always advertised their company as "Sharikat Baydafun al-Wataniyya" (The National Baidaphon Corporation). On their label, the company name was rendered in Arabic (Baydafun) and French (Baidaphon).

64. Lagrange, "Musiciens," 117–22.

65. There are debates over the origin of the word *ta'tu'a* (*taqtuqa*), with some claiming that it is a mispronunciation of the word *qatquta*, which means cute or miniature. See Zaki, *al-Tadhawuq al-Musiqi*, 117–28; Rachid, *al-Taqatiq al-Sha'biyya*, 4–8; and Lagrange, "Musiciens," 286–88.

66. Lagrange, "Musiciens," 147.

67. *Al-Zuhur* (Cairo), July 1911.

68. For an excellent expanded examination of the *taqatiq* phenomenon during the 1920s and 1930s, see Lagrange, "Women."

69. See *Ha-Ha-Ha*, March 8, 1907; and *Khayal al-Zil*, March 15, 1907. During those sixteen years, Ahmad Hafiz 'Awad opened and operated at least three other newspapers: *al-Minbar* (1909), *al-Ahali* (1919), and *Kawkab al-Sharq* (1924).

70. Jum'a, *Shahid 'Ala al-'Asr*, 58.

71. On the numbers of periodicals, see *Dar al-Kutub al-Misriyya*.

72. *Mu'alim* literally means teacher or master, although in a nineteenth- and twentieth-century Egyptian context, it is a title given to merchants and shop and small business owners (especially coffee shops).

73. See "al-Mu'alim Hanafi wa Nadim" in *al-'Ustadh*, September 6, 1892, and September 20, 1892.

74. Although Sannu' ruthlessly attacks the Khedive Ismail (1863–1879) and his successor Tawfiq (1879–1892), he does not attack 'Abbas II (1892–1914).

75. For a closer look at the representation of the fellah by Sannu', see Gasper, *Power of Representation*.

76. *Al-Kashkul al-Musawwar*, January 23, 1925. For more on the history of the Egyptian tobacco industry and tobacco advertisements in Egypt, see Shechter, *Smoking Culture*.

77. These types of advertisements filled the pages of nationalist newspapers such as *al-Liwa*, *al-Mu'ayid*, *al-Lata'if al-Musawwara*, and *al-Sa'ada*. For examples, see *al-Kashkul al-Musawwar*, September 12, 1924; October 10, 17, and 24, 1924; and January 23, 1925; and *al-Lata'if al-Musawwara*, October 16 and 23, 1922.

78. Blunt, *My Diaries*, v. 1, 33–35.

79. The colloquial Egyptian word *sarmaha* roughly means to frolic or to muck around.

80. *Al-bihim* literally means a farm animal, and in colloquial Egyptian it is used to indicate stupidity.

81. *Al-'Arghul*, October 1, 1894. *Al-'Arghul* was edited and owned by Muhammad al-Naggar and was dubbed a scientific, literary, comedic, and educa-

tional newspaper (*jarida 'ilmiyya, 'adabiyya, fukahiyya, tahdhibiyya*). It was published from 1894 until 1900.

82. For instance, almost every issue of *al-'Arghul* contained a moralistic *zajal* expressing the evils of gambling and drinking. See, for example, *al-'Arghul*, October 15, 1894; November 15, 1894; November 30, 1894; July 8, 1895; January 11, 1895; and January 25, 1895.

83. See the "Hanifa and Latifa" dialogue in *al-'Ustadh*, September 27, 1892.

84. *Al-'Ustadh*, October 4, 1892. *Yi-laghbat 'a'loh* literally means to mix up his brain. For the modern institutionalization of marriage and Egyptian national identity, see Kholoussy, *For Better, For Worse*.

85. *Al-'Arghul*, January 25, 1895.

86. *Al-'Arghul*, August 1, 1895.

87. *Al-'Ustadh*, September 27, 1892, and October 4, 1892.

88. See "Majliss Tibi 'ala-Musab bil-'Afrangi" (Medical consultation on those afflicted by "European" pronunciation), *al-Tankit wa al-Tabkit*, June 6, 1881.

89. These funny-sounding fictional names are not real Arabic names; however, they were familiar to most of Nadim's contemporaries because they were all featured in popular Egyptian proverbs.

90. All of Zi'ayt's dialogue is spoken in broken Arabic with several French words. All the French words in italics are transliterated into Arabic letters and used by Nadim throughout the dialogue.

91. *Al-Tankit wa al-Tabkit*, June 6, 1881; *Majalat Sarkis*, May 1, 1907.

92. For a more in-depth analysis of this sketch, see Gasper, *Power of Representation*, 84–87.

93. *Majalat Sarkis*, May 1, 1907.

94. *Al-Babaghlu al-Misri*, January 8, 1904.

95. *Al-Babaghlu al-Misri*, January 8, 1904.

96. Sharubim, *al-Kafi fi Tarikh Misr*, v. 5, bk. 1, pt. 2, 660.

97. Sharubim, *al-Kafi fi Tarikh Misr*, v. 5, bk. 1, pt. 2, 660.

98. Sharubim, *al-Kafi fi Tarikh Misr*, v. 5, bk. 1, pt. 2, 660–61.

99. 'Abduh did have a relatively close relationship with Lord Cromer and at the very least they respected each other. 'Abduh visited Cromer regularly in his office and counseled him on Islamic issues. For example, see Great Britain, Public Records Office, FO 141/367.

100. *Humarit Munyati* (The idiocy of my desires), *al-Babaghlu al-Misri* (The Egyptian parrot), and *al-Arnab* (The rabbit) regularly attacked 'Abduh for most of his tenure as Egypt's grand mufti. For example, see *Humarit Munyati*, May 28, 1901; July 8, 1901; October 3, 1901; December 20, 1901; January 16, 1902; and March 1, 1902.

101. Sharubim, *al-Kafi fi Tarikh Misr*, v. 5, bk. 3, 127–29.

102. Sharubim, *al-Kafi fi Tarikh Misr*, v. 5, bk. 3, 127–29.

103. Sharubim, *al-Kafi fi Tarikh Misr*, v. 5, bk. 3, 128.

104. See Shafiq Pasha, *Mudhakkirati fi Nisf Qarn*, v. 3, 40.

105. *Al-Babaghlu al-Misri*, January 15, 1904.

106. *Al-Babaghlu al-Misri*, January 15, 1904. These populist attacks on 'Abduh demonstrate the tensions between 'Abduh and his circle of bourgeois na-

tionalists, who advocate working within the structure of British colonialism, and the more "radical" nationalists, who demand immediate independence.

107. See Great Britain, Public Records Office, FO 371/3714, FO 141/781/8915, and Political Summary, Cairo, April 8, 1919.

108. *Al-Tijara*, June 3, 1879.

109. *Al-'Ustadh*, October 25, 1892.

110. For a debate on the use of colloquial Egyptian in Nadim's journal, see *al-'Ustadh*, October 25, 1892, and November 1, 1892.

111. *Al-'Ustadh*, November 1, 1892.

112. For more on Wilcocks, see Gasper, *Power of Representation*, 173; and Suleiman, *Arabic Language*, 185, 199.

113. *Al-'Ustadh*, January 3, 1892. However, in the February 21, 1893, issue, Nadim gradually returned to using *'ammiyya*.

114. 'Umar, *Hadir al-Misriyyin*, 34.

115. For an analysis of Muhammad 'Umar's book, see Lockman, "Imagining the Working Class," 164–70.

116. 'Umar, *Hadir al-Misriyyin*, 34.

117. United Kingdom, Parliamentary Papers, *Reports*, 1904, 32–33.

118. United Kingdom, Parliamentary Papers, *Reports*, 1905, 13.

119. Cromer to Lansdowne, Cairo, February 26, 1904, Great Britain, Public Records Office, FO 407/163, no. 4; United Kingdom, Parliamentary Papers, *Reports*, 1903, 31–32.

120. In the next year's (1904) report to Parliament, Cromer continued to defend his hands-off policy with regard to the Egyptian press: "I do not think that it is either necessary or desirable to interfere with the perfect freedom which the press in Egypt now enjoys. That freedom is accompanied by certain disadvantages may be readily admitted. . . . But I am very clearly of the opinion that the advantages far outweigh the disadvantages. . . . I do not think that, of recent years, a single instance can be quoted, connected with matters of public importance, where the least worthy portion of the local press have done any real harm." See United Kingdom, Parliamentary Papers, *Reports*, 1904, 32–33.

121. Sharubim, *al-Kafi fi Tarikh Misr*, v. 5, bk. 1, pt. 2, 660.

122. Sharubim, *al-Kafi fi Tarikh Misr*, v. 5, bk. 1, pt. 2, 1101.

123. Al-Rafi'i, *Mustafa Kamil*, 205–9; Shafiq Pasha, *Mudhakkirati fi Nisf Qarn*, v. 3, 99–101.

124. For an English translation of the entire Dinshaway trial, see "Mr. Findlay to Sir Edward Gray," July 15, 1906, Great Britain, Public Records Office, FO 407/167, no. 56; and United Kingdom, Parliamentary Papers, "Further Paper." See also Shafiq Pasha, *Mudhakkirati fi Nisf Qarn*, v. 3, 100–102.

125. Early in his career, Kamil began using an external strategy for swaying European public opinion toward the Egyptian nationalist cause. Working toward this goal, Kamil spent every summer from 1895 to 1907 in Europe publicizing Egyptian nationalist causes. For a more detailed look at Mustafa Kamil's propaganda campaign in Europe, see Z. Fahmy, "Francophone Egyptian Nationalists," 170–83.

126. *Le Figaro*, July 11, 1906. The article, which was titled "A la nation anglaise et au monde civilisé," is included in Adam, *L'Angleterre*, 151–59.

127. The speech was titled "Programme et vues du Parti National Egyptien" and is included in Adam, *L'Angleterre*, 160–72. See also Ghali, *L'Egypte nationaliste*, 58–63.

128. See Z. Fahmy, "Francophone Egyptian Nationalists," 181–83.

129. For example, in his book *Abbas II*, Cromer wrote, "Every feather-headed young Egyptian who thought himself of equal if not of superior mental caliber to his British official superior, rallied around the foolish youth, who—probably without being fully aware of it—had raised the standard of revolt against Western civilization. The Gallicised Egyptian, who posed as a reformer, joined hands with the retrograde Pasha." See Cromer, *Abbas II*, 34–35.

130. For example, see *al-Ahram*, June 28, 1906; and *al-Liwa*, June 28, 1906.

131. *Majalit Sarkis*, July 15, 1906, and August 15, 1906. See also al-Rafi'i, *Shu'ara' al-Wataniyya fi Misr*, 101–2.

132. Al-Rafi'i, *Shu'ara' al-Wataniyya fi Misr*, 35–36, 49–50.

133. For an Arabic transcript of this *mawwal*, see Kamal, *al-Ghina' al-Sha'bi al-Misri*, 92–94. For a more detailed analysis of the gendered discourse of this ballad, see Baron, *Egypt as a Woman*, 43–44. See also Cachia, *Popular Narrative Ballads*, 255–57.

134. *Al-Liwa*, July 12, 1906.

135. *Al-Liwa*, August 29, 1906.

136. *Al-Ahram*, July 22, 1908.

137. For an examination of the portrayal of the Egyptian peasant in *'Adhra' Dinshaway*, see Lockman, "Imagining the Working Class," 179–81; see also Gasper, *Power of Representation*, 206–7, 210–11.

138. See Yahya Haqqi's introduction to Haqqi, *'Adhra' Dinshaway*, i–xv. Thus Muhammad Husayn Haykal's *Zaynab*, first published in 1913, was not the first Egyptian novel. See Haikal, *Mohammed Hussein Haikal's Zainab*.

139. Haqqi, *'Adhra' Dinshaway*, i–xv, 2–6. See Mahmud Haqqi's original preface.

140. The Egyptian prosecutor assigned to the case was Ibrahim al-Hilbawi (1858–1940), who later resurrected his career as a wafdist nationalist.

141. Haqqi, *'Adhra' Dinshaway*, 79–80.

142. Partly because of this media campaign and the resulting national and international pressure, all of those imprisoned because of the Dinshaway debacle were released on January 7, 1908. See Sir Eldon Gorst to Ronald Graham, January 10, 1908, Great Britain, Public Records Office, FO 407/172.

143. Briggs and Burke, *Social History of the Media*, 22–23.

CHAPTER FIVE

1. See Anderson, *Imagined Communities*, 37–46.

2. Briggs and Burke, *Social History of the Media*, 22–23.

3. See Sharubim, *al-Kafi fi Tarikh Misr*, v. 5, bk. 3, 492.

4. Sharubim, *al-Kafi fi Tarikh Misr*, v. 5, bk. 3, 492.

5. For an examination of the reading aloud of newspapers in Egypt during this period and the intersection of print and oral communication, see Chapters 1 and

4. See also Ayalon, *The Press*, 56, 154–59; Booth, "Colloquial Arabic Poetry," 423–24; and Baron, *Women's Awakening*, 92.

6. Cromer and Muhammad 'Abduh, for instance, had a mutually respectful relationship. There is also evidence to suggest that before his retirement, Cromer encouraged the establishment of a moderate nationalist party, which would later become the 'Umma Party. See Owen, *Lord Cromer*, 361–62; and Shafiq, *Mudhakkirati fi Nisf Qarn*, v. 3, 129.

7. See Kamil, *'Awraq Mustafa Kamil: al-Khutab*, 301–38. Theaters were increasingly used as public gathering places for speeches and other political events in Egypt at the turn of the twentieth century. The role of theaters as public spaces for political discourse in Egypt has yet to be examined.

8. The leading figures of the 'Umma Party were Mahmud Sulayman Pasha (president), 'Ali Sha'rawi Pasha and Hassan 'Abd al-Raziq Pasha (vice-presidents), and Lutfi al-Sayyid (secretary). See al-Shiliq, *Hizb al-'Umma*, 72–73.

9. *Al-Jarida*, September 21, 1907.

10. Shafiq, *Mudhakkirati fi Nisf Qarn*, v. 3, 128–29.

11. See Kamil, *'Awraq Mustafa Kamil: al-Khutab*, 3, 12–13.

12. Lockman, "Imagining the Working Class," 183.

13. al-Saghir, *Al-Hizb al-Watani*, 154–55.

14. Sharubim, *al-Kafi fi Tarikh Misr*, v. 5, bk. 3, 500. Kamil's picture adorned the walls of many urban coffee shops and postcard-size pictures of him were printed and distributed.

15. Sharubim, *al-Kafi fi Tarikh Misr*, v. 5, bk. 3, 492.

16. Sharubim, *al-Kafi fi Tarikh Misr*, v. 5, bk. 3, 492–96.

17. For example, see 'Umar, *Hadir al-Misriyyin*.

18. Sharubim, *al-Kafi fi Tarikh Misr*, v. 5, bk. 3, 500.

19. Ronald Graham to Sir Eldon Gorst, May 3, 1910, Great Britain, Public Records Office, FO 141/492. For more on Jawish, see Lockman, "Exploring the Field," 141–42.

20. Great Britain, Parliamentary Papers, *Reports*, 1908, 3. See also Great Britain, Public Records Office, FO 371/660/12577.

21. Eldon Gorst, "The Press in Egypt," September 16, 1908, Great Britain, Public Records Office, FO 371/451/31779. As discussed in Chapter 4, Cromer was categorically against press censorship, and thus it was only after Eldon Gorst replaced him as consul-general that sterner methods were taken to muffle the satirical press.

22. This law was first instated on November 26, 1881, and established a number of restrictions on the local press. It continued to be partly enforced until it was shelved in 1894. Shafiq, *Mudhakkirati fi Nisf Qarn*, v. 3, 173–74.

23. According to *al-Zuhur* magazine, which used a post office survey to count 144 periodicals in Egypt in 1910, the percentage of periodicals deemed "acceptable" was roughly 38%. See *al-Zuhur*, April 1911. See also Great Britain, Parliamentary Papers, *Reports*, 1908, 5.

24. See *Al-Waqa'i' al-Misriyya*, March 27, 1909; Sharubim, *al-Kafi fi Tarikh Misr*, v. 5, bk. 3, 600–601; and Shafiq, *Mudhakkirati fi Nisf Qarn*, v. 3, 173–81. See also Great Britain, Public Records Office, FO 371/660/6829, FO 371/660/12577, and FO 371/660/13943.

25. Sharubim, *al-Kafi fi Tarikh Misr*, v. 5, bk. 3, 603. Graham to Sir Edward Grey, Cairo, April 4, 1909, Great Britain, Public Records Office, FO 371/660/12761.

26. Gorst to Grey, Cairo, February 11, 1909, Great Britain, Public Records Office, FO 371/660/6829.

27. Sharubim, *al-Kafi fi Tarikh Misr*, v. 5, bk. 3, 605–7, 611.

28. Sharubim, *al-Kafi fi Tarikh Misr*, v. 5, bk. 3, 605–7, 611. See also Graham to Grey, Cairo, April 4, 1909, Great Britain, Public Records Office, FO 371/660/12761.

29. This excerpt was quoted and translated in Ronald Graham to Sir Eldon Gorst, May 3, 1910, Great Britain, Public Records Office, FO 141/492. Also see Great Britain, Public Records Office, FO 371/664/30776, August 16, 1909.

30. Graham to Grey, Ramleh (Alexandria), August 8, 1909, Great Britain, Public Records Office, FO 371/664/30776.

31. See *al-Liwa*, August 7, 10, and 11, 1909; and Ronald Graham to Sir Eldon Gorst, May 3, 1910, Great Britain, Public Records Office, FO 141/492.

32. Ronald Graham to Sir Eldon Gorst, May 3, 1910, Great Britain, Public Records Office, FO 141/492; *Al-Liwa*, August 17, 1909.

33. Sharubim, *al-Kafi fi Tarikh Misr*, v. 5, bk. 3, 644.

34. Ronald Graham to Sir Eldon Gorst, May 3, 1910, Great Britain, Public Records Office, FO 141/492. In an article in *al-Liwa*, June 17, 1908, Jawish argued that only Muslims should hold important political positions in Egypt.

35. See *al-Watan*, June 15, 1908.

36. Sharubim, *al-Kafi fi Tarikh Misr*, v. 5, bk. 3, 485–86.

37. Sharubim, *al-Kafi fi Tarikh Misr*, v. 5, bk. 3, 485–86. Also see Cromer, *Modern Egypt*.

38. See Sir Edward Grey to Sir Eldon Gorst, March 10, 1911; Sir Eldon Gorst to Sir Edward Grey, March 11, 1911; and Sir Eldon Gorst to Sir Edward Grey, March 18, 1911. All in Great Britain, Public Records Office, FO 407/176.

39. Strapped for cash, the Egyptian government was considering extending the Suez Canal concessions for forty additional years. The outcry from the nationalists led to several large demonstrations, forcing the Egyptian General Assembly to vote the proposal down. For a detailed look at the Suez Canal concession crisis, see al-Sayyid Husayn Jalal, *Mu'ammarat Madd Imtiyaz Qanat al-Suways*.

40. Sharubim, *al-Kafi fi Tarikh Misr*, v. 5, bk. 3, 694.

41. Sir Eldon Gorst to Sir Edward Grey, March 25, 1911, Great Britain, Public Records Office, FO 407/176. Gorst wrote several long reports to the British Foreign Office statistically detailing the number of Copts in privileged government positions. He concluded that "Copts occupy a proportion of posts in the public service far in excess of anything to which their numerical strength would entitle them." Gorst ends one of his reports by stating that "no class has profited more" during the British occupation than the Copts and that "at the present moment, the Copts have no real grievance of any importance." See Sir Eldon Gorst to Sir Edward Grey, March 18, 1911, Great Britain, Public Records Office, FO 407/176.

42. See Sharubim, *al-Kafi fi Tarikh Misr*, v. 5, bk. 3, 700–701. Judging from the press coverage and the persistent editorial jousting, tension between Copts

and Muslims continued for at least two years after the assassination of Butrus Ghali.

43. Sir Eldon Gorst to Sir Edward Grey, July 17, 1910, Great Britain, Public Records Office, FO 141/492.

44. Sir Eldon Gorst to Sir Edward Grey, July 11, 1910, Great Britain, Public Records Office, FO 141/492.

45. Sir Eldon Gorst to Sir Edward Grey, July 11, 1910, Great Britain, Public Records Office, FO 141/492.

46. *Al-Jarida*, July 9, 1910; *al-Ahram*, July 10, 1910.

47. Saqr, *Diwan Amir Fan al-Zajal*, 34. 'Izat Saqr (d. 1932) was one of the most famous *zajjalun* of the early twentieth century and was referred to by colleagues and fans as *'amir al-zajal* (the prince of *zajal*).

48. See Cromer, *Modern Egypt*.

49. *Al-Sayf*, August 6, 1911. *Al-Sayf* (owned and edited by Husayn 'Ali), which described itself as a comedic, literary weekly newspaper, was a typical satirical magazine consisting of four large pages. About half of *al-Sayf*'s content was written in colloquial Egyptian.

50. *Al-Sayf*, September 24, 1911.

51. *Al-Sayf*, August 6, 1911.

52. *Al-Sayf*, August 6, 1911.

53. *Al-Sayf*, August 6, 1911.

54. See Cromer to Kitchener, London, July 25, 1912, Great Britain, Public Records Office, PRO 30/57/42.

55. Bourdieu, *Distinction*, 6–7. In the introduction to *Distinction*, Bourdieu elaborates: "Taste classifies, and it classifies the classifier. Social subjects, classified by their classifications, distinguish themselves by the distinctions they make, between the beautiful and the ugly, the distinguished and the vulgar, in which their position in the objective classifications is expressed or betrayed."

56. Naturally, taste is a uniquely individual characteristic, although what I mean by mass taste is a type of mass appreciation of certain cultural products by the majority of cultural consumers.

57. Racy, "Musical Change," 168–69. See also Danielson, "Artists and Entrepreneurs," 304. According to Omar Carlier, phonographs were also common in Algerian coffee shops. See Carlier, "Le café maure," 989.

58. Danielson, *Voice of Egypt*, 27–28.

59. *Al-Masrah*, June 14, 1927. See also Racy, "Record Industry," 43.

60. Gronow, "Record Industry," 255.

61. Racy, "Record Industry," 27–45.

62. Gronow, "Record Industry," 283–84. In 1929, Germany's record export to Egypt increased to more than 375,000 records. These figures do not include the records that were produced locally.

63. Khayri, *Mudhakkirat Badi' Khayri*, 16.

64. Booth, *Bayram al-Tunsi's Egypt*, 1.

65. Khayri, *Mudhakkirat Badi' Khayri*, 16.

66. See *al-Masrah*, May 24, 1926; and Riyad and al-Sabah, *Tarikh Adab al-Sha'b*, 177–85. Dawud Husni become famous for composing *taqatiq* because

of the music he had written for Qamar and Lila, two sisters who "performed in coffee shops specializing in singing and dancing, like Eldorado, al-Jadid, al-Qadim, and 'Alf Layla wa-Layla." The two sisters ended their careers working for the 'Ukasha theater troupe.

67. *Al-Zuhur* (Cairo), July 1911.

68. Gronow, "Record Industry," 266–67.

69. Racy, "Record Industry," 39.

70. Racy, "Record Industry," 39, 47.

71. Racy, "Record Industry," 39; *al-Masrah*, May 24, 1926.

72. There are conflicting accounts of al-Mahdiyya's birth date (from 1884 to 1898). Also, some claim that she was raised in Alexandria. See R. al-Hifni, *al-Sultana Munira al-Mahdiyya*, 84–85; Zaki, *'A'lam al-Musiqa*, 147–51; Qabil, *Mawsu'at al-Ghina' al-Misri*; and Danielson, "Artists and Entrepreneurs," 296. Also see *al-Masrah*, May 30, 1927.

73. Danielson, "Artists and Entrepreneurs," 296. See also *al-Minbar*, January 5, 1916.

74. Danielson, "Artists and Entrepreneurs," 296.

75. Yunis al-Qadi, who began his artistic career writing colloquial poetry for such satirical magazines as *al-Sayf* and *al-Lata'if al-Musawwara*, was hired by Baidaphon and wrote dozens of songs for them from 1912 until the mid-1920s. Early in his recording career, al-Qadi was paid 50 piasters per song, which was considerably more than he was making as a *zajal* writer for the colloquial press. See Riyad and al-Sabah, *Tarikh Adab al-Sha'b*, 237–44.

76. *Al-Masrah*, May 24, 1926.

77. *Al-Naqid*, February 20, 1928.

78. *Al-Naqid*, February 20, 1928.

79. *Al-Zuhur*, July 1911.

80. *Al-Masrah*, July 5, 1926. For more on Egyptian female singers, see Danielson, "Artists and Entrepreneurs," 296.

81. Danielson, "Artists and Entrepreneurs," 295–96.

82. M. al-Hifni, *Sayyid Darwish*, 34–35.

83. *Al-Masrah*, June 14, 1927. During World War I, Mechian, which was owned by an Armenian Egyptian, took advantage of the decrease in production by its foreign-based competitors. Because the other recording companies were based outside Egypt, they experienced a shortage of materials and recording engineers, who could not travel to Egypt during the war. See Racy, "Record Industry," 43.

84. *Al-Masrah*, August 29, 1927.

85. A *safiha* is a tin that holds approximately a gallon and half (5 liters).

86. *Min kan fakir 'ini da yigra / hata il-kabrit ba'a luh zikrah / Wi 'izazit il-lumba khadit shuhra / bi frank we nuss we shiwayya.* This song was also known as *Litr il-gaz bi-rubiyya* (The liter of kerosene now costs a rupee).

87. *'Ayshin fi wadi il-nil nishrab*
    *bil-'adadat 'ala mili wi santi*
    *Min gaz li-malh wa min sukar*
    *li-turmayat il-khawaga kiriyanti*

*Rabina ma yi-wariksh lusitna*
*il-gayb nidif 'amma il-bayt 'andaf*
*Wi il-hidmah di ili-'ala gititna*
*mahguz 'aliha . . . di 'isha ti'arraf*

For the version sung by Sayyid Darwish, see Odeon 171.

88. *Ana Munira al-Mahdiyya hubb al-watan 'andi ghiyya / 'Afdi biladi wil-huriyya bi-ruhi wa mali ana wa mal al-bakht.* For the original words of *Bassara Barraja*, see Maktabat al-'Iskandariyya, *Sayyid Darwish*, v. 1, 131. For the recorded version with the "improvised" lines, see *Bassara Barraja* by Munira al-Mahdiyya (Baidaphon 80–81/834). *Bassara* literarily means a woman who sees the future, and *barraja* means a female astrologer.

89. "*Salma ya Salama*" was also called "*al-'Umal wa al-Sulta*" (The workers and the British Authority). For the version sung by Sayyid Darwish, see Odeon 178:

*Salma ya salama*
*Ruhna wa gayna bil-salama*
*Safar ya wabur wa 'urbut 'andak*
*Nazilni fi il-bald di*
*Bala 'amrika bala 'uruba*
*Mafish 'ahsan min baladi*
*Di al-markib 'illy bitgib*
*'Ahsan mili-bitwadi*
. . .
*Salma ya salama*
*Ruhna we gayna bil-salama*
. . .
*Sulta ma sulta kullaha maksab*
*Hawishna maluw 'idayna*
*Shufna al-harb wa shufna al-darb*
*Wa shufna il-dinamit be 'inayna*
*Rabak wahid 'umrak wahid*
*'Adihna ruhna wa gayna*
. . .
*Salma ya salama*
*Ruhna we gayna bil-salama*

90. "*Salma Ya Salama*" is universally known in Egypt today. The song was remade and sung by many singers throughout the twentieth century. The most famous version was recorded in the late 1970s by the international star Dalida (the daughter of Italian émigrés, she was born and raised in Cairo). In Egypt, the chorus of this song has become a part of the popular musical repertoire. It is, for example, typically sung by children returning from school trips.

91. *Al-Shabab*, November 19, 1919.

92. For Anderson's discussion of print capitalism, see Anderson, *Imagined Communities*, 37–46.

93. See "Note by the Aga Khan and M. A. Ali Baig on the Situation in Egypt," January 12, 1915, Great Britain, Public Records Office, FO 371/2355/10934: "It

appears to us from what we have heard that under the combined operation of the Press Act and martial law, the Arabic Press has to a large extent ceased to reflect the trend of Egyptian feeling in all its aspects."

94. Sir Milne Cheetham to Sir E. Grey, December 28, 1914, Great Britain, Public Records Office, FO 141/545/4307.

95. Sir Milne Cheetham to Sir E. Grey, December 21, 1914, Great Britain, Public Records Office, FO 141/545/4307. Deposing 'Abbas Hilmi II was deemed essential for Britain's wartime efforts, because he not only disliked the British but had a close relationship with Germany as well as the Ottomans.

96. "Note by the Aga Khan and M. A. Ali Baig on the Situation in Egypt," January 12, 1915, Great Britain, Public Records Office, FO 371/2355/10934.

97. Sir Milne Cheetham to Sir E. Grey, December 28, 1914, Great Britain, Public Records Office, FO 141/545/4307.

98. See *Dar al-Kutub al-Misriyya*, 1996.

99. Salim, *Misr fi al-Harb al-'Alamiyya al-'Ula*, 150.

100. *Al-'Ahaly*, December 13, 1917; Riyad and al-Sabah, *Tarikh 'Adab al-Sha'b*, 69. For an in-depth analysis of Bayram al-Tunsi's poetry and *azjal* published in *al-'Ahali*, see Booth, *Bayram al-Tunsi's Egypt*, 41–56.

101. *Al-Masamir* was owned and edited by Sayyid 'Arif, one of Sayyid Darwish's closest friends. It had a similar format to many colloquial newspapers, consisting of four large pages with more than half its content written in colloquial Egyptian. See *al-Masamir*, May 6, 1918.

102. Traditionally, during the Muslim 'Id (the prophet's Muhammad's birthday), people, especially children, are accustomed to wearing new clothes and visiting their relatives. See *al-Masamir*, July 21, 1918:

> *Til'a il-fa'ir min hugtu*
> *'Al 'id yisalah hidmitu*
> *Wala yira'a' gizmitu*
> *Tarbush yighayar gilditu*
> *Wa ghayru mafish luh nasib*
> *Fi di il-hayah ya 'ammina*
> *Al-bu'us dah izay nimna'u 'ana*
> *Wa min rah yidfa'u*
> *Fi 'ardina il-khayr nizra'u*
> *Il-sharr bi-yigi yi'la'u*
> *Wa il-ghisn hata in kan ratib*
> *Til'ah nishif fi ardu*

103. *Al-Masamir*, July 21, 1918, and September 16, 1918.

104. *Al-Masamir*, September 16, 1918. *Mal'un abu sa'atak* literally means "may your eminence's father be cursed."

105. *Al-Masamir*, November 17, 1918.

106. *Al-Masamir*, July 21, 1918.

107. *Al-Masamir*, July 21, 1918, and September 16, 1918.

108. See *Al-Masamir*, December 15, 22, and 29, 1918; and January 5, 12, and 19, 1919.

109. *Al-'Afkar*, March 25, 1919.
110. *Al-Masamir*, December 8, 1918:

"'Andak lahma dani? . . . 'andi lahma 'ahssan [more horselike] min il-dani."

"'Intum bit-bi'u il-lahma bi'ay thamman dulwa'ti? . . . Baghla [mulelike] thamman."

111. *Al-Masamir*, December 15 and 22, 1918.
112. For an examination of some of the early Franco-Arab theater, see Abou-Saif, "Najib al-Rihani."
113. *Al-Masrah*, August 8, 1927.
114. *Al-Afkar*, January 12, 1917; February 16 and 23, 1917; March 2 and 18, 1917; and October 3, 1917; *Al-Muqatam*, March 5, 1918; *Misr*, September 4, 1918.
115. Al-Rihani, *Mudhakkirat Najib al-Rihani*, 81–82. To place these ticket prices in perspective, according to Nabawiyya Musa, schoolteachers in Egypt during the first decade of the twentieth century earned an estimated monthly salary of 6 to 12 Egyptian pounds. See Musa, *Tarikhi Biqalami*, 93.
116. *Al-Ahram*, January 17–24, 1917; February 23, 1917; March 1–5 and 22–26, 1917; and April 3–10, 1917; *Al-'Afkar*, January 19, 1917, and March 18, 1917.
117. *Al-Mu'ayid*, September 4, 1907; *al-Ahram*, September 14 and 21, 1907; *al-Watan*, October 4, 1907; *al-Mu'ayid*, September 4, 1907.
118. See *al-Tamthil*, April 1916; and al-Fil, *Ru'yat wa Bayan Halat al-Masrah al-'Arabi*, 401–3, 410–11. This probably means that for an unknown reason 'Id stopped making plays during those six years.
119. *Al-Adab wa al-Tamthil*, April 1916. For a detailed analysis of Ruz al-Yusuf's life, see Metcalf, "Morality Play."
120. Metcalf, "Morality Play," 152–57.
121. "Entering the public bath is easier than exiting it" is an Egyptian proverb that means that starting something is easier than finishing it.
122. *Al-Masrah*, August 8, 1927.
123. *Al-Masrah*, August 8, 1927.
124. *Al-Minbar*, February 18, 1917; *al-'Afkar*, January 5, 1917, and December 29, 1918. The 'Ukasha Brothers Troupe also performed plays in which the "proceeds were donated to the Red Cross and Crescent." See *al-Muqatam*, November 6, 1917.
125. *Al-'Afkar*, February 23, 1917.
126. Al-Rihani, *Mudhakkirat Najib al-Rihani*, 69.
127. *Al-Shabab*, November 19, 1919.
128. Khayri, *Mudhakkirat Badi' Khayri*, 33–34.
129. *Al-Minbar*, August 26, 1918.
130. *Al-Minbar*, March 10, 1919; the article was titled "*Tharwat Kishkish*" (Kishkish's fortune). See also *al-Shabab*, November 13, 1919.
131. Zaghlul, *Mudhakkirat Sa'd Zaghlul*, v. 7, 113.
132. Al-Rihani, *Mudhakkirat Najib al-Rihani*, 106.
133. *Al-Ahram*, May 16, 1919. This *Ahram* advertisement stressed that the music was by Sayyid Darwish. The nine hit songs were "*Shid al-Hizam*" (Odeon

171), "*Salma Ya Salama*" (Odeon 178), "*al-Bahr Biyidhak*" (Odeon 178), "*Da ba'f min ili yi'aliss*" (Odeon 47711), "*Til'it ya Mahla Nurha*" (Mechian 652), "*'Um ya Masri*" (Odeon 170), "*Khafif al-Ruh*" (Mechian 589), "*al-Qilal al-Qinawi*" (Mechian 797 and 665), and "*Ya Wild 'Ami*" (Mechian 827). Many of these songs are universally known in Egypt today.

134. *Al-Masrah*, August 29, 1927.

135. The names of some of these plays are taken from pure colloquial Egyptian expressions, and some contemporaries have said that 'Ali al-Kassar and Najib al-Rihani were actually using the titles of their plays to playfully communicate and tease each other in the classic *'afiyya* style (a colloquial Egyptian verbal duel).

136. For examples of the themes and discourses of *azjal* and the satirical press, see also Booth, "Colloquial Arabic Poetry," 423–33.

137. *Al-Muqattam*, January 15, 1919; *al-Ahram*, June 21, 1919.

138. See Maktabat al-'Iskandariyya, *Sayyid Darwish*, v. 1, 360.

> *Kharalambo shaf gaybi mi'ammar*
> *Rah dughri wa'if mitsammar*
> *'Al 'izbba 'aynu bidtawar*
> *Galli 'il'ab bartitit poker*
> *Ya bey ishrab da juni wukar*
> *Li'ibt sikirt khisirt*
> *Hatta wi'i't fi his bis*

139. See Maktabat al-'Iskandariyya, *Sayyid Darwish*, v. 1, 361:

> *Wa bukra harga' tani muhtaram*
> *'Akhdim 'ana biladi wa il-watan*
> *Hubb il-watan shi' ghandara*
> *Wa tubt 'ana mil-hankara*

140. Abu al-Kashakish is Kishkish's nickname. For the original version sung by Fathia 'Ahmad and Najib al-Rihani, see Mechian 651. See also Pathé records 35004/18007.

141. See "*Shaykh Qufa'a*" (Odeon 172 and Odeon 47714). For the lyrics of the song, see Maktabat al-'Iskandariyya, *Sayyid Darwish*, v. 1, 365.

142. See Maktabat al-'Iskandariyya, *Sayyid Darwish*, v. 1, 359.

143. This *taqtuqa* is also known as "*'Uw'a Liminak 'Uw'a Shimalak*" (Watch out to your right, watch out to your left). See "*Lahn al-Siyas*" (Odeon 181); and Maktabat al-'Iskandariyya, *Sayyid Darwish*, v. 2, 363.

144. See Maktabat al-'Iskandariyya, *Sayyid Darwish*, v. 2, 370.

145. *Al-Minbar*, January 21, 1917; *al-Ahram*, January 9 and 14–17, 1917; *al-Muqatam*, July 2 and August 8, 1917. Professional troupes who occasionally toured the Egyptian countryside included the theaters of al-Rihani, al-Kassar, Abyad, and al-Mahdiyya.

146. Ramzi, *Masrahuna 'Ayyam Zaman*, 10–11.

147. Ramzi, *Masrahuna 'Ayyam Zaman*, 10–11, 15, 43.

148. Al-Rihani, *Mudhakkirat Najib al-Rihani*, 32–33.

149. Ramzi, *Masrahuna 'Ayyam Zaman*, 38–39, 58–59. For an analysis of the

nationalist and racial implications of al-Kassar's theater, see Powell, "Burnt-Cork Nationalism."

150. *Al-Ahram*, June 8, 1915.

151. *Al-Minbar*, March 3, 1916.

152. See *al-Muqattam*, October 4, 1919; and *al-Ahram*, November 1, 1919.

153. *Al-Basir*, April 3, 1917.

154. *Al-Minbar*, August 20, 1918.

155. *Al-Ahram*, June 10, 1915.

156. Riyad and al-Sabah, *Tarikh Adab al-Sha'b*, 237–40. Some of these low songs written by al-Qadi include the famous "*Irkhi al-Sitara 'illi fi Rihna*" (Loosen the bind that is separating us), "*Ta'ala Ya Shatir Niruh al-'Anatir*" (Come on, kiddo, let's go to the park), and "*al-Hubb Dah Dah wa al-Hagr Kukh Kukh*" (Love is nice and parting is bad).

157. *Al-Masrah*, April 12, 19, and 26, 1926.

158. *Al-Masrah*, April 26, 1926. For a closer look at some of these sexualized *taqatiq*, see Lagrange, "Women."

159. *Misr*, February 22, 1919.

160. See Maktabat al-'Iskandariyya, *Sayyid Darwish*, v. 2, 378–79.

161. Ramzi, *Masrahuna 'Ayyam Zaman*, 110; al-Rihani, *Mudhakkirat Najib al-Rihani*, 113.

162. For a closer look at this phenomenon, see Racy, "Musical Change," 66.

163. *Al-Minbar*, September 3, 1918.

164. See Bakhtin, "Towards a Methodology," 169–72. This supports Mikhail Bakhtin's dialogical view of culture, which describes a dynamically ongoing dialogue between cultural producers and consumers.

165. Ramzi, *Masrahuna 'Ayyam Zaman*, 25.

166. See *al-Masrah*, July 25, 1927. Ramzi admits that he wrote into his plays many of the jokes that he heard in the coffee shop.

167. Khayri, *Mudhakkirat Badi' Khayri*, 10; al-Rihani, *Mudhakkirat Najib al-Rihani*, 26–27, 30.

## CHAPTER SIX

1. "Egyptian Unrest," April 1, 1919, Great Britain, Public Records Office, FO 371/3714/50207. The dispatch containing this song was titled "Translation of Song Now Popular in Egypt," and it clarifies that "this is the song which the little boys in the street in Cairo and the ladies in the harems have been singing lately." The Foreign Office intelligence report includes the entire song in Arabic and is accompanied by an English translation. However, because the translation is full of inaccuracies, I have retranslated parts of it to best capture the spirit of the song. Because this song was sung in the streets, there were many simultaneous versions of it, with slightly different lyrics. According to a contemporary, the first verses of the song went: "Pardon us, o Wingate! But our country is ruined (*khirbit*). . . . They killed our children, pillaged our country, and exiled our leader." See Mustafa Amin, *Min Wahid li-'Asharah*, 187.

2. Brown, *Peasant Politics*, 200.

3. Sir Milne Cheetham, "Egyptian Political Situation," March 9, 1919, Great Britain, Public Records Office, FO 371/3714/39690. For a detailed British analysis of what caused the revolt, see Great Britain, *Report of the Special Mission to Egypt*, 7–12.

4. The 'Umma Party favored a more gradual road to independence, advocating the need for consulting with and benefiting from the British whenever possible. Inherent in this policy was an aversion to any change in the stability of the status quo and a general distrust of the masses who were deemed unfit, so far, for political independence. For a look at the official platform of the Party, see *al-Jarida*, September 21, 1907. Many of the leading figures of the 'Umma Party, such as Zaghlul, Mahmud Sulayman Pasha, 'Ali Sha'rawi Pasha, and Lutfi al-Sayyid, would later form the new Wafd Party. See al-Shiliq, *Hizb al-'Umma*, 72–73.

5. Zaghlul's diary entries during this period reveal the story of a depressed man with an exaggerated sense of self-importance. He seems to have been increasingly aware of his own mortality and desperately in search of a cause to embrace. See Zaghlul, *Mudhakkirat Sa'd Zaghlul*, v. 7.

6. Terry, *The Wafd*, 7–8. Most of the early members of the Wafd Party were also members of the 'Umma Party.

7. Fahmi, *Mudhakkirat 'Abd al-Rahman Fahmi*, v. 1, 51, 59–60.

8. Ramadan, *Tatawwur al-Haraka*, 88.

9. For an account of the conversation between the Wafd leaders and Wingate, see Fahmi, *Mudhakkirat 'Abd al-Rahman Fahmi*, 47–48; 'Abd al-Nur, *Mudhakkirat Fakhri 'Abd al-Nur*, 39–50; and Ramadan, *Tatawwur al-Haraka*, 88–93.

10. Fahmi, *Mudhakkirat 'Abd al-Rahman Fahmi*, 51–52.

11. Ramadan, *Tatawwur al-Haraka*, 93–97; Terry, *The Wafd*, 82–84. Later, Mustafa al-Nahhas, Hafiz 'Afifi, Hamad al-Basil, Isma'il Sidqi, and Muhammad Abu al-Nasr were added to the party. Of the original seven members, only al-Sayyid was not a member of the Legislative Assembly.

12. Ramadan, *Tatawwur al-Haraka*, 6–7; Terry, *The Wafd*, 81.

13. Ghali, *L'Egypte nationaliste*, 169–70; Ramadan, *Tatawwur al-Haraka*, 106–7; al-Rafi'i, *Thawrat 1919*, 123–25.

14. This image of Woodrow Wilson as a potential "savior" of the colonized was quite prevalent at the time. See Manela, "Imagining Woodrow Wilson."

15. Sir Milne Cheetham to Curzon, Cairo, February 23, 1919, Great Britain, Public Records Office, FO 371/3714/38763.

16. Sir Milne Cheetham, "Egyptian Political Situation," March 6, 1919, Great Britain, Public Records Office, FO 371/3714/36312.

17. Sir Milne Cheetham, "Egyptian Political Situation," March 9, 1919, Great Britain, Public Records Office, FO 371/3714/39690.

18. Sir Milne Cheetham, "Egyptian Political Situation," March 9, 1919, Great Britain, Public Records Office, FO 371/3714/39198.

19. Sir Milne Cheetham, "Deportation of Egyptian Independence Leaders," March 10, 1919, Great Britain, Public Records Office, FO 371/3714/40278; Ghali, *L'Egypte nationaliste*, 173–75.

20. Sir Milne Cheetham, "Deportation of Egyptian Independence Leaders," March 10, 1919, Great Britain, Public Records Office, FO 371/3714/40278.

21. See *Misr*, March 12, 1919; and *al-Muqattam*, March 13, 1919.

22. Sir Milne Cheetham, "Military Report," March 15, 1919, Great Britain, Public Records Office, FO 371/3714/41569.

23. Sir Milne Cheetham, "Egyptian Unrest," March 15, 1919, Great Britain, Public Records Office, FO 371/3714/41615.

24. Sir Milne Cheetham, "Military Report," March 18, 1919, Great Britain, Public Records Office, FO 371/3714/43601.

25. General Officer Commanding, Royal Air Force, Cairo, to Sir Ronald Graham, March 17, 1919, Great Britain, Public Records Office, FO 371/3714/45524.

26. Ronald Graham, "Press Criticism of General Allenby," April 4, 1919, Great Britain, Public Records Office, FO 371/3714/52101.

27. *Al-'Afkar*, March 17, 1919; *al-Muqattam*, March 20, 1919; Sha'rawi, *Mudhakkirat Ra'idat al-Mar'ah al-'Arabiyya*, 166–86; Badran, *Feminists, Islam, and Nation*, 74–78. For an excellent analysis of the women's demonstrations and the press coverage of those events, see Baron, *Egypt as a Woman*, 107–34.

28. Col. F. H. Smith, "Intelligence Report," April 8, 1919, Great Britain, Public Records Office, FO 141/753/6/8952/2.

29. Terry, *The Wafd*, 110–22.

30. Beinin and Lockman, *Workers on the Nile*, 88–106; Gershoni and Jankowski, *Egypt, Islam, and the Arabs*, 54.

31. *Washington Post*, June 21, 1919. Because of British censorship, Ellis's editorials were not printed until a couple of months after the events. In May, Ellis was detained by the British authorities for more than a month; he was accused of sympathizing with and aiding the Egyptian nationalists. He was exonerated by Secretary of State Robert Lansing (1863–1928) in December 1919. See *New York Times*, August 18 and December 20, 1919.

32. Fahmi, *Mudhakkirat 'Abd al-Rahman Fahmi*, 220. Here, Fahmi is describing the April 7, 1919, demonstration held to celebrate the release of the Wafd leaders from Malta.

33. *Washington Post*, June 21, 1919.

34. *Washington Post*, June 21, 1919.

35. Fahmi, *Mudhakkirat 'Abd al-Rahman Fahmi*, 220–21. According to Fahmi, among the chants heard that day were "Long live Egypt, long live our independence, and long live our nationalist leaders."

36. "Intelligence Report on the Egyptian Situation," April 8, 1919, Great Britain, Public Records Office, FO 141/781/8915.

37. According to Mikhail Bakhtin, carnival culture allows for the "temporary suspension of all hierarchic distinctions and barriers among men." Bakhtin coined the term *carnivalesque* to refer to the carnivalizing that takes place in normal life. See Bakhtin, *Rabelais*, 15.

38. Baron, *Egypt as a Woman*, 140–41.

39. Badran, *Feminists, Islam, and Nation*, 81; Baron, *Egypt as a Woman*, 140–41.

40. Baron, *Egypt as a Woman*, 140.

41. Baron, *Egypt as a Woman*, 135–36.

42. "Intelligence Report on the Egyptian Situation," April 8, 1919, Great Britain, Public Records Office, FO 141/781/8915.

43. "Intelligence Report on the Egyptian Situation," April 8, 1919, Great Britain, Public Records Office, FO 141/781/8915.

44. "Intelligence Report on the Egyptian Situation," April 8, 1919, Great Britain, Public Records Office, FO 141/781/8915.

45. A translated copy of this pamphlet is included in Great Britain, Public Records Office, FO 141/781/8915, April 8, 1919.

46. Mubarak, *al-Khitat al-Tawfiqiyya*, v. 1, 218, 238. Mubarak also counted 532 bars and *buza* shops (*buza* is considered a "low-class" alcoholic drink and is made from fermented stale bread).

47. "Intelligence Report on the Egyptian Situation," May 5, 1919, Great Britain, Public Records Office, FO 141/781/8915. This report documents how illicit circulars were spread in urban coffee shops.

48. "Intelligence Report on the Egyptian Situation," April 8, 1919, Great Britain, Public Records Office, FO 141/781/8915.

49. "Intelligence Report on the Egyptian Situation," April 22, 1919, Great Britain, Public Records Office, FO 141/781/8915.

50. "Intelligence Report on the Egyptian Situation," May 6, 1919, Great Britain, Public Records Office, FO 141/781/8915. Groppi is a popular middle-class Cairene café/teahouse. It was opened in 1909 by an Italian man named Giacomo Groppi.

51. "Intelligence Report on the Egyptian Situation," May 3, 1919, Great Britain, Public Records Office, FO 141/781/8915.

52. Government employees began their strike on April 2, 1919, and most returned to their jobs on April 26. See *al-Akhbar*, April 26, 1919.

53. "Intelligence Report on the Egyptian Situation," April 26, 1919, Great Britain, Public Records Office, FO 141/781/8915.

54. *Al-Akhbar*, April 26, 1919.

55. "Intelligence Report on the Egyptian Situation," April 26, 1919, Great Britain, Public Records Office, FO 141/781/8915.

56. "Intelligence Report on the Egyptian Situation," May 30, 1919, Great Britain, Public Records Office, FO 141/781/8915.

57. The many cafés in the 'Imad al-Din Street theater district were the most notable exception to these "rules." Female singers and actresses frequented those cafés along with their male colleagues.

58. Sham al-Nasim, which literally means "inhaling the breeze," is a traditional nonsectarian Egyptian spring festival.

59. "Intelligence Report on the Egyptian Situation," April 24, 1919, Great Britain, Public Records Office, FO 141/781/8915.

60. "Intelligence Report on the Egyptian Situation," May 3, 1919, Great Britain, Public Records Office, FO 141/781/8915.

61. "Intelligence Report on the Egyptian Situation," May 5, 1919, Great Britain, Public Records Office, FO 141/781/8915.

62. "Intelligence Report on the Egyptian Situation," June 23, 1919, Great Britain, Public Records Office, FO 141/781/8915.

63. See "Intelligence Report on the Egyptian Situation," May 3, 1919, and June 23, 1919, Great Britain, Public Records Office, FO 141/781/8915.

64. "Intelligence Report on the Egyptian Situation," April 8, 1919, Great Britain, Public Records Office, FO 141/781/8915.

65. "Intelligence Report on the Egyptian Situation," April 7, 1919, Great Britain, Public Records Office, FO 141/781/8915.

66. See "Intelligence Report on the Egyptian Situation," April 5, 1919, Great Britain, Public Records Office, FO 141/781/8915. "With reference to this morning's meeting at Tulun Mosque, the road between Saida Zenab [Sayyida Zaynab] and Khaliba kism [qism] has been, it is reported, completely blocked by stones."

67. "Intelligence Report on the Egyptian Situation," April 28, 1919, Great Britain, Public Records Office, FO 141/781/8915.

68. "Intelligence Report on the Egyptian Situation," April 20, 1919, Great Britain, Public Records Office, FO 141/781/8915. See also *al-Ahram*, April 20, 1919; and *Misr*, April 19, 1919.

69. "Intelligence Report on the Egyptian Situation," June 2, 1919, Great Britain, Public Records Office, FO 141/781/8915.

70. "Intelligence Report on the Egyptian Situation," April 15, 1919, Great Britain, Public Records Office, FO 141/781/8915; 'Abd al-Nur, *Mudhakkirat Fakhri 'Abd al-Nur*, 57–60. Fakhri 'Abd al-Nur (1881–1942) was one of the key Coptic Christian Wafdist leaders.

71. "Intelligence Report on the Egyptian Situation," April 21, 1919, Great Britain, Public Records Office, FO 141/781/8915.

72. See, for example, *al-Watan*, March 10, 1919; and *al-Muqattam*, March 11, 1919.

73. *Al-Ahram*, March 11, 1919; *Misr*, March 11, 1919; *Wadi al-Nil*, March 11, 1919; *al-Mahrusa*, March 11, 1919.

74. Kamil, *al-Sahafa al-Wafdiyya*, 12–13, 17–18. Official press censorship laws were imposed again for fourteen months from March 6, 1920, until May 15, 1921.

75. *Al-Masamir*, March 30, 1919.

76. *Al-Masamir*, May 18, 1919.

77. "Intelligence Report on the Egyptian Situation," May 2, 1919, Great Britain, Public Records Office, FO 141/781/8915.

78. See *al-Ahram*, April 8, 1919; and *al-'Akhbar*, April 9, 1919.

79. "Intelligence Report on the Egyptian Situation," April 24, 1919, Great Britain, Public Records Office, FO 141/781/8915.

80. On June 25, 1919, the press censorship law was canceled, allowing the officially recognized press more flexibility. See *al-'Umma*, June 25, 1919.

81. "Intelligence Report on the Egyptian Situation," April 30, 1919, and September 20, 1919, Great Britain, Public Records Office, FO 141/781/8915.

82. "Intelligence Report on the Egyptian Situation," May 12, 1919, Great Britain, Public Records Office, FO 141/781/8915.

83. Khayri, *Mudhakkirat Badi' Khayri*, 43–44.

84. 'Abd al-Fattah, *al-Mas'ala al-Misriyya wa al-Wafd*, 174.

85. Amin, *Hayati*, 204–5.

86. See "Intelligence Report on the Egyptian Situation," May 21, 1919, Great Britain, Public Records Office, FO 141/781/8915.

87. Kamil, al-Sahafa al-Wafdiyya, 12.

88. "Intelligence Report on the Egyptian Situation," May 9, 1919, Great Britain, Public Records Office, FO 141/781/8915.

89. "Intelligence Report on the Egyptian Situation," September 20, 1919, Great Britain, Public Records Office, FO 141/781/8915.

90. For an analysis of this zajal, see Booth, Bayram al-Tunsi's Egypt, 594–95; and al-Tunsi, Mudhakkirati, 119–20. Al-Tunsi called these Qasa'id al-Bamiyya al-Sultani wa al-'Ar' al-Muluki wa al-Bitingan al-'Arusi (The sultan-like okra, kingly squash, and bride-like eggplant poems).

91. Al-Tunsi, Mudhakkirati, 121; al-'Azab, 'Azjal Bayram al-Tunsi, 24–25.

92. Khazuq in colloquial Egyptian literally means "getting screwed" or to be taken advantage of.

93. Booth, Bayram al-Tunsi's Egypt, 61. During his exile, al-Tunsi spent most of his time in France and Tunisia, although he returned clandestinely to Egypt and stayed there for a year from March 27, 1922, to May 25, 1923.

94. See "Intelligence Report on the Egyptian Situation," May 16, 1919, Great Britain, Public Records Office, FO 141/781/8915.

95. "Intelligence Report on the Egyptian Situation," April 30, 1919, Great Britain, Public Records Office, FO 141/781/8915.

96. "Intelligence Report on the Egyptian Situation," May 2, 1919, Great Britain, Public Records Office, FO 141/781/8915. Edith Cavell was a British nurse who was shot by the Germans in Belgium in 1915. After the incident, she became a celebrated hero for the Allies during World War I.

97. "Intelligence Report on the Egyptian Situation," May 12, 1919, Great Britain, Public Records Office, FO 141/781/8915.

98. "Intelligence Report on the Egyptian Situation," April 23, 1919, Great Britain, Public Records Office, FO 141/781/8915.

99. "Intelligence Report on the Egyptian Situation," April 23, 1919, Great Britain, Public Records Office, FO 141/781/8915.

100. Busta was taken from the Italian word posta.

101. "Intelligence Report on the Egyptian Situation," April 24, 1919, Great Britain, Public Records Office, FO 141/781/8915.

102. "Intelligence Report on the Egyptian Situation," May 2, 1919, Great Britain, Public Records Office, FO 141/781/8915.

103. "Intelligence Report on the Egyptian Situation," May 5, 1919, Great Britain, Public Records Office, FO 141/781/8915.

104. "Intelligence Report on the Egyptian Situation," April 15, 1919, Great Britain, Public Records Office, FO 141/781/8915.

105. Anderson, Imagined Communities, 35.

106. "Intelligence Report on the Egyptian Situation," April 9, 1919, Great Britain, Public Records Office, FO 141/781/8915.

107. Quoted in "Intelligence Report on the Egyptian Situation," July 15, 1919, Great Britain, Public Records Office, FO 141/781/8915.

108. "Intelligence Report on the Egyptian Situation," July 31, 1919, Great Brit-

ain, Public Records Office, FO 141/781/8915. Enver Pasha was the Ottoman minister of war during World War I. See also Booth, "Colloquial Arabic Poetry," 424.

109. "Intelligence Report on the Egyptian Situation," June 9, 1919, Great Britain, Public Records Office, FO 141/781/8915. "Seditious pamphlets are being widely distributed throughout the East Delta Area. They are said to be brought from Cairo by messengers who conceal the papers in their boots."

110. "Intelligence Report on the Egyptian Situation," July 15, 1919, Great Britain, Public Records Office, FO 141/781/8915.

111. "Intelligence Report on the Egyptian Situation," July 15, 1919, Great Britain, Public Records Office, FO 141/781/8915. See "'*Um ya Masri*" (Odeon 170).

112. "Intelligence Report on the Egyptian Situation," April 8, 1919, Great Britain, Public Records Office, FO 141/781/8915.

113. Riyad and al-Sabah, *Tarikh 'Adab al-Sha'b*, 232–33.

114. Riyad and al-Sabah, *Tarikh 'Adab al-Sha'b*, 231–37.

115. See Riyad and al-Sabah, *Tarikh 'Adab al-Sha'b*, 233–35.

> *Ya talbin al-'isti'lal*
> *Yahiya al-watan ya masryin*
> *Bil darb 'an kul al-a'mal*
> *Wa sakk abwab al-dawawin*
> *Ya rayis al-wizara—ma'sur*
> *'Arif hu'u'u bikul yaqin*
> *'Ahrar nitalbak bil-dustur*
> *Wi rad kayd al-muhtalin.*

116. For an excellent study on the impact of song culture on revolutions and the printing and distribution of songs, see Mason, "Songs."

117. al-Rihani, *Mudhakkirat Najib al-Rihani*, 113. This sum was a fortune by the standards of the day.

118. *Al-Minbar*, March 10, 1919; the article was titled "*Tharwat Kishkish*" (Kishkish's fortune). See also *al-Shabab*, November 13, 1919: "Today you see the Egyptian masses literally singing in the streets the songs of Kishkish and others like it from the theater."

119. 'Amin Sidqi used to write the words to al-Rihani's plays until a falling-out over money forced Sidqi to work for 'Ali al-Kassar's troupe.

120. *Al-Masrah*, July 18, 1927.

121. *Al-Masrah*, July 5, 1926.

122. A *buza* is an Egyptian drinking den where people drink *buza*, a cheap and potent beerlike alcoholic drink made from fermented bread. *Buza* was, and still is, especially popular in Upper Egypt, Nubia, and Sudan.

123. *Al-Masrah*, July 5, 1926.

124. Al-Rihani, *Mudhakkirat Najib al-Rihani*, 113. Amin, *Min Wahid li-'Asharah*, 188, 190.

125. *Al-Minbar*, March 15, 1919; *al-'Afkar*, March 30, 1919. *Al-Minbar* simply announced that the "theaters are still temporarily closed."

126. See Amin, *Min Wahid li-'Ashara*, 190–93.

127. Khayri, *Mudhakkirat Badi' Khayri*, 42–43. For Najib al-Rihani's description of these events, see al-Rihani, *Mudhakkirat Najib al-Rihani*, 115.

128. *'U'bal 'andukum* is a colloquial Egyptian phrase that is equivalent to saying "You're welcome." It is used to respond to a congratulatory remark. *Al-Watan* (April 1, 1919) and *al-Ahram* (April 9, 1919) advertised the play.

129. For an analysis of the nationalist and racial implications of al-Kassar's theater, see Powell, *Different Shade of Colonialism*, 185–95.

130. The earliest advertisement I could find for al-Rihani's plays after the British shutdown of theaters in March was dated May 5, although he probably reopened his theater earlier than that. See *Misr*, May 5, 1919.

131. *Al-'Ikspress*, July 6, 1919.

132. Many of the songs from *'Ululuh* were recorded by the record companies, including "*Shid al-Hizam*" (Odeon 171), "*Salma Ya Salama*" (Odeon 178), "*al-Bahr Biyidhak*" (Odeon 178), "*Da Ba'f Min 'Ili yi'Alis*" (Odeon 47711), "*Ya Wild 'Ami, Til'it ya Mahla Nurha*" (Mechian 652), "*'Um ya Masri*" (Odeon 170), "*Khafif al-Ruh*" (Mechian 589), and "*al-Qilal al-Qinawi*" (Mechian 797 and 665).

133. Al-Rihani, *Mudhakkirat Najib al-Rihani*, 117–18.

134. *Al-Ahram*, May 16, 1919; May 23, 1919; May 27, 1919. These *Ahram* advertisements emphasized that the music was by Sayyid Darwish.

135. "*'Um ya Masri*" (Odeon 170).

> *'Um Ya masri*
> *Masr dayman bitnadik*
> *Khud bi nasri*
> *Nasri dayn wagib 'alayk*
> *Yum ma Sa'di*
> *Rah hadar 'udam 'inayk*
> *'Idli magdi*
> *'Illi daya'tu bi'dayk*
> . . .
> *Shuft 'ayy*
> *Bilad ya masri fi il-gamal*
> *Tigi zayy*
> *Biladak 'illi turabha mal*
> *Nilha Gayy*
> *Al-Sa'd minu halal zalal*
> . . .
> *Hib garak*
> *'Abl ma tihib il-wugud*
> *'Ayh nasarah*
> *Wi muslimin 'al 'ayh wi yahud*
> *Di al-'Ibarah*
> *Nasl wahid mil-gudud*

The song is also known as "*Lahn al-Kashafa*" (The Boy Scouts tune). For the printed lyrics of this song, see Maktabat al-'Iskandariyya, *Sayyid Darwish*, v. 2, 415–16. The line in the song that declared, "What's the difference—Christian, Muslim, or Jew," has been changed (censored) in the recently printed addition. The word Jew (*yahud*) has been changed to soldiers (*gunud*).

136. Zaghlul dates are one among several varieties of dates native to Egypt.

137. See "*Balah Zaghlul*" (Mechian 687½ and Mechian 923).

*Ya balah zaghlul ya hiliywa*
*Ya balah, ya balah zaghlul*
*Allahu 'Akbar 'alayk ya sukkar*
*Ya gabir 'agbar—zaghlul ya balah*
*'Alayk 'anadi fi kul wadi*
*'Asdi muradi—zaghlul ya balah*
*Ya zar' baladi 'alayk ya wa'di*
*Ya bakht sa'di—zaghlul ya balah*
*Ya ruh biladak layh tal bi'adak*
*Ta'ala sun wiladak—zaghlul ya balah*

138. See "*Shaal al-Hamam*" (Baidaphon 83468).

*Shaal al hamam hatt al hamam*
*Min masr lil-Sudan*
*Zaghlul we 'albi mal 'ilayh*
*'Andahlu lama 'ahtag 'ilayh*
*Yifham lughaa 'illi yilaghih*
*Wi yi'ul hamayham ya hamam*
*'Ish' al-zaghalil ghiyyiti*
*Wi hubuhum min 'ismmiti*

139. Several successful songs from *Kullaha Yumayn* were recorded by Baidaphon, including "*al-Zibda*" (Baidaphon 64-63/823 and Baidaphon 82864), "*Nam ya Khufu*" (Baidaphon B82492), "*Yahiyya al-'Adl*" (Baidaphon 93-94/824), "*Gana al-Farah*" (Baidaphon 93-94/824), "*Intisarik ya Munira*" (Baidaphon 61-62/823), and "*al-Sibirtuh*" (Baidaphon 43-44/824).

140. The hose (*al-Khartum*) refers to the capital of Sudan, alluding to the fact that the British at the time were planning to annex all of Sudan in potential "deals" with the Egyptian nationalists.

141. See Maktabat al-'Iskandariyya, *Sayyid Darwish*, v. 2, 477–78.

*'Ihgim 'al nar 'awwy 'albak*
*'Iw'a il-khartum layruh minak*
*Dahhi hayatak lagl 'ikhwatak*
*Il-nar, il-nar ahsan mil-'ar*
*'Um ya masri ba'a wi sa'id*
*Di il-'id 'al 'id bitsa'id*
*'Iwhib nafsak lihayat baladak*
*'Inta wi 'ikhwatak tingid watanak*
*Dahi hayatak lagl 'ikhwatak*
*Il-nar, il-nar 'ahsan mil-'ar*
*'Adi al-rigal il-masryyin*
*'Illi bitihfaz 'arwahna*
*Naguna min fi'l il-zalimin*
*Khatru biruhum 'alashanna*
*Wi il-nar ma tihra'sh mukhliss*
*Wi masr di narha ganna*

142. For other representations of Egypt as a woman, see Baron, *Egypt as a Woman*.

143. Al-Mahdiyya's nationalistic "country butter" song, first performed in this play, was quite popular and sold thousands of copies with Baidaphon records. See *"al-Zibda"* (Baidaphon 64-63/823). Metaphorically, country butter, pigeons, and dates also symbolized the fruitfulness and bounty of the Egyptian countryside as an authentic manifestation of the Egyptian nation. *Baladi* also means "my nation."

144. *"Nam ya Khufu"* (Baidaphon B82492). For the written lyrics of the song, see Maktabat al-'Iskandariyya, *Sayyid Darwish*, v. 2, 481.

> Nam ya khufu wi 'istarih fi 'aman
> 'It-hadayna wi il-'adhab shufnah wi han
> Min ha yinsah il-darss dah tul il-zaman
> Ya 'azim al-magd ya bani il-haram
> Il-misihiyyin wayya il-muslimin kuluhum fi khidmitak mutatawi'in
> Wi 'itihadhum 'itihad lakin matin bukra nisbah 'arqa 'Umma fi il-'Ummam

145. For a synopsis of the play, see Maktabat al-'Iskandariyya, *Sayyid Darwish*, v. 2, 475.

146. Bakhtin, *Rabelais*, 15.

147. Bakhtin, *Dostoevsky's Poetics*, 128.


## CONCLUSION

1. It is worth noting that when the novels written by the mentioned authors were later "vernacularized" and adapted into films and radio and television serials, their "audience" and hence their impact were exponentially increased.

2. Briggs and Burke, *Social History of the Media*, 5, 22–23.

3. See Booth, "Colloquial Arabic Poetry," 423. Booth describes how *azjal* and colloquial satirical newspapers connected the masses and the nationalist elites.

4. Anderson, *Imagined Communities*, 6–7.

5. Briggs and Burke, *Social History of the Media*, 22–23.

6. Billig, *Banal Nationalism*, 15–16.

7. Billig, *Banal Nationalism*, 8.

8. This is similar to what was happening in France during roughly the same time period. See Weber, *Peasants into Frenchmen*, 486–88.

9. Briggs and Burke, *Social History of the Media*, 30.

10. See Ramzi, *Masrahuna 'Ayyam Zaman*, 25. At least three major cafés on Imad al-Din Street were frequented by actors, singers, writers, and musicians: Qahwat al-Fan (The Arts Café), Qahwat Barun (The Baron Cafés), and Qahwat Misr (The Egypt Café).

11. Bakhtin, *Dialogic Imagination*, 259. See also Bakhtin, "Towards a Methodology," 169–72.

12. Bakhtin, *Dostoevsky's Poetics*, 293.

13. See Charles D. Smith, "Crisis of Orientation"; Gershoni and Jankowski, *Redefining the Egyptian Nation*, 54–78.

14. Mahfuz's comment in the epigraph to this section is quoted in Cachia,

"Use of Colloquial," 20. All of Mahfuz's novels including the dialogue and speech of his fictional characters—from pashas to peasants—were unrealistically written in a form of Fusha.

15. For an analysis of the linguistic breakdown of Egyptian mass media today, see Haeri, *Sacred Language*, 30–34.

16. Haeri, *Sacred Language*, 150.

17. Armbrust, *Mass Culture*, 48. For an excellent overview of diglossia in Egypt, see the chapter titled "The Split Vernacular."

18. Beinin, "Writing Class," 192.

19. For an examination of the proliferation of cassette tapes in Cairo and the importance of recorded sermons, see Hirschkind, *Ethical Soundscape*. For *sha'bi* music and cassette tape dissemination, see Armbrust, *Mass Culture*, 173–84; Gordon, "Singing"; Swedenburg, "Sa'ida Sultan/Danna International"; and Danielson, "New Nightingales."

# References

ARCHIVAL AND UNPUBLISHED SOURCES

*Great Britain, Public Records Office, Kew Gardens*

FO 141        Embassy and Consular Archives, Egypt, Correspondence
FO 371        General Correspondence, Political
FO 407        Confidential Print, Egypt and the Sudan
PRO 30/57/42  Kitchener Papers

*Egypt, Dar al-Kutub al-Misriyya (Egyptian National Library), Cairo*
Arab-language periodicals (1877–1920)
Arabic phonograph records (1904–1920)

PUBLISHED GOVERNMENT SOURCES AND INDEXES

*Egypt*

*Annuaire statistique de l'Egypte* [Statistical yearbook of Egypt], 1909, 1914, 1918, and 1928–29. Ministère de Finance, Départment de la Statistique Générale. Cairo: National Printing Department.

*Dar al-Kutub al-Misriyya: Fihris al-Dawriyat al-'Arabiyya 'Alati Taqtaniha al-Dar* (Index of the periodicals contained in the Egyptian National Library). Cairo: Dar al-Kutub al-Misriyya, 1996.

Dar al-Kutub wa al-Watha'iq al-Qawmiyya. *Fihris al-Musiqa wa al-Ghina' al-'Arabi al-Qadim: al-Musajala 'Ala 'Istiwanat* (Index of all the musical records contained in the Egyptian National Library). Cairo: Matba'at Dar al-Kutub al-Misriyya, 1998.

Maktabat al-'Iskandariyya. *Sayyid Darwish: Mawsu'at 'I'lam al-Musiqa al-'Arabiyya*, 2 vols. Cairo: Dar al-Shuruq, 2003.

Mubarak, 'Ali Pasha. *al-Khitat al-Tawfiqiyya al-Jadida li Misr wa al-Qahira wa-Muduniha wa-Biladiha al-Qadima wa al-Shahira*, vols. 1–7. Cairo: Matba'at Dar al-Kutub wa al-Watha'iq al-Qawmiyya, 2005.

Sami Pasha, Amin. *Taqwim al-Nil*, v. 3. Cairo: Matba'at Dar al-Kutub al-Misriyya, 1936.


## Great Britain

Great Britain. *Report of the Special Mission to Egypt*. Egypt no. 1 (1921).

United Kingdom, Parliamentary Papers. *Further Paper Respecting the Attack on British Officers at Denshawai*. Egypt nos. 3 and 4 (1906).

United Kingdom, Parliamentary Papers. *Reports by His Majesty's Agent and Consul-General on the Finances, Administration, and Condition of Egypt and the Sudan* [annual reports], various years. London: Harrison & Sons.


## DISCOGRAPHY:
### RECORDED MUSIC AND COMEDIC SKETCHES

*Abu al-Kashakish* (Mechian 651 and Pathé Records 35004/18007)
*'Afiyit al-Fiqi* (Zonophone 102706)
*'Afiyit al-Turk* (Columbia Records 3339 and Odeon 47881)
*al-Bahr Biyidhak* (Odeon 178)
*Gana al-Farah* (Baidaphon 93-94/824)
*Intisarik ya Munira* (Baidaphon 61-62/823)
*Nam ya Khufu* (Baidaphon B82492)
*al-Qilal al-Qinawi* (Mechian 797 and 665)
*Salma Ya Salama* (Odeon 178)
*Shaykh Qufa'a* (Odeon 172 and Odeon 47714)
*Shid al-Hizam* (Odeon 171)
*al-Sibirtu* (Baidaphon 43-44/824)
*Til'it ya Mahla Nurha* (Mechian 652)
*'Um ya Misri* (Odeon 170)
*Yahiyya al-'Adl* (Baidaphon 93-94/824)
*al-Zibda* (Baidaphon 64-63/823)


### ARABIC PERIODICALS

All periodicals were printed in Cairo, unless otherwise indicated.

*'Abu-al-Hul*                          *al-'Alam al-Misri*
*Abu-Naddara Zarqa' [Zar'a]* (Paris)   *al-Arghul*
*al-Adab wa al-Tamthil*                *al-'Arnab*
*al-'Afkar*                            *al-Babaghlu al-Misri*
*al-'Afrit*                            *Baghlit al-'Ishar*
*'Afrit al-Hammara*                    *al-Bahbaha*
*'Afrit al-Muqawalin*                  *al-Bahlul*
*al-'Aga'ib*                           *al-Basass*
*al-'Ahram*                            *al-Bo'bo'*

al-Dabba
Did al-Khala'a
al-Dik
al-Fil al-Abyyad
al-Fukaha
al-Ghazala
Ghazl al-Banat
Guhha
Ha Ha Ha
al-Hammara
al-Hawanim
al-Hilal
Humarat Munyati
al-Ibtisam (Alexandria)
al-'Ikspras (The Express)
Jaridat Misr
al-Kashkul
al-Kashkul al-Musawwar
al-Kawkab al-Misri
al-Khala'a
al-Khala'a al-Misriyya
al-Khala'a al-Wataniyya
Khayal al-Zil
al-Khila al-Kadaba
al-Lata'if (Cairo)
al-Lata'if al-Musawwara
al-Ligam
al-Magnun
al-Mahbub
Majallat Sarkis
al-Maqsud
al-Masala
al-Masamir

al-Masrah
al-Mirzaba
Misr
al-Missih al-Dagal
al-Mu'ayid
al-Muftah
al-Muhit
al-Muqattam
al-Nukta
al-Qahira
al-Ra'd
Rawdat al-Madaris al-Misriyya
Ruz al-Yusuf
al-Sa'iqa
al-Sanf
al-Sarukh
al-Sayf
Sayf al-'Adala
al-Shaga'a
Silsilat al-Fukahat
al-Surur (Alexandria)
al-Tamthil (Alexandria)
al-Tankit wa al-Tabkit (Alexandria/Cairo)
al-Tara'if
al-Tijara
al-Timsah
al-Ustadh
al-Waqa'i' al-Misriyya
al-Watan
al-Zara'if
al-Zuhur
al-Zumar (Alexandria)

## ENGLISH AND FRENCH PERIODICALS

Le Figaro (Paris)
L'Illustration (Paris)
New York Times

The Times (London)
L'Univers Musulman (Paris)
Washington Post

## PUBLISHED DIARIES, MEMOIRS, LETTERS, AND SPEECHES

'Abd al-Nur, Fakhri. *Mudhakkirat Fakhri 'Abd al-Nur, Thawrat 1919: Dawr Sa'd Zaghlul wa al-Wafd fi al-Haraka al-Wataniyya*. Cairo: Dar al-Shuruq, 1992.

Amin, Ahmad. *Hayati*. Cairo: Matabi' al-Hay'a al-Misriyya al-'Amma lil-Kitab, 2003 [1950].

Amin, Mustafa. *Min Wahid li-'Ashara*. Cairo: al-Maktab al-Misri al-Hadith Lil-Tiba'a wa al-Nashr, 1977.

Fahmi, 'Abd al-Rahman. *Mudhakkirat 'Abd al-Rahman Fahmi: Yawmiyat Misr al-Siyasiyya*, pt. 1. Cairo: al-Hay'a al-Misriyya al-'Amma lil-Kitab, 1988.

Jum'a, Muhammad Lutfi. *Shahid 'Ala al-'Asr: Mudhakkirat Muhammad Lutfi Jum'a, 1886–1937*. Cairo: al-Hay'a al-Misriyya al-'Amma lil-Kitab, 2000.

Kamil, Mustafa. *'Awraq Mustafa Kamil: al-Khutab*, ed. and comp. Yuaqim Rizq Murqus. Cairo: al-Hay'a al-Misriyya al-'Amma lil-Kitab, 1984.

———. *'Awraq Mustafa Kamil: al-Murasalat*. Cairo: al-Hay'a al-Misriyya al-'Amma lil-Kitab, 1982.

———. *What the National Party Wants: Speech Delivered on 22nd October 1907 in the Zizinia Theater at Alexandria*. Cairo: Egyptian Standard, 1907.

Khayri, Badi'. *Mudhakkirat Badi' Khayri: Khamsa wa Arbi'un Sana 'ala Adwa' al-Masrah*. Beirut: Dar al-Thaqafa, n.d.

Musa, Nabawiyya. *Tarikhi Biqalami*. Cairo: Multaqa al-Mar'a wa al-Dhakira, 1999.

al-Naqash, Salim Khalil. *Misr li al-Misriyyin*, v. 4. Cairo: al-Hay'a al-Misriyya al-'Amma lil-Kitab, 1986 [1884].

al-Rafi'i, 'Abd al-Rahman. *Mudhakkirati: 1889–1951*. Cairo: Dar al-Hilal, 1952.

Ramzi, Ibrahim. *Masrahuna 'Ayyam Zaman wa Tarikh al-Fananin al-Qudama'*. Cairo: Matba'at al-Salam, 1984.

al-Rihani, Najib. *Mudhakkirat Najib al-Rihani*. Cairo: Dar al-Hilal, 1959.

al-Sayyid, Ahmad Lutfi. *Qisat Hayati*. Cairo: Dar al-Hilal, 1982.

Shafiq Pasha, Ahmad. *Mudhakkirati fi Nisf Qarn*, v. 3. Cairo: al-Hay'a al-Misriyya al-'Amma lil-Kitab, 1998 [1934].

———. *Mudhakkirati fi Nisf Qarn: min Sanat 1873 ilá Sanat 1923*, v. 2. Cairo: al-Hay'a al-Misriyya al-'Amma lil-Kitab, 1994.

Sha'rawi, Huda. *Mudhakkirat Ra'idat al-Mar'a al-'Arabiyya*. Cairo: Dar al-Hilal, 1981.

Sharubim, Mikha'il. *al-Kafi fi Tarikh Misr al-Qadim wa al-Hadith*, v. 4. Cairo: Maktabat Matbuli, 2004 [1898–1900].

———. *al-Kafi fi Tarikh Misr al-Qadim wa al-Hadith*, v. 5. Cairo: Matba'at Dar al-Kutub wa al-Watha'iq al-Qawmiyya bil-Qahira, 2003.

al-Tunsi, Mahmud Bayram. *Mudhakkirati: al-Majmu'a al-Kamila*. Tunis: Dar al-Janub lil-Nashr, 2001.

Zaghlul, Sa'd. *Mudhakkirat Sa'd Zaghlul*, vols. 1–8, comp. 'Abd al-'Aziz Ramadan. Cairo: al-Hay'a al-Misriyya al-'Amma lil-Kitab, 1996.

## ARABIC SECONDARY SOURCES

'Abd al-Fatah, Mahmud. *al-Mas'ala al-Misriyya wa al-Wafd.* Cairo: n.p., 1921.

'Abduh, Ibrahim. *A'lam al-Sahafah fi Misr.* Cairo: Maktabat al-'Adab, 1948.

'Abu Buthayna. *al-Zajal wa al-Zajalun.* Cairo: n.p., 1962.

al-'Allati, Hasan. *Kitab Tarwih al-Nufus wa Mudhik al-'Ubus*, 2 vols. Cairo: Matba'at Jaridat al-Mahrusa, 1889.

'Anus, Najwa Ibrahim. *Masrah Ya'qub Sannu'.* Cairo: al-Hay'a al-Misriyya al 'Amma lil-Kitab, 1984.

al-'Azab, Yusri. *'Azjal Bayram al-Tunsi: Dirasa Fanniyya.* Cairo: al-Hay'a al-Misriyya al-'Amma lil-Kitab, 1981.

Baibars, Ahmed Samir. *al-Masrah al-'Arabi fi al-Qarn al-Tasi' 'Ashr.* Cairo: Sa'id Ra'fat lil-Tiba'a, 1985.

Darwish, Hasan. *Min 'Ajl 'Abi: Sayyid Darwish.* Cairo: al-Hay'a al-Misriyya al-'Amma lil-Kitab, 1990.

al-Fil, Muhammad. *Ru'yat wa Bayan Halat al-Masrah al-'Arabi: Ta'sis al-Kumidiyya.* Cairo: al-Hay'a al-Misriyya al-'Amma lil-Kitab, 2004.

Ghonaim, 'Abd al-Hamid. *Sannu': Ra'id al-Masrah al-Misri.* Cairo: al-Dar al-Qawmiyya lil-Taba'a wa al-Nashr, 1966.

al-Hadidi, 'Ali. *'Abdallah al-Nadim: Khatib al-Wataniyya.* Cairo: Maktabat Misr, 1986.

Haqqi, Mahmud Taher. *'Adhra' Dinshaway.* Cairo: al-Maktaba al-'Arabiyya lil-Nashr, 1964 [1909].

al-Hifni, Mahmud Ahmad. *Sayyid Darwish: Hayatuhu wa Athar 'Abqariatuhu.* Cairo: Dar Misr Lil-Tiba'a, 1962.

al-Hifni, Ratiba. *al-Sultana Munira al-Mahdiyya: Wa al-Ghina' fi Misr Qablaha wa fi Zamanaha.* Cairo: Dar al-Shuruq, 2001.

Hijazi, 'Amina. *al-Wataniyya al-Misriyya fi al-'Asr al-Hadith: Nash'atuha wa Numuwaha hata 'Am 1914.* Cairo: al-Hay'a al-Misriyya al-'Amma lil Kitab, 2000.

Isma'il, Sayyid 'Ali. *Masirat al-Masrah fi Misr 1900–1935: al-Masrah al-Ghina'i.* Cairo: al-Hay'a al-Misriyya al-'Amma lil Kitab, 2003.

———. *Tarikh al-Masrah fi Misr fi al-Qarn al-Tasi' 'Ashr.* Cairo: al-Hay'a al-Misriyya al-'Amma lil Kitab, 1998.

Jabr, Mustafa al-Nahas. *Siyasat al-'Ihtilal Tijah al-Haraka al-Wataniyya min 1914–1936.* Cairo: al-Hay'a al-Misriyya al-'Amma lil-Kitab, 1985.

Jalal, al-Sayyid Husayn. *Mu'ammarat Mad Imtiyaz Qanat al-Suways.* Cairo: al-Hay'a al-Misriyya al-'Amma lil-Kitab, 1990.

Jalal, 'Uthman. *al-Riwayat al-Mufida fi 'Ilm al-Trajida.* Cairo: n.p., 1892.

al-Jumay'i, 'Abd al-Min'im. *'Abdallah al-Nadim wa-Dawruh fi al-Haraka al-Siyasiyya wa al-'Ijtima'iyya.* Cairo: Dar al-Kitab al-Jami'i, 1980.

Kamal, Safwat. *al-Ghina' al-Sha'bi al-Misri: Mawawil wa Qisas Ghina'iyya Sha'biyya.* Cairo: al-Hay'a al-Misriyya al-'Amma lil-Kitab, 1994.

Kamil, Najwa. *al-Sahafa al-Wafdiyya wa al-Qadiyya al-Wataniyya, 1919–1936.* Cairo: al-Hay'a al-Misriyya al-'Amma lil-Kitab, 1989.

Khurshid, Faruq. *al-Judhur al-Sha'biyya lil-Masrah al-'Arabi.* Cairo: al-Hay'a al-Misriyya al-'Amma lil-Kitab, 1991.

Najm, Muhammad Yusuf. *al-Masrah al-'Arabi: Dirasat wa Nusus*, v. 3, *Ya'qub Sannu'*. Beirut: Dar al-Thaqafa, 1963.

———. *al-Masrah al-'Arabi: Dirasat wa Nusus*, v. 4, *Muhammad 'Uthman Jalal*. Beirut: Dar al-Thaqafa, 1964.

Nussayr, 'Ayda 'Ibrahim. *al-Kutub al-'Arabiyya 'Allati Nusharat fi Misr Bayn 'Am 1900–1925*. Cairo: Qism al-Nashr bil-Jami'a al-'Amrikiyya bil-Qahira, 1983.

———. *Harakat Nashr al-Kutub fi Misr fi al-Qarn al-Tasi' 'Ashr*. Cairo: al-Hay'a al-Misriyya al-'Amma lil-Kitab, 1994.

———. *al-Kutub al-'Arabiyya Allati Nusharat fi Misr fi al-Qarn al-Tasi' 'Ashr*. Cairo: Qism al-Nashr bil-Jami'a al-'Amrikiyya bil-Qahira, 1990.

Qabil, Muhammad. *Mawsu'at al-Ghina' al-Misri fi al-Qarn al-'Ishrin*. Cairo: al-Hay'a al-Misriyya al-'Amma lil-Kitab, 1999.

Rachid, Bahija. *al-Taqatiq al-Sha'biyya*. Cairo: al-Lajna al-Musiqiyya al-'Ulya, 1968.

al-Rafi'i, 'Abd al-Rahman. *'Asr Isma'il*, v. 1. Cairo: Dar al-Ma'arif, 1987.

———. *'Asr Muhammad 'Ali*. Cairo: Dar al-Ma'arif, 2001.

———. *Mustafa Kamil: Ba'ith al-Haraka al-Wataniyya*, 5th ed. Cairo: Dar al-Ma'arif, 1985.

———. *Shu'ara' al-Wataniyya fi Misr: Tarajimahum wa Shi'rihum al-Watani wa al-Munasabat 'Allati Nazamu fiha Qasa'idahum*. Cairo: Dar al-Ma'arif, 1992 [1954].

———. *al-Thawra al-'Urabiyya wal-'Ihtilal al 'Injilizi*, 2 vols. Cairo: n.p., 1949.

———. *Thawrat 1919: Tarikh Misr al-Qawmi min 1914 'ila 1921*. Cairo: Dar al-Ma'arif, 1987 [1946].

al-Ra'i, 'Ali. *Funun al-Kumidiyya: Min Khayal al-Zil 'ila Najib al-Rihani*. Cairo: Dar al-Hilal, 1971.

———. *al-Kumidiyya al-Murtajila fi al-Masrah al-Misri*. Cairo: Dar al-Hilal, 1968.

Ramadan, 'Abd al-'Azim. *Tatawwur al-Haraka al-Wataniyya fi Misr, 1918–1936*. Cairo: al-Hay'a al-Misriyya al-'Amma lil-Kitab, 1998.

Riyad, Husayn Mazlum, and Mustafa Muhammad al-Sabah. *Tarikh 'Adab al-Sha'b: Nash'atuhu, Tatawiratuhu, A'lamuhu*. Cairo: Matba'at al-Sa'ada, 1936.

al-Saghir, 'Isam Diya' al-Din al-Sayyid 'Ali. *al-Hizb al-Watani wa al-Nidal al-Siri, 1907–1915*. Cairo: al-Hay'a al-Misriyya al-'Amma lil-Kitab, 1987.

al-Sahm, Sami Sulayman Muhammad. *al-Ta'lim wa al-Taghiyir al-'Ijtima'i fi Misr fi al-Qarn al-Tasi' 'Ashr*. Cairo: al-Hay'a al-Misriyya al-'Amma lil-Kitab, 2000.

Sa'id, Naffusa Zakariyya. *'Abdallah al-Nadim Bayna al-Fusha wa al-'Ammiyya*. Alexandria: al-Dar al-Qawmiyya lil-Tiba'a wa al-Nashr, 1966.

———. *Tarikh al-Da'wah 'Ila al-'Ammiyya wa-'Atharaha fi Misr*. Alexandria: Dar Nashr al-Thaqafah, 1964.

Salih, Ahmad Rushdi. *al-'Adab al-Sha'bi*. Cairo: al-Hay'a al-Misriyya al-'Amma lil-Kitab, 2002 [1956].

Salim, Latifah Muhammad. *Misr fi al-Harb al-'Alamiyya al-'Ula*. Cairo: al-Hay'a al-Misriyya al-'Amma lil-Kitab, 1984.

Sami Pasha, Amin. *al-Ta'lim fi Misr fi Sanat 1914–1915*. Cairo: Matba'at al-Ma'arif, 1917.

Saqr, 'Izat. *Diwan Amir Fan al-Zajal*. Cairo: n.p., 1933.

al-Shiliq, Ahmad Zakariyya. *Hizb al-'Umma wa Dawruha fi al-Siyasa al-Misriyya*. Cairo: Dar al-Ma'arif, 1979.

al-Shirbini, Ahmad. *Tarikh al-Tijara al-Misriyya fi 'Asr al-Hurriyya al-'Iqtisadiyya, 1840–1914*. Cairo: al-Haiy'a al-Misriyya al-'Amma lil-Kitab, 1995.

Tawfiq, Najib. *'Abdallah al-Nadim: Khatib al-Thawra al-'Urabiyya*. Cairo: Maktabat al-Kuliyyat al-Azhariyya, 1970.

Taymur (Pasha), Ahmad. *al-'Amthal al-Sha'biyya*. Cairo: Markaz al-'Ahram lil-Targamma wa al-Nashr, 1986.

'Umar, Muhammad. *Hadir al-Misriyyin 'Aw Sirr Ta'akhkhurihum*. Cairo: Matba'at al-Muqtataf, 1902.

Zaki, 'Abd al-Hamid Tawfiq. *'A'lam al-Musiqa al-Misriyya 'Abr 150 Sana*. Cairo: al-Hay'a al-Misriyya al-'Amma lil Kitab, 1990.

———. *al-Tadhawuq al-Musiqi wa Tarikh al-Musiqa al-Misriyya*. Cairo: al-Hay'a al-Misriyya al-'Amma lil-Kutub, 1995.

Zaydan, Jurji. *Tarajim Mashahir al-Sharq fi al-Qarn al-Tasi'ashr*. Cairo: Dar al-Hilal, 1922.

## WORKS IN ENGLISH AND FRENCH

Abdel-Malek, Kamal. *A Study of the Vernacular Poetry of Ahmad Fu'ad Nigm*. Leiden: Brill, 1990.

Abou Saif, Laila. "Najib al-Rihani: From Buffoonery to Social Comedy." *Journal of Arabic Literature* 4 (1973): 1–17.

———. "The Theatre of Naguib al-Rihani: The Development of Comedy in Modern Egypt." Ph.D. dissertation, University of Illinois at Urbana-Champaign, 1969.

Abul Naga, Atia. *Les sources françaises du théâtre Egyptien (1870–1839)*. Madrid: Altamira-Rotopress, 1972.

Abu-Lughod, Lila. "Bedouins, Cassettes, and Technologies of Public Culture." *Middle East Report* (July–August 1989): 25–30.

———. "Writing Against Culture." In *Recapturing Anthropology: Working in the Present*, ed. Richard G. Fox. Santa Fe, NM: School of American Research Press, 1991.

Adam, Juliette. *L'Angleterre en Egypte*. Paris: Imprimerie du Centre, 1922.

Ahmed, Jamal Mohammed. *Intellectual Origins of Egyptian Nationalism*. London: Oxford University Press, 1960.

Anderson, Benedict. *Imagined Communities: Reflections on the Origins and Spread of Nationalism*, 2nd ed. New York: Verso Press, 1991.

Armbrust, Walter. "The Formation of National Culture in Egypt in the Interwar Period: Cultural Trajectories." *History Compass* 7(1) (2009): 155–80.

———. *Mass Culture and Modernism in Egypt*. Cambridge: Cambridge University Press, 1996.

———. *Mass Mediations: New Approaches to Popular Culture in the Middle East and Beyond*. Berkeley: University of California Press, 2000.

Armstrong, John. *Nations Before Nationalism*. Chapel Hill: University of North Carolina Press, 1982.

Asma, A., and M. Zahniser, eds. *Humanism, Culture, and Language in the Near East: Studies in Honor of Georg Krotkoff*. Baltimore: Eisenbrauns, 1997.

Ayalon, Ami. *The Press in the Arab Middle East: A History*. London: Oxford University Press, 1995.

Badawi, M. M. *Early Arabic Drama*. Cambridge: Cambridge University Press, 1988.

Badran, Margot. *Feminists, Islam, and Nation: Gender and the Making of Modern Egypt*. Princeton, NJ: Princeton University Press, 1995.

Badrawi, Malak. *Political Violence in Egypt, 1910–1924: Secret Societies, Plots, and Assassinations*. London: Curzon Press, 2000.

Bakhtin, Mikhail. *The Dialogic Imagination: Four Essays*. Austin: University of Texas Press, 2006.

———. *Problems of Dostoevsky's Poetics*, ed. and trans. Caryl Emerson. Minneapolis: University of Minnesota Press, 1984.

———. *Rabelais and His World*. Bloomington: Indiana University Press, 1984.

———. "Towards a Methodology of the Human Sciences." In *Speech Genres and Other Late Essays*, ed. C. Emerson and M. Holquist, 159–72. Austin: University of Texas Press, 1986.

Baron, Beth. *Egypt as a Woman: Nationalism, Gender, and Politics*. Berkeley: University of California Press, 2005.

———. *The Women's Awakening in Egypt: Culture, Society, and the Press*. New Haven, CT: Yale University Press, 1994.

Beinin, Joel. *The Dispersion of Egyptian Jewry: Culture Politics and the Formation of a Modern Diaspora*. Berkeley: University of California Press, 1998.

———. "Writing Class: Workers and Modern Egyptian Colloquial Poetry (Zajal)." *Poetics Today* 15(2) (summer 1994): 191–215.

Beinin, Joel, and Zachary Lockman. *Workers on the Nile: Nationalism, Communism, Islam, and the Egyptian Working Class, 1882–1954*. Cairo: American University in Cairo Press, 1998.

Berdine, Michael D. *The Accidental Tourist, Wilfrid Scawen Blunt, and the British Invasion of Egypt in 1882*. London: Routledge, 2005.

Berque, Jacques. *Egypt: Imperialism and Revolution*, trans. John Stewart. London: Faber & Faber, 1972.

Billig, Michael. *Banal Nationalism*. London: Sage, 1995.

Blunt, Wilfrid Scawen. *My Diaries: Being a Personal Narrative of Events, 1888–1914*, 2 vols. New York: Knopf, 1922.

Boktor, Amir. *School and Society in the Valley of the Nile*. Cairo: Elias' Modern Press, 1936.

Booth, Marilyn. *Bayram al-Tunsi's Egypt: Social Criticism and Narrative Strategies*. Exeter, UK: Ithaca Press, 1990.

———. "Colloquial Arabic Poetry, Politics, and the Press in Modern Egypt." *International Journal of Middle East Studies* 24 (1992): 419–40.

———. *May Her Likes Be Multiplied: Biography and Gender Politics in Egypt*. Berkeley: University of California Press, 2001.

Bourdieu, Pierre. *Distinction: A Social Critique of the Judgment of Taste.* Cambridge, MA: Harvard University Press, 2000.

———. *Language and Symbolic Power.* Cambridge, MA: Harvard University Press, 1991.

Boyd, Douglas. *Broadcasting in the Arab World: A Survey of the Electronic Media in the Middle East.* Ames: Iowa State University Press, 1999.

Brass, Paul R. *Ethnicity and Nationalism: Theory and Comparison.* New Delhi: Sage, 1991.

Breuilly, John. *Nationalism and the State.* Chicago: University of Chicago Press, 1994.

Briggs, Asa, and Peter Burke. *A Social History of the Media: From Gutenberg to the Internet.* Cambridge: Polity Press, 2002.

Brown, Nathan J. *Peasant Politics in Modern Egypt: Struggle Against the State.* New Haven, CT: Yale University Press, 1990.

Browne, Ray B. "Popular Culture: Notes Towards a Definition." In *Popular Culture Theory and Methodology: A Basic Introduction*, ed. Harold E. Hinds, Marilyn Motz, and Angela Nelson, 15–22. Madison: University of Wisconsin Press, 2006.

Burckhardt, John Lewis. *Arabic Proverbs and the Manners and Customs of Modern Egyptians.* London: Bernard Quaritch, 1875.

Burke, Peter. *Popular Culture in Early Modern Europe.* London: Maurice Temple Smith, 1978.

Cachia, Pierre. *Popular Narrative Ballads of Modern Egypt.* Oxford: Clarendon Press, 1989.

———. "The Use of Colloquial in Modern Arabic Literature." *Journal of American Oriental Studies* 87(1) (1967): 12–22.

Carlier, Omar. "Le café maure: Sociabilité masculine et effervescence citoyenne (Algérie, XVIIᵉ–XXᵉ siècles)." *Annales: Histoire, Sciences Sociales* 45(4) (1990): 975–1004.

Chalcraft, John T. *The Striking Cabbies of Cairo and Other Stories: Crafts and Guilds in Egypt, 1863–1914.* Albany: State University of New York Press, 2004.

Chatterjee, Partha. *The Nation and Its Fragments: Colonial and Postcolonial Histories.* Princeton, NJ: Princeton University Press, 1993.

Clifford, James. *The Predicament of Culture: Twentieth-Century Ethnography, Literature, and Art.* Cambridge, MA: Harvard University Press, 1988.

Cole, Juan R. I. *Colonialism and Revolution in the Middle East: Social and Cultural Origins of Egypt's 'Urabi Movement.* Cairo: American University in Cairo Press, 1999.

———. "Printing and Urban Islam in the Mediterranean World, 1890–1920." In *Modernity and Culture from the Mediterranean to the Indian Ocean*, ed. Leila Fawaz and C. A. Bayly, 344–64. New York: Columbia University Press, 2002.

Colla, Elliott. *Conflicted Antiquities: Egyptology, Egyptomania, Egyptian Modernity.* Durham, NC: Duke University Press, 2007.

Connor, Walker. "A Nation Is a Nation, Is a State, Is an Ethnic Group, Is a . . ." *Ethnic and Racial Studies* 1(4) (1978): 378–400.

Corbin, Alain. *Time, Desire, and Horror: Towards a History of the Senses.* Cambridge: Polity Press, 1995.

———. *Village Bells: Sound and Meaning in the 19th-Century French Countryside.* New York: Columbia University Press, 1998.

Cromer, Evelyn Baring. *Abbas II.* London: Macmillan, 1915.

———. *Modern Egypt.* New York: Macmillan, 1908.

Cuno, Kenneth M. *The Pasha's Peasants: Land, Society, and Economy in Lower Egypt, 1740–1858.* Cambridge: Cambridge University Press, 1992.

Danielson, Virginia. "Artists and Entrepreneurs: Female Singers in Cairo During the 1920s." In *Women in Middle Eastern History: Shifting Boundaries in Sex and Gender,* ed. Nikki Keddie and Beth Baron, 292–309. New Haven, CT: Yale University Press, 1991.

———. "New Nightingales of the Nile: Popular Music in Egypt Since the 1970s." *Popular Music* 15(3) (1996): 299–312.

———. *The Voice of Egypt: Umm Kalthum, Arabic Song, and Egyptian Society in the Twentieth Century.* Chicago: University of Chicago Press, 1997.

Darnton, Robert. "An Early Information Society: News and the Media in Eighteenth-Century Paris." *American Historical Review* 105(1) (2000): 1–35.

Deeb, Maurius. *Party Politics in Egypt: The Wafd and Its Rivals, 1919–1939.* London: Ithaca Press, 1979.

Delanoue, Gilbert. "'Abd Allah Nadim (1845–1896): Les idées politiques et morales d'un journaliste Egyptien." *Bulletin d'Etudes Orientales* 17 (1961–1962): 75–120.

Deny, J. *Sommaire des archives turques du Caire.* Cairo: Société royale de géographie d'Egypte, 1930.

Di-Capua, Yoav. *Gatekeepers of the Arab Past: Historians and History Writing in Twentieth-Century Egypt.* Berkeley: University of California Press, 2009.

Dickie, John. *Darkest Italy: The Nation and the Stereotypes of the Mezzogiorno, 1860–1900.* New York: St. Martin's Press, 1999.

Edensor, Tim. *National Identity, Popular Culture, and Everyday Life.* Oxford: Berg Press, 2002.

Fahmy, Khaled. *All the Pasha's Men: Mehmed Ali, His Army, and the Making of Modern Egypt.* Cambridge: Cambridge University Press, 1997.

Fahmy, Ziad. "Francophone Egyptian Nationalists, Anti-British Discourse, and European Public Opinion, 1885–1910: The Case of Mustafa Kamil and Ya'qub Sannu'." *Comparative Studies of South Asia, Africa, and the Middle East* 28(1) (2008): 170–83.

———. "Media Capitalism: Colloquial Mass Culture and Nationalism in Egypt, 1908–1918." *International Journal of Middle Eastern Studies* 42(1) (2010): 83–103.

Ferguson, Charles A. "The Arabic Koine." *Language* 35 (1959): 616–30.

———. "Diglossia." *Word* 15 (1959): 325–40.

Fine, Gary Alan. "Popular . . . Culture: Sociological Issues and Explorations." *Journal of Popular Culture* 11(2) (1977): 381–84.

Fyfe, H. Hamilton. *The New Spirit in Egypt.* London: William Blackwood & Sons, 1911.

Gasper, Michael Ezekiel. *The Power of Representation: Publics, Peasants, and Islam in Egypt*. Stanford, CA: Stanford University Press, 2009.

Geertz, Clifford. *The Interpretation of Cultures*. New York: Basic Books, 1973.

———, ed. *Old Societies and New States: The Quest for Modernity in Asia and Africa*. New York: Collier-Macmillan, 1963.

Gellner, Ernest. *Nations and Nationalism*. Oxford: Blackwell Press, 1983.

Gendzier, Irene. *The Practical Visions of Ya'qub Sanu'*. Cambridge, MA: Harvard University Press, 1966.

Gershoni, Israel, and James P. Jankowski. *Egypt, Islam, and the Arabs: The Search for Egyptian Nationhood, 1900–1930*. New York: Oxford University Press, 1986.

———. "Print Culture, Social Change, and the Process of Redefining Imagined Communities in Egypt." *International Journal of Middle East Studies* 31 (1999): 81–94.

———. *Redefining the Egyptian Nation, 1930–1945*. New York: Cambridge University Press, 1995.

Ghali, Ibrahim. *L'Egypte nationaliste et libérale de Moustapha Kamel à Saad Zaggloul, 1892–1927*. The Hague: Martinus Nijhoff, 1969.

Goldberg, Ellis. "Peasants in Revolt: Egypt 1919." *International Journal of Middle East Studies* 24(2) (1992): 261–80.

Goldschmidt, Arthur. *Biographical Dictionary of Modern Egypt*. London: Lynne Rienner, 2000.

———. "The Egyptian Nationalist Party, 1892–1919." In *Political and Social Change in Modern Egypt*, ed. P. M. Holt, 308–33. London: Oxford University Press, 1968.

Goldschmidt, Arthur, Amy Johnson, and Barak Salmoni, eds. *Re-Envisioning Egypt, 1919–1952*. Cairo: American University in Cairo Press, 2005.

Gordon, Joel. "Singing the Pulse of the Egyptian-Arab Street: Shaaban Abd al-Rahim and the Geo-Pop-Politics of Fast Food." *Popular Music* 22(1) (2003): 73–88.

Gorman, Anthony. *Historians, State, and Politics in Twentieth-Century Egypt: Contesting the Nation*. London: Routledge Curzon, 2003.

Gramsci, Antonio. *The Southern Question*, trans. Pascquale Verdicchio. Lafayette, IN: Bordighera Inc., 1995.

Gran, Peter. *Islamic Roots of Capitalism: Egypt, 1760–1840*. Syracuse, NY: Syracuse University Press, 1998.

———. "Upper Egypt in Modern History: A 'Southern Question'?" In *Upper Egypt: Identity and Change*, ed. Nicholas Hopkins and Reem Saad, 79–96. Cairo: American University in Cairo Press, 2004.

Gronow, Pekka. "The Record Industry Comes to the Orient." *Ethnomusicology* 25(2) (1981): 251–84.

Habermas, Jürgen. *The Structural Transformation of the Public Sphere: An Inquiry into a Category of Bourgeois Society*. Cambridge, MA: MIT Press, 1991.

Haeri, Niloofar. *Sacred Language, Ordinary People: Dilemmas of Culture and Politics in Egypt*. New York: Palgrave Macmillan, 2003.

Haikal, Mohammed Hussein. *Mohammed Hussein Haikal's Zainab: The First Egyptian Novel*, trans. John Mohammed Grinsted. London: Darf, 1989.

Hanna, Nelly. *In Praise of Books: A Cultural History of Cairo's Middle Class, Sixteenth to the Eighteenth Century*. Syracuse, NY: Syracuse University Press, 2003.

Hartmann, Martin. *The Arabic Press of Egypt*. London: Luzac, 1899.

Hechter, Michael. *Internal Colonialism: The Celtic Fringe in British National Development, 1536–1966*. Berkeley: University of California Press, 1975.

Heyworth-Dunne, J. *An Introduction to the History of Education in Modern Egypt*. London: Frank Cass, 1968.

Hilmi, Abbas. *Khedive of Egypt: Memoirs of Abbas Hilmi II*, ed. and trans. Amira Sonbol. Beirut: Ithaca Press, 1998.

Hinds, Harold E. "Popularity: The Sine Qua Non of Popular Culture." In *Popular Culture Theory and Methodology: A Basic Introduction*, ed. Harold E. Hinds, Marilyn Motz, and Angela Nelson, 359–70. Madison: University of Wisconsin Press, 2006.

Hinds, Harold E., Marilyn Motz, and Angela Nelson, eds. *Popular Culture Theory and Methodology: A Basic Introduction*. Madison: University of Wisconsin Press, 2006.

Hirschkind, Charles. *The Ethical Soundscape: Cassette Sermons and Islamic Counterpublics*. New York: Columbia University Press, 2006.

Hobsbawm, Eric. "Introduction: Inventing Traditions." In *The Invention of Traditions*, ed. Eric Hobsbawm and Terence Ranger. London: Cambridge University Press, 1983.

Holes, Clive. *Modern Arabic: Structures, Functions, and Varieties*. Washington, DC: Georgetown University Press, 2004.

Hopkins, Nicholas, and Reem Saad, eds. *Upper Egypt: Identity and Change*. Cairo: American University in Cairo Press, 2004.

Hourani, Albert. *Arabic Thought in the Liberal Age, 1798–1939*. Cambridge: Cambridge University Press, 1983.

Hunter, F. Robert. *Egypt Under the Khedives, 1805–1879: From Household Government to Modern Bureaucracy*. Cairo: American University in Cairo Press, 1999.

Jacob, Wilson. "Working Out Egypt: Masculinity and Subject Formation Between Colonial Modernity and Nationalism, 1870–1940." Ph.D. dissertation, New York University, 2005.

Jankowski, James, and Israel Gershoni, eds. *Rethinking Nationalism in the Arab Middle East*. New York: Columbia University Press, 1997.

Keddie, Nikki R. *Sayyid Jamal ad-Din "al-'Afghani": A Political Biography*. Los Angeles: University of California Press, 1972.

Khalidi, Rashid, Lisa Anderson, Muhammad Muslih, and Reeva S. Simon, eds. *The Origins of Arab Nationalism*. New York: Columbia University Press, 1991.

Kholoussy, Hanan. *For Better, For Worse: The Marriage Crisis That Made Modern Egypt*. Stanford, CA: Stanford University Press, 2010.

Khouri, Mounah A. *Poetry and the Making of Modern Egypt (1882–1922)*. Leiden: Brill, 1971.

al-Khozai, Mohamed A. *The Development of Early Arabic Drama, 1847–1900*. London: Longman, 1984.

Khuri-Makdisi, Ilham. "Levantine Trajectories: The Formulation and Dissemination of Radical Ideas In and Between Beirut, Cairo, and Alexandria, 1860–1914." Ph.D. dissertation, Harvard University, 2003.

Lagrange, Frédéric. "Une Egypte libertine? Taqâtîq et chansons légères au début du XXe siècle." In *Paroles, Signes, Mythes, Mélanges offerts à Jamel Eddine Bencheikh*, ed. Floréal Sanagustin, 257–300. Damascus, Syria: IFEAD, 2001.

———. "Musiciens et poètes en Egypte au temps de la nahda." Ph.D. dissertation, Université de Paris à Saint-Denis, 1994.

———. "Women in the Singing Business, Women in Songs." *History Compass* 7(1) (2009): 226–50.

Landau, Jacob. "Abu Naddara: An Egyptian Jewish Nationalist." *Journal of Jewish Studies* 3(1) (1952): 30–44.

———. "Popular Arabic Plays, 1909." *Journal of Arabic Literature* 17 (1986): 120–25.

———. "Prolegomena to a Study of Secret Societies in Modern Egypt." *Middle Eastern Studies* 1(2) (January 1965): 135–86.

———. *Studies in the Arab Theater and Cinema*. Philadelphia: University of Pennsylvania Press, 1969.

Lane, Edward William. *An Account of the Manners and Customs of the Modern Egyptians: Written in Egypt During the Years 1833–1835*. London: East West, 1978.

Lockman, Zachary. "Exploring the Field: Lost Voices and Emerging Practices in Egypt, 1882–1914." In *Histories of the Modern Middle East: New Directions*, ed. Israel Gershoni, Hakan Erdem, and Ursula Wokock, 137–53. London: Lynne Rienner, 2002.

———. "Imagining the Working Class: Culture, Nationalism, and Class Formation in Egypt, 1899–1914." *Poetics Today* 15(2) (1994): 157–91.

Manela, Erez. "Imagining Woodrow Wilson in Asia: Dreams of East-West Harmony and the Revolt Against Empire in 1919." *American Historical Review* 111(5) (2006): 1–39.

Marçais, William. "La diglossie arab." *L'Enseignement Public* 97 (1930): 401–9.

Marsot, Afaf Lutfi al-Sayyid. *Egypt and Cromer: A Study in Anglo-Egyptian Relations*. New York: Praeger, 1969.

———. *Egypt in the Reign of Muhammad Ali*. Cambridge: Cambridge University Press, 1984.

Mason, Laura. "Songs: Mixing Media." In *Revolution in Print: The Press in France, 1775–1800*, ed. Robert Darnton and Daniel Roche, 252–69. Berkeley: University of California Press, 1989.

McLuhan, Marshall. *The Gutenberg Galaxy: The Making of Typographic Man*. Toronto: University of Toronto Press, 1962.

———. *Understanding Media: The Extensions of Man*. New York: McGraw-Hill, 1964.

El-Messiri, Sawsan. *Ibn al-Balad: A Concept of Egyptian Identity*. Leiden: Brill, 1978.

Metcalf, Cynthia Gray-Ware. "From Morality Play to Celebrity: Women, Gender, and Performing Modernity in Egypt: c. 1850–1939." Ph.D. dissertation, University of Virginia, 2008.

Miller, Catherine. "Between Myth and Reality: The Construction of a Sa'idi Identity in Cairo." In *Upper Egypt: Identity and Change*, ed. Nicholas Hopkins and Reem Saad, 25–54. Cairo: American University in Cairo Press, 2004.

Mitchell, T. F. *Colloquial Arabic: The Living Language of Egypt*. London: English Universities Press, 1962.

———. "Some Preliminary Observations on the Arabic Koine." *Bulletin of the British Society for Middle Eastern Studies* 2(2) (1975): 70–86.

Mitchell, Timothy. *Colonizing Egypt*. Berkeley: University of California Press, 1991.

———. *Rules of Experts: Egypt, Techno-Politics, Modernity*. Berkeley: University of California Press, 2002.

Moore, Barrington, Jr. *Social Origins of Dictatorship and Democracy: Lord and Peasant in the Making of the Modern World*. Boston: Beacon, 1966.

Moosa, Matti. "Ya'qub Sanu' and the Rise of Arab Drama in Egypt." *International Journal of Middle Eastern Studies* 5 (1974): 401–33.

Mukerji, Chandra, and Michael Schudson, eds. *Rethinking Popular Culture: Contemporary Perspectives in Cultural Studies*. Berkeley: University of California Press, 1991.

Nairn, Tom. *The Break-Up of Britain: Crisis and Neo-Nationalism*. London: Verso, 1981.

Nieuwkerk, Karin van. *A Trade Like Any Other: Female Singers and Dancers in Egypt*. Austin: University of Texas Press, 1995.

Ninet, John. *Arabi Pacha*. Berne: Imprimerie J. Moureau et Fils, 1884.

———. *Lettres d'Egypte 1879–1882*, ed. Anouar Louca. Paris: Centre National de la Recherche Scientifique, 1979.

———. "Origins of the National Party in Egypt." *The Nineteenth Century* 13 (January 1883): 117–34.

Ong, Walter. "Oral Residue in Tudor Prose Style." *Publications of the Modern Language Association* 80(3) (1965): 145–54.

Owen, Roger. *Cotton and the Egyptian Economy, 1820–1914: A Study in Trade and Development*. Oxford: Clarendon Press, 1969.

———. *Lord Cromer: Victorian Imperialist, Edwardian Proconsul*. Oxford: Oxford University Press, 2004.

———. *The Middle East in the World Economy, 1800–1914*. London: Methuen, 1981.

Piterberg, Gabriel. "The Tropes of Stagnation and Awakening in Nationalist Historical Consciousness: The Egyptian Case." In *Rethinking Nationalism in the Arab Middle East*, ed. James P. Jankowski and Israel Gershoni, 42–61. New York: Columbia University Press, 1997.

Pollard, Lisa. "The Family Politics of Colonizing and Liberating Egypt, 1882–1919." *Social Politics* 7(1) (2000): 47–79.

———. "The Habits and Customs of Modernity: Egyptians in Europe and the Geography of Nineteenth-Century Nationalism." *Arab Studies Journal* 7(2)–8(1) (fall 1999–spring 2000): 52–74.

———. *Nurturing the Nation: The Family Politics of Modernizing, Colonizing, and Liberating Egypt, 1805–1923.* Berkeley: University of California Press, 2005.

Powell, Eve M. Troutt. "Burnt-Cork Nationalism: Race and Identity in the Theater of Alî al-Kassâr." In *Colors of Enchantment: Theater, Dance, Music, and the Visual Arts of the Middle East,* ed. Sherifa Zuhur, 27–38. Cairo: American University in Cairo Press, 2001.

———. *A Different Shade of Colonialism: Egypt, Great Britain, and the Mastery of the Sudan.* Berkeley: University of California Press, 2003.

Racy, Ali Jihad. *Making Music in the Arab World: The Culture and Artistry of Tarab.* Cambridge: Cambridge University Press, 2003.

———. "Musical Change and Commercial Recording in Egypt, 1904–1932." Ph.D. dissertation, University of Illinois at Urbana-Champaign, 1977.

———. "The Record Industry and Egyptian Traditional Music: 1904–1932." *Ethnomusicology* 20(1) (1976): 23–48.

Reid, Donald M. *Cairo University and the Making of Modern Egypt.* New York: Cambridge University Press, 1990.

———. *Whose Pharaohs? Archaeology, Museums, and Egyptian National Identity from Napoleon to World War I.* Berkeley: University of California Press, 2002.

Russell, Mona. *Creating the New Egyptian Woman: Consumerism, Education, and National Identity, 1863–1922.* New York: Palgrave Macmillan, 2004.

Ryzova, Lucie. *L'effendiyya ou la modernité contestée.* Cairo: CEDEJ, 2004.

———. "Egyptianizing Modernity Through the 'New Effendiya': Social and Cultural Constructions of the Middle Class in Egypt Under the Monarchy." In *Re-Envisioning Egypt, 1919–1952,* ed. Arthur Goldschmidt, Amy Johnson, and Barak Salamoni, 124–63. Cairo: American University in Cairo Press, 2005.

Sabry, Mohammed [Muhammad Sabri]. *La genèse de l'esprit national Egyptien, 1863–1882.* Paris: Librairie Picart, 1924.

Sadgrove, P. C. *The Egyptian Theater in the Nineteenth Century: 1799–1882.* Berkshire, UK: Ithaca Press, 1996.

Safran, Nadav. *Egypt in Search of Political Community: An Analysis of the Intellectual and Political Evolution of Egypt, 1804–1952.* Cambridge, MA: Harvard University Press, 1961.

Schmidt, H. D. "The Idea and Slogan of 'Perfidious Albion.'" *Journal of the History of Ideas* 14 (October 1953): 604–16.

Schmidt, Leigh Eric. *Hearing Things: Religion, Illusions, and the American Enlightenment.* Cambridge, MA: Harvard University Press, 2000.

Schölch, Alexander. *Egypt for the Egyptians: The Social-Political Crisis in Egypt, 1878–1882.* London: Ithaca Press, 1981.

Scott, James C. *Domination and the Arts of Resistance: Hidden Transcripts.* New Haven, CT: Yale University Press, 1990.

Selim, Samah. *The Novel and the Rural Imaginary in Egypt, 1880–1985.* New York: Routledge, 2004.

Shakry, Omnia. *The Great Social Laboratory: Subjects of Knowledge in Colonial and Postcolonial Egypt.* Stanford, CA: Stanford University Press, 2007.

Shechter, Relli. *Smoking Culture and Economy in the Middle: The Egyptian To-bacco Market, 1850–2000.* Cairo: American University in Cairo Press, 2006.

Shryock, Andrew. *Nationalism and the Genealogical Imagination: Oral History and Textual Authority in Tribal Jordan.* Berkeley: University of California Press, 1997.

Sladen, Douglas. *Oriental Cairo: The City of the "Arabian Nights."* Philadelphia: Lippincott, 1911.

Smith, Anthony D. *The Ethnic Origins of Nations.* Oxford: Blackwell Press, 1986.

———. "Gastronomy or Geology? The Role of Nationalism in the Reconstruction of Nations." *Nations and Nationalism* 1(1) (1994): 3–23.

———. *National Identity.* Las Vegas: University of Nevada Press, 1991.

Smith, Charles D. "The 'Crisis of Orientation': The Shift of Egyptian Intellectuals to Islamic Subjects in the 1930s." *International Journal of Middle East Studies* 4 (1973): 382–410.

———. "'Cultural Constructs' and Other Fantasies: Imagined Narratives in *Imagined Communities*—Surrejoinder to Gershoni and Jankowski's 'Print Culture, Social Change, and the Process of Redefining Imagined Communities in Egypt.'" *International Journal of Middle East Studies* 31 (1999): 95–102.

———. "Imagined Identities, Imagined Nationalisms: Print Culture and Egyptian Nationalism in Light of Recent Scholarship." *International Journal of Middle Eastern Studies* 29 (1997): 607–22.

———. "The Intellectual and Modernization: Definitions and Reconsiderations—The Egyptian Experience." *Comparative Studies in Society and History* 22 (1980): 513–33.

———. *Islam and the Search for Social Order in Modern Egypt: A Biography of Muhammad Husayn Haykal.* Albany: State University of New York Press, 1983.

Smith, Jacob. *Vocal Tracks: Performance and Sound Media.* Berkeley: University of California Press, 2008.

Smith, Mark M. *Sensing the Past: Seeing, Hearing, Smelling, Tasting, and Touching in History.* Berkeley: University of California Press, 2007.

Sonbol, Amira el-Azhary. *The New Mamluks: Egyptian Society and Modern Feudalism.* Syracuse, NY: Syracuse University Press, 2000.

Starr, Deborah. *Remembering Cosmopolitan Egypt: Literature, Culture, and Empire.* London: Routledge, 2009.

Storey, John. *Inventing Popular Culture: From Folklore to Globalization.* Oxford: Blackwell, 2003.

Suleiman, Yasir. *The Arabic Language and National Identity: A Study in Ideology.* Washington, DC: Georgetown University Press, 2003.

Swedenburg, Ted. "Sa'ida Sultan/Danna International: Transgender Pop and the Polysemiotics of Sex, Nation, and Ethnicity on the Israeli-Egyptian Border." In *Mass Mediations: New Approaches to Popular Culture in the Middle East and Beyond*, ed. Walter Armbrust, 88–119. Berkeley: University of California Press, 2000.

Terry, Janice J. *The Wafd: Cornerstone of Egyptian Political Power.* London: Third World Center for Research and Publishing, 1982.

Tignor, Robert L. *Modernization and British Colonial Rule in Egypt, 1882–1914.* Princeton, NJ: Princeton University Press, 1966.

Tilly, Charles. "Major Forms of Collective Action in Western Europe, 1500–1975." *Theory and Society* 3(3) (1976): 365–75.

Van den Berghe, Pierre L. "Race and Ethnicity: A Socio-Biological Perspective." *Ethnic and Racial Studies* 1(4) (1978): 401–14.

Van Nieuwkerk, Karen. *Female Singers and Dancers in Egypt.* Austin: University of Texas Press, 1995.

Vatikiotis, P. J. *The History of Modern Egypt: From Muhammad Ali to Mubarak.* Baltimore: Johns Hopkins University Press, 1991.

Vitalis, Robert. *When Capitalists Collide: Business Conflict and the End of Empire in Egypt.* Berkeley: University of California Press, 1995.

Weber, Eugen. *Peasants into Frenchmen: The Modernization of Rural France, 1870–1914.* Stanford, CA: Stanford University Press, 1976.

Wendell, Charles. *The Evolution of the Egyptian National Image: From Its Origins to Ahmad Lutfi al-Sayyid.* Berkeley: University of California Press, 1972.

Wogan, Peter. "Imagined Communities Reconsidered: Is Print-Capitalism What We Think It Is?" *Anthropological Theory* 1(4) (2001): 403–18.

Woidich, Manfred. "Egyptian Arabic and Dialect Contact in Historical Perspectives." In *Humanism, Culture, and Language in the Near East: Studies in Honor of Georg Krotkoff,* ed. A. Asma and M. Zahniser, 185–97. Baltimore: Eisenbrauns, 1997.

Zuhur, Sherifa, ed. *Colors of Enchantment: Theater, Dance, Music, and the Visual Arts of the Middle East.* Cairo: American University in Cairo Press, 2001.

———, ed. *Images of Enchantment: Visual and Performing Arts of the Middle East.* Cairo: American University in Cairo Press, 1998.

# Index

CPSIA information can be obtained
at www.ICGtesting.com
Printed in the USA
JSHW021051030120
3352JS00001B/8